A History of Tavistock Cricket Club 1849 – 1999

Tavistock Cricket Club,
the author, and the publishers
gratefully acknowledge the following
whose generous donations
contributed towards the production of this book:

Dot Avery
Peter Anderson
Bill Antrobus
Peter Ayres
Piers Bickley
Bob Carr
Maurice Craze
Mike Crocker
Peter Earl
Dave Ewings
Andrew Gauler
John Gosling Sen.
John Gosling Jun.
Sir Robert Hicks
Geoff Husband
Stuart Munday
John Perkin
Derek Pethick
Robert Quick

A History of Tavistock Cricket Club 1849 – 1999

150 YEARS OF CRICKET AT THE RING

Gerry Woodcock

Northcote House

First published in 1999 by Northcote House Publishers Ltd, Plymbridge House, Estover Road, Plymouth PL6 7PY, United Kingdom.
Tel: +44 (01752) 202368 Fax: +44 (01752) 202330.

British Library Cataloguing-in-Publication Data
A catalogue record for this book is available from the British Library

ISBN 0 7463 0935 X

Typeset by PDQ Typesetting, Newcastle-under-Lyme
Printed and bound by The Baskerville Press, Salisbury, Wiltshire.

Contents

Contents

Foreword

by
David Shepherd MBE

I was very pleased to be asked to provide a few words as a foreword to Gerry Woodcock's most interesting book on the history of Tavistock Cricket Club. The club has a special place in my affections, and in January 1994 it did me the honour of electing me to Honorary Life Membership.

As a North Devon CC player, I enjoyed our matches against Tavistock, both home and away. They were usually played very competitively, but always in good spirit. Lasting friendships were made between members of each club. One of the best Tavistock bowlers I encountered in those early days was Jack Davey. We were soon to become great friends and colleagues when we went to play first-class cricket for Gloucestershire. Jack and I were mates on the county scene for over ten years, and when we were awarded a joint benefit in the late seventies it was great to bring the full Gloucestershire side down to play Tavistock at The Ring. As usual, the hospitality was magnificent. The lads were greatly impressed by the unique setting of The Ring – surely one of the better places to play one's cricket on a fine day. Even when it is not so good you can see the rain coming from a long way off, so players can get off the field before getting soaked!

Such was the friendliness between the Tavistock and North Devon clubs, three of us from North Devon, Bill Walter, my brother Bill, and I, were invariably invited to play in the Tavistock President's XI against the club side. It was always, and still is, the last fixture of each season. The President who started this tradition was that wonderful character Maurice Avery, and it continued until the three of us felt that our playing days should be but fond memories. Sadly, Maurice is no longer with us but it is always a pleasure to see his widow, Dot, whenever we get to visit the club.

We had some wonderful President's Days. Our friend, Graham, would collect the three of us from Instow at six o'clock in the morning, and we would set off for an early morning round of golf at Launceston Golf Club en route to The Ring. Once in Tavistock we would make for the Cornish Arms where we enjoyed a pie and a pint. Then it was up to the ground for the President's game, traditionally always followed by a wonderful post-match liquid social evening. The long homeward journey usually involved a stop-off for a snack at the Dartmoor Inn, Lydford, returning to North Devon in the early hours. Happy days!!

I remember playing in one match a few years ago when, after about half an hour, we discovered that a certain club member who shall remain nameless (Stuart Munday) had marked the pitch at a length of 23 yards instead of 22. I was asked what should be done, and I suggested that we should carry on since the pitch would be the same for both sides. Shortly after, I set off for a quick single having quite forgotten that there is no such thing as a quick single on a 23 yard pitch. You will have guessed it – I was run out by a clear yard!

150 not out this year, in 1999. Congratulations to 'Tavvy', but don't let it end there. It is so important that the game flourishes at club level. Cricket is so much more competitive nowadays with most teams playing league cricket, and many clubs engaging overseas players to achieve success. It seems that we are now as a finishing school, grooming overseas players to become Test cricketers. I am not sure that I agree with this modern trend. Our clubs must provide facilities and opportunities for local players. Long may Tavistock continue to do so.

Enjoy your 150th anniversary. You've earned it!

D R Shepherd MBE *January 1999*

Introduction

by
Clifford Alford,
President, Tavistock Cricket Club

When Gerry Woodcock first mentioned to me that he would like to research and record the history of Tavistock Cricket Club, I had little idea that it would be possible for him to unearth such a wealth of detail on so many personalities and events stretching back to the club's very beginning 150 years ago. His proposal, nevertheless, sounded an exciting one. Gerry, as local readers in particular will know, is highly regarded for his eminently readable and popular series of books detailing the history of his lovely market town on the western fringe of Dartmoor. In the summer of 1978, whilst the Senior Sixth-Form Tutor of Tavistock College (later to be known as Head of the Sixth-Form) Gerry wrote and had published, a book of full length which he entitled *Tavistock School – The First Thousand Years.*

With that background and so much experience behind him, Tavistock Cricket Club is indeed fortunate that Gerry, with his unbounding passion for the game, was so keen to mark the 150th anniversary of the club's foundation in 1849 in this way. I know only too well of the many hours, and undoubted considerable personal expense he has given freely to make his dream for this book become a reality. He has gone to great lengths to locate former players now living in places near and far, and their recollections of times past are reflected in the events which he has now recorded for our interest and pleasure. The archives, which have been under the careful management of club archivist, John Montgomery, have been examined and many of today's playing membership and officials, too, have been consulted.

That the book now appears in print is due in no small measure to the generous support of club trustee Mrs Dot Avery whose name, with that of her late husband, Maurice, is synonymous with that of Tavistock Cricket Club. On the very day that I write this introduction, which I am delighted to do at Gerry Woodcock's request, Dot is celebrating her 90th birthday. Still displaying considerable energy and alertness, she continues to hold the club very dear to her heart. It is a remarkable record that she has given outstanding and constant support to the club for more than sixty-five years. Long may she be able to do so.

I would like to take this opportunity to pay tribute to another stalwart benefactor and friend of the club. Bob Noakes, is known to everyone, and it seems like everywhere, as 'Nocker'. Bob hails from St Leonards-on-Sea in Sussex. Older members of the club first came across Nocker during their tour of Sussex county many years ago. If I remember it correctly, in each of the matches we played over the week's tour, the opposition had the same wicket keeper. It was Nocker. He is a man skilled in the making of cricket bats of fine quality. He produces them not only for club players, but also for men in the county game too. Nocker and his wife, Maureen, make an annual pilgrimage to Tavistock for a week or two's holiday during August, usually armed with fulfilled bat orders which vie for space in the car with their luggage. Nocker never fails to visit The Ring as often as he can be spared from visits to the beach, and we are most grateful to him for his yearly gift of a quality match ball for use in the President's Day match. For that we are indeed indebted, but we were doubly appreciative when three years ago he presented the club with a marble-mounted cricketing figurine as a trophy to be competed for on that special last playing day in each season. In recognition of its gratitude to Bob Noakes for his friendship and support, the club was delighted to make him an Honorary Vice-President in December, 1995, so linking his name to those of Bill Shepherd and Bill Walters of North Devon CC, who already held that distinction.

It is, of course, a matter of great pride to the club, as well as being a tribute to Gerry Woodcock, that David Shepherd so willingly agreed to write the foreword to this book. Few, if any, would dispute that David is the number one umpire in world cricket today. England has produced many outstanding umpires in the past, and without a shadow of a doubt David ranks at the top of the ladder with the very best.

I am delighted that David has very recently been joined by Gerry Woodcock as one of the club's Honorary Life Members. The committee and members of Tavistock Cricket Club are greatly indebted to both of them for their contribution to the history of the club in this notable year, and especially to Gerry for producing this splendid record of 150 years of cricket at The Ring.

Clifford Alford — *January 1999*
President

Preface

It is five years since I decided I would like to pay a tribute to Tavistock Cricket Club as it approached its 150th birthday. During that period I have, in putting together this history, received much help, and pleasure, from talking to a large number of members of the club, past and present. I offer my grateful thanks to all those who have given generously of their time, and have provided me with valuable material. They include: Roy Acton, Clifford Alford, Margaret Alford, Dot Avery, Bill Colling, Don Connett, Maurice Craze, Mike Crocker, Jack Davey, Andrew Gauler, John Gosling, Geoff Husband, Eric Jarman, John Montgomery, Stuart Munday, Gerry Parsons, Alec Pethick, Bob Quick, Jack Taylor, and Bill Tucker. Peter Wynne-Jones, the Secretary of the Association of Cricket Statisticians and Historians, gave me some helpful information. Valuable source material was provided in Edward Chilcott's diary, and in a collection of memorabilia covering the careers of Eric and Jack Davey. I am very grateful to the Chilcott family and to Jack Davey for putting this information at my disposal. A collection of material compiled by Frank Millman also became available and provided much useful data on the inter-war period. Jack Taylor's published reminiscences offered an affectionate insight into some more recent events and personalities. John Montgomery, the club's archivist, was kind and helpful in introducing me to many boxes of minute books, scorebooks, and other records, covering much of the twentieth century, and I owe him a particular debt.

The search for older photographs to supplement the more recent ones in the possession of the club was greatly helped by the following, who either put illustrative material in my way or gave their permission for its use: Roy Acton, Clifford Alford, Dot Avery, Frank Bond, Jack Davey, Edward Garnier, Tavistock Golf Club, Brian Jones, Simon May, Tony Miller, John Montgomery, and Bill Tucker. I am grateful to Peter Miatt for making copies of some pictures found in unexpected settings.

The absence of club records before the First World War meant that I had to lean heavily on the reports of local newspapers. This proved to be a rich field. The files of the following papers were consulted: *Exeter and Plymouth Gazette*, *Exeter Flying Post*, *Plymouth and Devonport Weekly Journal*, *Tavistock Gazette*, *Tavistock Times*, *Western Daily Mercury*, *Western Evening Herald*, *Western Morning News*, *Western Times*. Reference books like *Wisden* and *Who's Who of Cricketers* proved useful on the relationship between local cricket and the wider scene. There is, however, very little about cricket in the books written about this area. Authors seem to prefer less important subjects like politics, education, industry, or trade. This is a mystery to me. If I have restored the balance a little, I am well satisfied.

The book is dedicated to the members of the Tavistock Cricket Club past and present. Each one played a part in the story of the last century and a half. And, because cricket is a great, and in a sense a timeless, game, there is the certainty that the story is nowhere near its end. The Ring is a field of dreams and a place of spirits. And dreams and spirits belong, and find a home, in the future, as much as they do in the past.

Gerry Woodcock

Part One: 1849–1888

The Age of Uncertainty

'A most healthy exercise'

In 1846 the Tavistock authoress Rachel Evans wrote an account of some interesting walks in and around her native town. In one chapter she takes her readers to Crowndale, and suggests that on the way back 'before leaving the banks of the canal' they should note:

> 'some pleasant fields, closely cropped by the nibbling sheep, which in the fine summer evenings have been used as a cricket ground'.

These fields, which belonged to the Fitzford estate, may lay claim to having been Tavistock's first cricket ground. The site is now occupied by Tavistock College. It offered one of the few flat and open areas suitable for ball games, and, cricket being an old game, it is reasonable to suppose that matches had been played at Crowndale for many years before Rachel Evans recorded her observations.

It is, however, clear that no cricket club existed in 1846. The assumption must be that the fields off the Crowndale Road were the setting for impromptu matches between teams of locals, or for occasional organised fixtures against sides from the district around. It may be that it was the haphazard nature of these arrangements, or perhaps the failure of the local cricketers of the 1840s to have exclusive rights to the use of the Crowndale grounds, that led to the formation of the Tavistock Cricket Club in 1849. Certain it is that the club was founded in that year, and that it established its first, and as it was to prove its enduring, home, not in the Tavy valley, but perched spectacularly on the exposed uplands of Whitchurch Down.

Few details of that first season have survived. The *Plymouth and Devonport Weekly Journal* reported on August 23rd that:

> 'The club had a grand field day on Thursday last on Whitchurch Down. The play was excellent and attracted a large number of spectators. Mr Gribbell of the Exeter Inn had a tent on the ground, and spread a capital dinner, which was done ample justice to by many of those present.'

William Gribbell had recently taken over the Exeter Inn after a spell as the proprietor of the Union Inn. He could well have been the brother of Richard

Gribbell, the grocer who was the club's first president and treasurer. Another report, this time in the *Exeter and Plymouth Gazette*, appeared at the end of the season. Under the headline 'Tavistock Cricket Club', it read:

> 'The players of this club held their last field day for the season on Wednesday. The weather in the morning was anything but fine, which deterred a great many from attending. The afternoon, however, brought better weather, and the result was a large party. The play was excellent. At seven o'clock the members and their friends, to the number of forty, sat down to an excellent dinner at the Exeter Inn, and the evening was spent in the most agreeable manner by all present'.

The piece appeared on Saturday October 20th. The 'last field day' must, therefore, have taken place on Wednesday October 17th. The pioneers were obviously reluctant to bring their first season to an end! It is assumed that 'field days' consisted of practice activities and of contests organised within the club between teams of home players. The incidence of such events in the early years may indicate the difficulty in arranging fixtures when there were comparatively few potential opponents within horse-and-carriage distance of Tavistock, or it may simply illustrate that the club saw the organisation of in-house activity as one of its principal functions.

On March 24th 1850 the *Plymouth and Devonport Weekly Journal* announced that:

> 'The Tavistock Cricket Club, having been revived, will commence playing at Whitchurch on Easter Monday next. We understand a large number have joined the party, and no doubt the game will be carried on with some spirit, at least for the present season. As it is a most healthy exercise, we shall be glad to find that it may continue'.

The use of the word 'revived' and of the phrase 'at least for the present season', suggest quite clearly that the club was operating on a season-to-season basis. As the second season opened there were the rudiments of an organisation but no fixture list and no pavilion. The *Exeter and Plymouth Gazette* carried two brief reports of the 1850 season, but as yet there was no sign of inter-club competition. It reported the Easter Monday relaunch as 'the first field day of the season', when 'the attendance was large and the play excellent'. On July 6th there was another grand field day. This time there had been a good deal of publicity before the day, with the result that 'a large concourse of persons assembled to witness this manly and noble game'. The club had bought a marquee, in which, on the day, lunches that included 'all the delicacies of the season' were provided. Although 'spacious', it was 'not sufficiently large to accommodate the party present'. As to the cricket:

> 'The fine bowling which was displayed would have done credit to first rate players, yet, notwithstanding the determined feeling of the bowlers, the batsmen, with equal determination, made long scores; the fielding also was not without frequent calls for admiration, showing in every point the feasibility of this club to compete with any other in this or adjoining counties'.

The eulogistic tone was, of course, the work of the anonymous local correspondent, who contributed the piece. What a pity that, in the midst of all that purple prose, he did not get round to mentioning a name or two.

The game that Rachel Evans saw being played in the 1840s, and that was first played on the Down by the newly-formed club in 1849, bore close resemblances to contemporary cricket. The modern design of the bat was already established. It was still commonly made in one piece, but its length and width had been regulated since 1835. Similarly, the design of the ball would have been familiar to a modern player, except that in 1849 the laws allowed for a maximum circumference of nine-and-a-quarter inches rather than the current nine inches. A wicket consisted of three stumps and two bails, although it was one inch less in both height and width than the present laws provide for. The length of the pitch, twenty-two yards, the medieval chain, has remained untouchable.

Scoring was similar to today, except that there were no boundaries. Wides had already been introduced, and the controversial leg-byes had appeared in 1849. One significant change was afoot, and that was in bowling technique. Round-arm bowling grew in popularity from 1822, although the laws did not recognise it until 1835. By then, a new generation of bowlers had begun to experiment with over-arm actions, although, like their round-arm predecessors, they were, in their early years, regularly no-balled. Over-arm was legalised in 1863, but the style did not become prevalent until the 1890s. The six-ball over was not instituted until 1900. The laws in 1849 provided for four-ball overs, although the Tavistock club had decided before the end of the century that five was the right number. This divergence between what the game's authorities said and what a local club might do, is a useful reminder that the writ of the M.C.C., the lawmakers, was not absolute. We can assume that edicts from Lord's provided clubs with a framework within which to operate, but the regulations were not always rigorously applied.

In the summer of 1849, when the story began, the first M.C.C. overseas tour was still ten years away, the first *Wisden* was not to appear for fifteen years, the first organised county championship was forty-six years into the future, and one of the features of the Grace family's summer, at their home just outside Bristol, was the celebration of the first birthday of their fourth son. The Prime Minister was Lord John Russell, who had once been M.P. for Tavistock, and whose brother, the Seventh Duke of Bedford, owned most of the town. Whitchurch Down was just one small part of the Duke's vast estate. He agreed that a part of it could be used for cricket. The infant club entered into a contract with the Bedford Office as a tenant of the Duke, and thus began a relationship which was to endure to this day, with the Duke, and then with his successor as landlord, the Tavistock Town Council.

One of the main features of The Ring, as the ground was eventually to be universally called, was the range of granite posts marking the boundary. They were provided by the Duke, and have been there throughout the life of the cricket ground. The presence of a boundary was not required by the laws of the game, for fours and sixes did not then exist. The posts, originally linked by chains, served two purposes, in delineating the area for which the club took responsibility, and in helping to keep both spectators and straying animals off the main playing area. If, during play, the ball went beyond the boundary, a fielder would jump over the chain to retrieve it, while the batsmen ran. In June 1874, playing for the 11th Regiment, Lieutenant Smith, opening the innings, ran nine off one ball in the first over of the innings.

The original playing area was rather uneven. Around 1860 some necessary improvements were carried out, £40 being spent in one year alone for this purpose. This had the immediate effect of attracting unauthorised usage, so that at the beginning of the 1862 season the club had to issue the following request:

> 'The members of the club having from time to time spent large sums of money in getting the ground into good condition, the committee earnestly entreat that no persons who are not members of the club will use the ground without having first obtained permission'.

In 1873 there was further extensive levelling and turf-laying. The wickets tended to be variable in quality, and this helps to explain the record of rather erratic scoring in the early years of the club. These, and other problems, were to remain the concerns of successive committees. The Ring was not the most accessible of grounds. Visiting teams were occasionally to seek the help of relief parties as they misread their maps. And having got there, there were May afternoons when the wind across the Down penetrated even a third sweater. But there surely can never have been a more charming or beguiling setting. The catch to long-on which dropped safely out of reach because the fielder was enjoying the ravishing view of the town below was no isolated example. Over a period of a century-and-a-half The Ring has captured the hearts of countless visitors and of generations of players.

Gentlemen and Players

Among the pioneers who played in the early seasons of the club's history were Henry Barnett and his son William. Henry was a storekeeper at the Devon Great Consols copper mine, and lived in Madge Lane. Before he retired from the game he played for some seasons in the 1850s alongside his son. William, who had been born in 1831, was an accountant. The first in a long line of all-rounders at The Ring, he had a playing career that stretched to the late 1860s. Unfortunately records survive of only 42 games in which he played. In these, his haul was 162 wickets at an average of 3.5. For many summers he shared the brunt of the attack with Thomas Youren, another accountant, who lived above his office in West Street. Like Barnett, he made useful runs, but his main value to the side was as an opening bowler. Said to be 'terribly destructive' on hard pitches, he bowled under-arm at medium pace, and, in the 44 innings for which records have survived, he took 167 wickets at an average of 3.8. This must have been only a small proportion of the games that he played, for he did not retire until the mid 1870s, and was thereafter to claim that he 'had had the pleasure of playing in every match through every season for a period of something like a quarter of a century'.

Two dynasties have, between them, spanned the greater part of the club's history. More recently it was the Daveys. In the nineteenth century it was the Chaves. Thomas Chave was the son of the man who established, in 1797, the first printing press in Tavistock since the dissolution of the Abbey two and a half centuries before. Thomas followed his father into the business, and in turn passed it on to his son James. Tom was the club's first secretary, and he held the office for twenty-one years. In the middle of this long period, at the annual dinner in 1857 at the Queen's Head, he was presented with a silver watch and chain 'in appreciation of all he has done for Tavistock cricket'. On the field he was a useful all-rounder, who played consistently until the mid 1860s. One of his last games was on June 6th 1864, when his son James made his debut at the age of eleven. The young man was to become a regular member of the side in 1871. In the early years he bowled a bit, and also enjoyed being an occasional wicket keeper, but his strength was his batting. He had a fine range of strokes, was particularly strong on the leg side, and was described by his captain, in a season in which he averaged 34.3, as 'one of the most stylish players in the west of England.' The only significant chink in his armour was a tendency to play across the line and to fall lbw. It was a fault shared by his brother. In 1874 James was honoured by the club, as his father had been seventeen years earlier. This time to a watch and chain was added a bat. He married the daughter of the proprietor of the Commercial Inn, who did a lot of the catering at The Ring. And he carried on the family business in Taylor Square well into the present century. He died in 1936 at the age of eighty-three.

The Chaves, Barnetts, and Yourens of the cricketing world could, of course, have been expected to provide the backbone of a club like Tavistock. What they could not have been expected to provide was captaincy. Cricket in the nineteenth century reflected, at every level, the prevailing set of class attitudes. Captaining a cricket team, like leading a battalion, occupying a vicarage, or chairing a bench, was a task for a gentleman.

Successive occupants of the post fitted the mould perfectly. By the end of the century there had been eight captains. They were in turn, a vicar, a landed gentleman, an army officer, another vicar, a schoolmaster, a banker, and two lawyers. The first of these eight, and the man with the distinction of being Tavistock's first club captain, was Richard Sleeman. Born in 1813, he was the son of the vicar of Whitchurch. Richard himself was destined for the church, and his first job was as curate to Jack Russell, the well-known hunting parson. In 1848 he succeeded his father as vicar of Whitchurch. In the following year, at the age of thirty-six, he was one of the pioneers who established the cricket club in its home on Whitchurch Down, only a few minutes walk from the vicarage in the centre of the village. His playing career took him through to the age of fifty-five, but he retired from the captaincy eleven years earlier, in 1857.

Thereafter, as well as playing, he took over responsibility for 'the management of the ground', and thus became The Ring's first curator. He died in 1870 at the age of fifty-seven, only two years after hanging up his cricket boots. His Whitchurch career, stretching over twenty-two years, had been dedicated to his two great concerns, the interest of the souls of his parishioners and the welfare of the cricket club. Over the years he spent a lot of time at The Ring reflecting his deep love of the game. There was though another factor at work. Summer days on Whitchurch Down must have afforded some respite from the noise, not only from the pack of hounds that he maintained at the vicarage, but also from the fifteen children that he reared within its walls. As a cricketer, he could perhaps be described as no more that a steady middle-order batsman. Of his qualities as a captain we have no idea. His position in the annals of the club remains secure. He was the first captain.

After nine seasons in charge, the good vicar retired from the captaincy, though not, perhaps, with the intention of spending more time with his family, since he continued as both player and groundsman. His successor was nineteen years old. John Carpenter had been born the son and heir of the owner of Mount Tavy. Educated at Harrow and Oxford, he was to succeed to the local estates when he came of age in 1860. Four years later he benefited under a family will by inheriting large properties in Hampshire in return for agreeing to add his uncle's name to own. As John Carpenter-Garnier he was to be squire, benefactor, patron, magistrate, and member of parliament. His career was to follow a conventional pattern down to its lengthy last phase in the depths of Hampshire and his death in 1926 at the age of eighty-six. There was cricket in the family, and two of his cousins played at county level. He himself played at Lord's as both a Harrow schoolboy and an Oxford undergraduate. As a teenager in the 1850s he made a lot of runs playing for Tavistock in late-season fixtures while he was on holiday from boarding school or university.

Of the many innings that he must have played for the club, records of only 26 have survived. In these he scored 526 runs at an average of 23. In 1858, at the age of nineteen, his achievement in winning a blue was marked by his appointment as both captain and president of the club. The former post he was to hold for twelve years and the latter for twenty-nine years. From 1864, when he succeeded to the Hampshire property, his appearances at The Ring grew increasingly infrequent, and had ceased altogether by the time he entered parliament in 1873. His link with the club through the presidency continued until 1887, by which time he had sold Mount Tavy and become firmly settled in Hampshire.

His political career had been curiously foreshadowed by an incident concerning a cricket match in 1863. In preparing for their match against Tavistock on August 5th, the Okehampton club was deprived of the services of its best-known player, a man called Holley. Holley had already agreed to play elsewhere on that day. He wrote to Carpenter to enquire whether the Tavistock captain would consider missing the game, so as to even things up. Carpenter, ever the gentleman, agreed. He had already come to understand the accepted parliamentary convention of pairing.

Carpenter's predecessor as president was Richard Gribbell, a town-centre grocer, who had held office since the birth of the club. Gribbell, in the later stages of a successful business career, may well have helped the infant club financially. He was also the club's first treasurer, holding this post until 1861. At the A.G.M. in that year his health forced him to resign. The meeting thanked him for his services and offered him 'deepest sympathy in his affliction'. He was dead within a month.

The first generation of Tavistock club cricketers also included George Doidge, butcher and fearsome opening bat, and Joe Mathews, a partner in one of the local iron foundries, who is, perhaps, now best remembered for laying the foundation stone of the Freemasons' Hall in Pym Street. There was Dr. Richard Sleman, general practitioner, participant in many town activities and pillar of tetotalism, and G.H. Smith, the chief clerk in the Duke of Bedford's Office and superintendent of the market. And there was Henry Spry, a popular and companionable team-member, who played for the club for the first twenty years of its life, at the end of which he was still sharp and enthusiastic, and, according to a colleague, still 'bounded about like a deer'. These were the pioneers. The administration of the club during these early years, technically in the hands of a committee elected by the A.G.M., fell largely to the secretary and treasurer. Tom Chave filled the former post from 1849 to 1870. Two long-serving treasurers after Richard Gribbell, Henry Allen, a West Street painter, and Robert Luxton, solicitor and clerk to the magistrates, took the club from the 1850s to the 1880s.

'A commodious building'

In April 1860 a pre-season meeting over which Joe Mathews presided declared an intention to 'erect a wood house on the ground to accommodate members'. It was ready for the first match of the season, which did not take place until July 8th. On that day the visitors, Okehampton, were entertained to lunch in the new pavilion. The building was a modest affair, and it was not to last long. Gales in the winter of 1872 blew it down. At the A.G.M. in April of that year it was resolved that the committee 'endeavour to raise money to rebuild or repair the pavilion'. Twelve months passed and nothing happened. When the 1873 A.G.M. was told that the club faced a second consecutive pavilionless season, there was an angry response, and a determination to take action. Negotiations with the Duke's office led to an agreement by which the landlord provided a building measuring thirty-six feet by seventeen-and-a-half feet with a small ante-room attached, and the tenants accepted the need to raise £30 to furnish it. The builder was Daniel Westaway of Brook Street. It was completed in July 1873. The *Tavistock Gazette* was able to report that:

> 'the old weather-beaten structure which graced, or rather disgraced, the cricket ground, has now been replaced by a commodious building, which again gives our club a local habitation'.

The new house was not to escape for long the attentions of young vandals. Within months the *Tavistock Gazette* was to report angrily that:

> 'the skylight has been broken once or twice, and very likely the building would have been down altogether had the means of destruction been within reach'.

Tavistock in the 1870s was plagued by such juvenile capers as throwing stones through windows, removing brass plates from office doors, and hurling live hedgehogs at passers-by.

Both the 'old weather-beaten structure', and the 'commodious building' that replaced it, served a triple purpose. They provided changing facilities, storage space for equipment, and somewhere to take refreshment on match days. The remoteness of The Ring from the town, or, in the early years, from any buildings of any kind, put particular pressure on the club to make adequate arrangements to discharge all three functions on the ground. The contract to provide lunches in the pavilion was held, for many years, by William Yelland of the Commercial Inn in Bedford Square. The arrangement appears to have proved mutually satisfactory; one particularly happy consequence was the marriage between William's daughter and the club's star batsman, James Chave. Such problems as arose over the catering related, not to the quality or quantity of the fare, but to the question of how long the lunch break should be. Before a game started, at perhaps eleven o'clock, there would be an agreement between the two sides on a time at which stumps would be drawn, say seven o'clock. An attempt would be made to play a two-innings-a-side game, and if, by seven o'clock, this had not been concluded, the result would be decided on the basis of first-innings scores, so long as such an arrangement had been agreed before the start of play. It can be seen that there may have been circumstances in which the players of one side might have felt that there was an advantage to be gained by eating their lunches slowly. Such a situation occurred on August 24th 1863, in a match against Okehampton. The visitors had batted first and made 86. In reply, Tavistock were all out for 78, at which point lunch was taken. Relations between the two sides were at that point a little strained, and not only because of the long history of rivalry between the two towns going back, some said, to the Civil War, if not earlier. An incident during the morning had soured the atmosphere. When Tavistock batted they lost their opener, William Barnett, for a duck. Henry Nicholls came in at Number 3 and was bowled first ball. He complained loudly that he had not been ready, the umpire upheld his claim, and Nicholls remained to make 29, the top score. The incident rankled, and the Okehampton players decided to prolong the lunch adjournment so that it would not be possible to complete a further innings for each side, and they would be left having won by 8 runs. Disaster, in the event, overtook them. They were all out in their second innings, when it eventually got under way, for 22, which included eight ducks, and Tavistock sailed home by 10 wickets, with Barnett and Carpenter knocking off the required runs. Certain morals could have been drawn from the story. The occasion, sadly, did nothing to improve relations between the two rivals.

Another source of occasional annoyance and frustration was the late arrival of a visiting team. For the local club there was, in this respect, as much sinning as being sinned against. In the pre-railway age, and for Tavistock this meant up to 1859, there were particular transport problems, and scores of excuses for delays. The coming of the railway helped a good deal, though journeys might still entail a decent walk from station to ground, as was the case in Tavistock, where visitors arriving at the station off the Whitchurch Road had to face the stiff climb up to The Ring.

In spite of the length of the journey, when Tavistock visited Hatherleigh on September 8th 1851, they concluded a full match of two innings a side. The game is significant because the details found their way into the columns of the Exeter-based *Western Times*. This was therefore the first Tavistock fixture to be given a full report in the press. Hatherleigh had a strong side, and had, it seems, defeated Tavistock earlier in the season, presumably at The Ring. For the return match they joined forces with the Okehampton club to put out a combined team. 'Okeleigh' scored 75 and 116, and Tavistock replied with 84 and 83, to lose a close-fought encounter by 24 runs. For the visitors, Weekes scored 3 and 5, Taylor 15 and 17, Honey 1 and 2, Doidge 0 and 33, Chave 24 and 1, Thynne 13 and 1, Barnett 8 and 4, Sleeman 4 and 5, Spry 5 and 3, Allen 0 and 1, Monk 1 and 0, and Extras 10 and 11. The paper reported 'the gentlemen of Tavistock' as saying that 'there was not much room for triumph' on the part of the Hatherleigh gents, since the latter:

> 'were provided with spiked shoes, but the Tavistock club were not, which rendered their fielding much less effective than it usually is, the ground being very hard and slippery'.

There were, however, no hard feelings, and after the game:

> 'the Hatherleigh gentlemen entertained their friends from a distance with a cold collation on the ground, after which the greatest harmony and conviviality prevailed'.

Almost a year later, on August 12th 1852, an away game against Launceston also provided a record of scorecard details which has survived. The visitors were dismissed for 16. Barnett scored 12 of them, and there were eight ducks. After Launceston had replied with 74, the Tavistock batting was again swept away, this time for 28, leaving the hosts to celebrate a victory by an innings and 30 runs. Two weeks later there was another journey, and another defeat, this time at the hands of the Devon Central Clubs at Inwardsleigh. The hosts made 58 and 56. Youren took 8 wickets, Chave 3, Barnett Senior 4, and Barnett Junior 3. Of the 18 wickets taken by bowlers, 17 were bowled and 1 caught. The 2 wickets that were not claimed by bowlers were a Run Out and a Hit Wicket, the latter form of dismissal not then being credited to the bowler. Tavistock scored 52 and 33, with 9 bowled, 6 caught, and 5 run out. No one reached double figures. There were 9 extras in the two innings: 3 byes, 3 wides, and 3 leg byes. During this period reports and details of matches are very sparse and spasmodic, offering only occasional glimpses of the club's playing fortunes. Misfortune against Launceston continued, with a 100 run defeat on September 2nd 1855. Carpenter and Doidge scored between them 66 of Tavistock's two-innings aggregate of 117, while Barnett and Youren took 17 Launceston wickets. The *Exeter and Plymouth Gazette* commended Carpenter for 'the scientific manner in which he played', and described also as 'extremely good' the performance, behind the wicket, of Mr Gunning. He is the first identifiable Tavistock wicket keeper. The evening was, apparently, spent at the King's Arms Inn, 'in social conviviality and good fellowship'. It was not always to be so.

On August 22nd 1857, at the Brickfields in Devonport, Keyham entertained Tavistock in a game that attracted a crowd estimated at 4000. Players and officials had difficulty throughout the day in keeping spectators at some distance from the wicket. Keyham won the toss, put the visitors in, and dismissed them for 126. In reply they made 116. By the time the closure came Tavistock had made 208 for 8 in their second innings. They therefore won on the basis of first innings scores. Or, as the press report quaintly put it:

> 'it was now seven o'clock, and the Keyham party, seeing they had no chance, admitted themselves partly beaten, and retired from the match'.

When the teams dined together at the Royal Hotel after the game, Henry Clark, Tavistock's vice president, made a speech in which he told his hosts that they had no need to feel ashamed of their defeat,

> 'since Mr Carpenter was in the habit of playing at Lord's against some first-rate bowlers, and Mr Doidge had long been considered one of the first crack batters in Devon'.

For young John Carpenter, who had top-scored with 37, the reference was to his participation, earlier in the summer, in the Eton-Harrow match, in which he had batted Number 4 for Harrow and made 41, the highest innings on either side. In the following year he was to make another Lord's appearance, this time for Oxford in the varsity match. For George Doidge, the compliment was made in spite of an off-day when he fell LBW for 4. Clark himself had enjoyed the game, making 48 in the rather pointless second innings.

Two weeks before this encounter the same two sides had met at The Ring. On that day Tavistock won by 51 runs. The home side's first innings total of 102 had, astonishingly, included 43 extras, of which 21 were wides, 12 byes, and 10 leg byes. Between them, Messrs Doidge and Extras contributed 91 runs, 40 more than the winning margin. Here, in the record of two matches close together between the two clubs, is an example of the practice that caught on in the 1850s of a return fixture at the other ground a fortnight after the original game. From 1859, for example, reports survive of two games against Okehampton, played at the end of July and the beginning of August, and both won by Tavistock, by 55 runs and by 9 wickets.

Games against Keyham proved to be, during these early seasons, particularly popular with players and spectators alike. A large crowd assembled at The Ring on Monday June 28th 1858 to witness such a contest. Umpires Doidge and Ball pitched stumps at eleven o'clock, and Tavistock batted first. With 37 from Carpenter, 31 from all-rounder William Cator, and 40 extras, it needed little from everyone else to reach a respectable total of 139. The Services side was then shot out for 66, Barnett taking 5 wickets and Cator 3. The rules at that time not only allowed for, but insisted on, a follow-on, and the relevant margin was 60 runs. Keyham therefore batted again, making 106, with the wickets shared between Cator, Gill, and Youren. Tavistock's winning target of 34 was reached for the loss of 4 wickets, and to the accompaniment of some predictable juggling with the batting order. The day ended with a dinner at the Bedford Hotel. The visitors were late getting home to Plymouth; the railway line which was to revolutionise transport between the two towns did not open until 1859.

A number of clubs in Devon were founded at about the same time as the one at Tavistock. Their common experience was that it was one thing to assemble an interested squad, to acquire a ground, and to gather the basic range of equipment, but quite another to produce a programme of competitive fixtures. This resulted partly from inexperience and natural self-doubt about relative standards. It was, for instance, three years before the Isca Club, established in Exeter in 1849, felt that sufficient improvement had taken place to 'embolden the members to try their powers with the other clubs of the county'. More fundamental were the practical problems of communication. The railway did not reach Tavistock until 1859. In the early years of the club, journeys to and from matches were long, costly, and difficult to organise. These factors, together with the relative scarcity of clubs within a reasonable radius, meant that there were too few fixtures to fill the season, or even to keep the players in some condition of match-fitness. This was understood, and presented no problems, because it was assumed that, as for instance would be the case with a bowling or a tennis club, a significant part of the regular pattern was the organisation of cricket within the club. The over 25s might play the under 25s, or the married men might take on the single men. These were not beer games, or selection exercises, but real contests, often referred to as field days, which formed part of the club's programme. A remnant of this feature survives in such occasions as President's Days.

'Meeting Neighbours in Friendly Rivalry'

The scores and reports that were carried, somewhat sporadically in the early years, in the local press, were contributed by correspondents of varying degrees of reliability. Some felt the need to put a highly personal gloss on the proceedings that they were reporting. And some certainly went too far for the ever-cautious editor. A report in the *Exeter Flying Post* of a game in July 1860 in which Tavistock beat Okehampton by 16 runs contained a suitably high-minded admonition:

> 'We would remind the gentleman who favoured us with the score, and some comments thereupon, that the office of umpire is a most thankless one, and that, however conscientious his decisions may be, he must displease some parties'.

There were also the local reporters who thought that cricket could best be described in flowery prose. Here is what happened when, on the afternoon of July 15th 1864, Okehampton's Balcomb bowled to Tavistock's Chowen:

> 'Balcomb caused a disagreeable rattle behind Chowen, and, on his looking round, he found the symmetry of his wicket was sadly interfered with, and he had to retire from the field of play'.

In the main, however, it was a question of reporting a victory or a defeat, with perhaps some outstanding individual achievement, even if you felt bound to point out that the visitors arrived an hour late.

All these elements were present on July 11th 1864 in a Tavistock V Okehampton derby. The game finally got under way at noon, and then H. Scobell, one of two brothers who played for Tavistock in the 1860s, scored 78 not out in a total of 175, and then took 4 wickets with his fast round-armers as Okehampton crashed to defeat.

It was to be another three years before the first century in the club's history was recorded. On Tuesday August 27th 1867, in a match at Plymouth against the Royal Marines, A. Henley, who appears to have played for the club for only one season, scored 144 out of a total of 267. He could well have been Anthony Henley, who played for Dorset for a number of seasons, and had one first-class game for Hampshire. It was usual, after a game either home or away, for the teams to dine together, the Bedford Hotel being a frequent venue. One can imagine the celebrations that took place at the Plymouth hotel on the evening of Henley's match. They would certainly not have caught the last train home, which left Plymouth at 7.45!

The Marines were one of the forces teams that provided regular opposition during the early decades. There were also the established town clubs, like Okehampton, Launceston, and Plymouth, who quickly set a pattern of offering both a home and an away fixture each season. And there were a handful of local schools, such as Tavistock Grammar School and Kelly College, who put out strong sides composed jointly of masters and senior boys.

Stronger village sides, such as Milton Abbot, were also given fixtures. Smaller clubs, like Gulworthy, which could not provide the same level of competition, were offered games against club players who, usually because of extreme age or youth, could not make the team. In these circumstances a Second Eleven was born. It was operating in 1863, although its existence thereafter was not continuous and its fixture list was often thin.

If matches against Okehampton often produced an extra edge of competitiveness which resulted in occasional friction, then this rivalry was overshadowed by the one that developed between Tavistock and Launceston. A number of matches between the clubs were played in the early years, but it was not until 1861 that Tavistock recorded a victory by bowling Launceston out for less than the 50 that they needed to continue their run of success. In the following year the fixture was played at The Ring in August. Tavistock made 112, and dismissed their opponents for 53. In the second innings the home side scored 122, leaving Launceston a target of 182 for victory. When they had reached 34 for 5 an incident, sadly unrecorded, occurred, which led to a quarrel and to the premature end of the game. Fences had, it seemed, been mended by the next summer, 1863, when the two sides managed to play out a tight and exciting match, which Tavistock won by 9 runs, Carpenter top-scoring in both innings and Youren and Barnett taking the wickets between them. It may be that feelings had gone deeper than some imagined. At any event, there is no record of a fixture between the two clubs between 1863 and 1872, when two games were played, apparently without major incident. In 1873 Launceston hosted a game on July 10th, and were humiliated when, in reply to Tavistock's 165, they scored 47 and 13 for 6. A short anonymous report in the *Tavistock Gazette* spoke of the Launceston batsmen 'disappearing rather with the rapidity of shadows than of men', and ended with the observation that:

> 'a few of the Launceston men may be seen hovering in the dusk of the evening over the scene of their defeat, but they have not been seen either to play or to smile since'.

In the next edition there was an angry response from an anonymous Launcestonian who thought that the report had been 'ridiculous, illogical, absurd, and cowardly'. He went on to raise one of those contentious issues that have continued to affect relationships in local sport down the years, by claiming that:

> 'a perusal of the list of names of the Tavistock eleven reveals the fact that four were not inhabitants'.

The guilty men were named as:

> 'B.F. Edyvean, being a native of Bodmin; the Hon. C.H. Butler and J. Adams, being members of the Plympton club; and Bewes, being a native of Plymouth'.

In subsequent correspondence, attention focused on young Edyvean, who had scored 43 in the Tavistock innings. He had, indeed, been born in Bodmin, although he had attended Tavistock Grammar School. No attempt was made to establish any particular local links for Butler, Adams, or Bewes, and, in fact, none of them played for the club after the 1873 season. Cannon fire continued across the Tamar for some time, and the smoke was to take a long time to clear. The Tavistock club received some unfortunate publicity as a result of the incident. One correspondent acidly told the club that if they:

> 'could not venture to meet their neighbours in friendly rivalry without resorting for aid to an indefinite number of players, connected with no one knows who and coming from no one knows where, they will earn a far more creditable reputation by remaining at home and by practising until they are in a position to do so'.

So there!

Such hiccups apart, relations between the club and its rivals were generally amicable. The one playing regulation that continued to cause occasional annoyance was the one that related to unconcluded matches. The normal convention was that, if by the time stumps were drawn a two-innings-a-side game had not been concluded, the issue should be decided on the basis of first innings scores. However, this had to be agreed by the captains before the start of play. In July 1863, in a home game against the Plymouth Garrison, the visitors made 134 and 112, and the hosts 120 and 44 for 2. A Plymouth newspaper claimed a victory for the soldiers. The Tavistock club insisted that, no prior agreement having been made, the game had been drawn. The latter view prevailed. But such differences were rare. More typical was the kind of occasion when a large happy crowd watched a friendly contest which was punctuated by a wholesome lunch provided by Mr Yelland and by a sociable dinner at the Bedford when stumps were drawn.

September 6th 1873 saw even more in the way of attractions. The opponents were the Eleventh Regiment, and they brought their band with them to play throughout the proceedings. There was a large gathering, and the ground was encircled by refreshment booths and ice cream vendors. The new pavilion was in use, and Tavistock won the game. God indeed was in his heaven. And, of course, there were showers.

Bigwigs, Brothers, and Professionals

From its beginnings the club attracted the support of many of the leading figures in the professional and commercial life of the town. Often this support was expressed in financial terms, in giving a donation or becoming a vice-president, or in attendance at matches. The occasion of the game against the Eleventh Regiment, for example, was adorned by the presence of a large gathering of city fathers, churchmen, and leaders of society, with their wives and daughters. Occasionally, such figures were found among the playing members of the club. William Northway, the long-time proprietor of the Bedford Hotel and a founder-member of the Urban District Council, played from the 1850s to the 1870s. So did Christopher Bridgmen, a well-known solicitor, who on one occasion in 1864, in a game against Devonport, hit the first three balls that he received for 5, 6, and 6, all run of course. And so did Reginald Gill, member of a very illustrious local family, under the terms of whose will the Gill Wing was to be added to the town's hospital. The Gill family, in fact, provided Tavistock with more than one player, and there were other dynasties, like the Barnetts and the Chaves, who served the club well. The Edyvean whose exploits against Launceston caused such a furore was one of three brothers who played during the 1870s. The same decade saw the appearances of three Clarke brothers, the most effective of who, P. T., was a very free hitter, but was, according to a contemporary observer, prone to become 'undone on an untrue wicket', a judgment that would surely apply to all but a very few players at any level in any age. The two Scobells played together. One of them bowled round-armers at such a fearsome pace that every delivery that passed the bat seemed to go for byes, however many long-stops were posted. Byes from his bowling top-scored for Liskeard in their one-wicket victory in August 1865. One delivery travelled so far that six had been run before the ball, presumably by some relay arrangements, found its way back to the wicket keeper.

Then there were the brother Toop, who were regulars in the mid 1860s. The Hammicks, who played together a few years later, were the sons of the Vicar

Tavistock Cricket Club's first captain.
Richard Sleeman was thirty-six when the club was founded. In the previous year he had succeeded his father as Vicar of Whitchurch. He was photographed in about 1860 during one of his rare visits to his vicarage. He was more often seen at The Ring, where he was not only first captain but the pioneer ground curator.

TAVISTOCK v. ROYAL ARTILLERY.

This match was played on Monday on the Plymouth ground, ending, it will be seen, triumphantly for the Tavistock Club.

ROYAL ARTILLERY.

First Innings.		Second Innings.	
Lieut. Williams, b J. F. Scobell	4	c Clark, b. Burd	5
Bombardier Smith, c J. F. Scobell	5	c Voules, b Clark	2
Sergt. Shoesmith, b Burd	1	not out	24
Capt. Richardson, b J. F. Scobell	0	c Garnier, b Scobell	0
Capt. Ryan, b Scobell	0	b Scobell	0
Lieut. Bent, b Burd	1	b Burd	0
Capt. Duncan, b Scobell	0	b Burd	0
Capt. Franklin, b Scobell	11	b Burd	0
Sergt. Knibbs, b Burd	5	c Voules, b Burd	8
Bombardier Knibbs, run out	3	run out	5
Gunner Bedford, not out	0	b Burd	4
Extras	16	Extras	23
Total	46	Total	71

TAVISTOCK.

W. Clark, c Ryan, b Smith	7
A. Henley, l b w, b Ryan	35
J. C. Garnier, b Smith	0
Rev. S. Voules, c and b Ryan	41
J. F. Scobell, run out	6
Rev. Mr Walker, b Bent	17
C. V. Bridgman, c and b Bent	6
Rev. R. Sleeman, l b w, b Bent	2
H. Scobell, c Smith, b Shoesmith	22
Tanner, b Bent	0
Burd, not out	9
Extras	12
	157

TAVISTOCK v. ROYAL MARINES.

This match was played on the Plymouth ground on Tuesday, when there was a magnificent display of cricket. Mr Henley's 144 for Tavistock was a glorious innings.

ROYAL MARINES.

First Innings.		Second Innings.	
T. M. Whale, b. Burd	1	c Burd, b Tanner	12
H. A. Peake, c. Garnier, b Burd	16	c Garnier, b Henley	34
J. F. Luxmore, b Burd	0	b Bennett	13
A. B. Liardet, c Henley, b Burd	7	l b w, b Henley	0
A. F. Blyth, c Sleeman, b Burd	0	b Henley	0
F. M. Eden, b Voules	2	b Burd	34
A. Hill, c. Scobell, b Burd	0	c Garnier, b Bennett	2
C. A. Masters, b Voules	5	c Henley, b Bennett	0
Capt Forbes, b Burd	0	b Henley	41
C. G. Harston, b Voules	0	not out	0
E. A. M. Liardet, not out	0	run out	0
Extras	3	Extras	22
Total	34	Total	158

TAVISTOCK.

A. Henley, s Eden, b Peake	144
W. Clark, c Whale, b Peake	4
Rev. S. Voules, c Peake, b Liardet	33
J. Carpenter-Garnier, c Liardet, b Peake	25
H. Scobell, l b w, b Peake	16
E. A. Bennett, s Eden, b Peake	5
E. Burd, c Masters, b Peake	6
F. Tanner, run out	4
Rev. R. Sleeman, not out	0
C. V. Bridgman, c Eden, b Peake	1
Capt Duncan, run out	0
Extras	29
Total	267

Among the earliest surviving match details are these two cards, printed in the *Tavistock Gazette*, for games played on 26th August and 27th August 1867. Sleeman was by now nearing the end of his career, and was slipping down the batting order. Henley's century against the Marines was, as far as it is known, the first in the club's history. A certain Anthony Henley had played for Hampshire in the previous season, and the evidence suggests that this was the same man, in which case he was the first first-class cricketer to play for Tavistock.

The original pavilion, erected in 1860 was blown down in the gales of 1872, and no picture of it survives. It was replaced by this building, which was completed in July 1873, and was to remain, largely unchanged, through much of the next century of the club's life. The builder was Daniel Westaway. A stone set high in the northern wall carries the date, and thus commemorates the opening.

Dead or strayed away,

THE TAVISTOCK CRICKET CLUB,

that for some years has been accustomed to
Play at Playing
On Whitchurch Down.

When last seen, the Club exhibited in its few remaining members, all the symptoms of weakness
that precede final dissolution ;
among which may be enumerated
long fits
of absence from the ground,
feeble, wild play when on it ; striking at empty space,
mistaking the earth for the ball, and any point
of the compass for the wicket.

Such a state filled its friends with solicitude, and induced them to make vigorous efforts for its recovery. It was thought desirable it should be put on a tonic course of bowling, and a professor was engaged to administer, but after a few applications the patient refused the bolus. Under the impression that the club might have something on its mind steps were taken to induce a confession ; but nothing could be elicited but a declaration of belief that "Cricket came by nature," and an incoherent reference to the "professional bowler," as though his mere presence would make it "all right ole fellah."

Of course the confessor retired.

Since the beginning of this season the few faithful officials of the club have been seen wandering about in a disconsolate manner over the ground, making "night hideous," and themselves especially so, by
their cries and gesticulations.

Should any one hear of the club and will communicate
with its officers,
they will be rewarded for their trouble,
not indeed by any gift of money,
but by the presentation of the last cricket ball
used by the club,
which will be found on inspection
to be as good as new.

A supporter of the club, probably the paper's editor, entered this 'obituary' in the columns of the *Tavistock Gazette* on 28th June 1867. This was fifteen years before the famous spoof obituary of English cricket that appeared in *The Sporting Times* and gave birth to the idea of The Ashes.

of Milton Abbot, and the Tancocks, three of them, were the sons of the Rev. Osborne Tancock, who became Vicar of Tavistock in 1857. One of them, in 1860, made the highest score hitherto recorded for the club, 82 out of a total of 136. Another, called after his father and also destined for the church, played in 1858 for the Gentlemen of Devon and Cornwall against an All England Eleven, a side which included John Wisden, the founder of the great cricketing almanack. Two of the brothers scored between them in the 1859 season 301 of the 770 runs that the club scored it that season.

The interesting relationship between the Church of England and the game of cricket, which has been expressed at every level from test matches to village cricket, was clearly seen at work in Victorian Tavistock, and not only with the Hammicks and the Tancocks. A particular link was forged between Whitchurch Rectory and The Ring by the Rev. Sleeman, the first captain. The path that over the years he wore between the two places was to be frequently trodden by one of his successors, the Rev. Sammy Featherstone.

It was quite common in the middle of the nineteenth century for clubs like Tavistock, as well as those with larger resources or ambitions, to hire professionals. A 'pro' would be recruited, on a one-season contract, and would be required to play, to coach, and to prepare wickets. The first record of such an engagement by the local club came in a *Tavistock Gazette* report of May 6th 1859:

> 'Last Tuesday was the first playing day of the season, and was inaugurated by the arrival of Newham, the professional. Owing to the boisterous state of the weather, there was not so large a gathering as was expected, but those who did attend were speedily "nowhere" by the smart bowling of Mr Newham. We are glad to hear that so many of the younger members are showing signs of taking a respectable stand'.

The new arrival did, at least, get one 'Mr'. Normally, cricket protocol required that a professional's name appeared without style or initial. Some will remember the remnants of such conventions in the Gentlemen V Players matches at Lord's. Whatever they called Newham, it is not clear what happened to him. He features in none of the eight scorecards for the 1859 season that have survived, and, after that May evening in the wind, when he got so many of the young bloods 'nowhere', he is not mentioned again. At the beginning of the following season, 1860, there was a resolve to have a professional, but nothing came of it. No further initiative in that direction appears to have been taken until 1866, when a J. Jackson was recruited from Lancashire. He may have been the John Jackson who, having been born in Lancaster in 1841, played once for his native county in 1867. He arrived in Tavistock at the beginning of May, and began a pattern of coaching sessions, though no record has survived of his achievements on the field. The cost of him to the club, in payments and expenses, was just over £30, and since this was almost exactly the average level of annual income, there had to be a special subscription to pay his costs. It is not clear whether members felt that they had got their money's worth out of Jackson. There was to be no similar appointment until 1882.

An Early Death?

Occasional attempts were made, in the early years, to encourage boys to take up cricket at an early age. In 1862, for example, fixtures were arranged to match a youth team against colts from Milton Abbot and from Gulworthy. The initiative suffered from two weaknesses. One was that the representative side tended to be limited to sons, or other relatives, of senior players, rather than to be seen as reaching out to the wider community. And secondly there was no attempt to establish a colts team as a permanent feature of the club's activities. At the Annual General Meeting in April 1860, some disquiet was expressed at the level of support which was being given by the young men of the town. One member feared that the recently-formed Rifle Corps 'would materially injure the cricket club' by offering an alternative channel for the direction of surplus energy at the end of a week's work.

Whether because of the existence of counter-attractions, or for other reasons, there began to grow, during the 1860s, an atmosphere, in and around the club, of decline. Supporters began to look back on the 1850s as a golden age, to be contrasted with a period of waning interest and diminishing commitment. In 1864 criticism began to focus on the performance of the team, and particularly on the fielding, the poor quality of which, it was said, reflected lack of practice.Tuesdays throughout the season had been set aside as practice days, with a two o'clock start. There had, it seems, been a falling-off in attendance in recent years. Not everyone, of course, found it as easy as the student, the parson, or the solicitor, to get a Tuesday afternoon off. Individual voices became a chorus in 1865, when one supporter echoed what had become a prominent theme:

> 'We don't know whether Tavistock has a desire to keep up its cricket club. If it has, a very different course must be pursued and the players must meet regularly for practice. We frequently go to The Down of a practice day and find only two or three of the members present, and this being so it cannot be wondered at that they are beaten'.

They were, in fact, to be beaten in every match throughout the season. On August 1st they lost to Okehampton by an innings and 55 runs, after being dismissed in their second innings for 15, a performance that drew from the *Tavistock Gazette* the despairing reflection that 'of all the cricket we have ever witnessed, we never saw anything so bad'. At the end of the season, Tom Chave felt that he ought to defend the players and the club. He admitted that distractions such as 'The Volunteer fete, the election, and the Royal Agricultural Exhibition' might have affected attendances at practices. But he claimed that the playing record was not as bad as it appeared. Some of the games had been close. Liskeard, for example, in spite of the advantage of having a professional, had only squeezed home by 1 wicket. The defeat by Okehampton had, indeed, been degrading, but it needed to be pointed out that out of 12 games between the two rivals, Tavistock had won 9. Certainly the season had been a difficult one, but it should be seen in the wider context of earlier successes. There was an acid response from a correspondent in the *Gazette*. Of the distractions offered as explanations by the hapless Chave, he commented that:

> 'It has come to this, that a cricketer can regard politics as more important than his own proper game!'

The year 1866 began with declarations from officers, committee, and players, that the fortunes of the club were to be turned round. The bold decision to employ a professional may have had some effect on the playing record, but, in the absence of other measures to improve the situation, it was not long before the old complaints were being heard again. In June some wag inserted the following notice in the columns of the local paper:

> 'Lost, not stolen or strayed, the senior members of the Tavistock Cricket Club. Whoever has found the same, and would bring them to Whitchurch Down on Tuesdays and Saturdays shall be rewarded for their trouble'.

The malaise that had affected the playing performance now appeared to spread to the organisation. The fixture list contracted. In 1868 the first game of the season was played on August 8th. An observer commented on:

> 'the nearly extinct marks of ancient popping creases, the holes where wickets once stood, and the other evidences of a generation of cricketers now passed away, but nothing to assure him that the game is still followed'.

In 1869 the rituals, like the A.G.M., were observed, but little else occurred, and, in all probability, no cricket was played. 'Cricket at Tavistock', mused one correspondent, 'is already a mere recollection – a shadow and phantom of the past'. The critical point came in June 1870 when a number of members, facing another barren summer, decided that the exercise was pointless and urged a voluntary winding-up. A number of younger players called for a reprieve and for the summoning of a special meeting. This was held on July 4th. It proved to be a turning point in the club's fortunes. Tom Chave and Henry Allen, sensing the need for new blood, resigned as secretary and treasurer, and were promptly offered life membership in recognition of their long service. They were replaced by Henry Trigg and Robert Luxton, and, before the season was out, there was a resumption of fixtures, albeit on a limited scale, together with a commitment to do something about improving the ground. John Carpenter had by then disappeared from the scene as a player, and had, at the beginning of the season, formally relinquished the captaincy after some seasons in which his involvement had been increasingly spasmodic. No successor was appointed.

The 1871 season saw a continuation of the modest recovery, but a report of an early-season game against the Naval Officers suggested that there was a long way to go:

> 'In days gone by the Tavistock Eleven carried with them a prestige which materially helped in their encounters, and they frequently returned with increased laurels. Although some interest has been manifested in the club this

> season, and the wickets have been fairly manned on practising days, there has not been anything like the number of old experienced hands seen with the bat, and the field has consequently had to be taken by young blood.'

The young blood on that particular day went under by an innings and 14 runs. The feeling that the club was offering little leadership, either on or off the field, was widely expressed in 1873, in spite of the extended fixture list, the relative success in playing terms, and the opening of the new pavilion. A letter to the *Gazette* made a plea for strong captaincy:

> 'To such as remember the club some twelve years ago, it is now a pitiful sight to see the same club engaged in a match. The fielding is slovenly, the bowling erratic, and the batting remarkable only for its want of form'.

The captaincy issue was at the centre of the correspondence that ensued. 'What we want', one member argued, 'is an energetic cricketer, resident in the town, who shall as captain regulate the working of the club'. There was criticism of the practice of appointing captains on a match basis, which made continuity, in playing terms, very difficult. Equally it was felt that a strong skipper would provide the leadership off the field which was not offered by a president whose only function was 'to carve the beef at match dinners'.

This side-swipe at President Carpenter produced a reply which was anonymous but probably came from Mount Tavy. The president's work had covered more than mere joint-carving. Who, for instance, had persuaded the Bedford Office to provide a new pavilion? What came out of all this was general support for the principle of appointing, at the A.G.M., a strong captain with wide powers, to serve for the season. All that remained was to find him. He did not immediately emerge. In spite of that, there seemed to be a renewed confidence flowing through the veins. A plan for a cricket week in August proved to be a little over-ambitious, but a three-day festival, limited in the event to two days, proved a success, and spirits remained sufficiently high for the season to continue until Saturday October 3rd.

In 1875, with the appointment of a strong captain, the club could be said to have emerged from the long period of depression, which, at some points over the previous fifteen years, had threatened its very existence.

For many years the club was able to peg the level of the subscription at the original rate. Members paid five shillings (25p) a year, with those under the age of seventeen paying half a crown (12½p). The club's accounts were always in balance, thanks mainly to the careful stewardship of successive treasurers, Henry Allen and Robert Luxton. No evidence survives of membership numbers, but it appears that the club was able to hold a firm nucleus of committed support throughout the difficult years. And with a limited playing programme there were, of course, fewer expenses. The 1866 accounts, when income was reported as £37 and expenditure as £20, were a record of a fairly typical year. Significantly, in 1875, with a general revival of activity and therefore an increase in costs and expenses, the balance was only £3.

Approving the accounts was one of the regular functions of the Annual General Meeting, held each year in March or April. There was also the question of electing a president, vice-presidents, a treasurer, a secretary, and a committee of six. More often than not, particularly in the age of such stalwarts as Chave, Allen, and Carpenter, it was a question of re-election. The meetings would usually end with arrangements for weekly, or twice-weekly, practice sessions. Pious hopes would be expressed about regular and full attendances at practice, but everyone assumed that it would be a struggle to get people there, as it always had been. At the other end of the season came the annual dinner, a permanent fixture in the club's calendar from the first season, and held in one of the town's hotels each autumn. It was generally well-attended, and provided opportunities for endless toasts and speeches, in which a captain's review of the playing season might follow a civic dignatory's tribute to the country's armed forces. It was most of all, and quite rightly, the occasion for self-congratulation. Another annual occasion that stretched out more widely to the local community was the sports festival that the club organised at The Ring at the end of each season. A reference in 1866 to this being held 'following a commendable custom' suggests that the tradition was already well established by then.

Because so little evidence of the playing record of the club in the early years has survived, it is impossible to judge whether the view, commonly expressed in the 1860s and 1870s, that there had been a golden age of success in the 1850s, was a correct one. In the first ten seasons, from 1849 to 1858, we know of only 10 games, 5 of which were won and 5 lost. In the next decade, from 1859 to 1868, we have the results of 39 games, of which 25 were won, 13 lost, and 1 drawn. For the five years from 1869 to 1873, a period that included the blank season of 1869, we know of a further 19 matches, which brought 9 victories and 9 defeats. All that can be said, therefore, of the playing record in the first quarter of a century of the life of the club is that if the results that have survived are a fair reflection of that record, then the club won 59% of its matches. That so few were drawn is an indication that the convention relating to the first innings lead in unfinished matches seemed to have been widely respected, and that most matches provided at least an innings a side. We do not, of course, know how many games were abandoned because of the weather.

'A Task for a Gentleman'

Between 1874 and 1888 details of the playing record become much more plentiful. This is almost entirely due to the reporting of games by the *Tavistock Gazette*, which now became a more frequent exercise as the club increasingly saw the advantages to be derived from a close relationship with the local press. In those fifteen years, the results of 183 games were reported. This is almost certainly the great majority of the matches that were played. There were 108 victories, 59 defeats, and 16 draws, giving a success rate of 59% and a tally of wins that was nearly double the number of losses. It was an impressive achievement, particularly in the light of the difficulties of the preceding years. It would be right to turn first to captaincy in the search for the causes of this renaissance.

Arthur Hill was an officer in the Royal Marines. (The Christian name was, of course, only used by his parents; to everyone else he was Captain A. M. Hill.) He began playing for the club in 1874, and was appointed captain in 1875. After two seasons in charge, he left the area, when his regiment was posted away from its Plymouth base. Returning in 1879, by which time he had reached the rank of major, he resumed his cricket career at The Ring, including the captaincy, which he held, alongside the post of secretary, for a further four years. He last led out a Tavistock side in 1883, the year in which he retired from the service. As a player, his strength lay in his steady batting, based on a sound technique and a useful range of off-side shots. He was also an agile fielder in the covers. But his most important contribution to the side, and to the club, was his strong, firm leadership on and off the field. He was responsible for the purchase of nets and for essential repairs to the pavilion. More generally, he brought the necessary element of discipline at a crucial time.

During the two years that he was away, 1877 and 1878, the duties of captaincy were taken over by the Rev. Samuel W. Featherstone, affectionately known as Sammy, who was, in 1883, to succeed his father as Vicar of Whitchurch. His long playing career, which began in 1876, was one of the most consistently successful in the club's history. Though predominantly a bowler, he made a lot of runs, topping the averages, for example, in 1880, with an average of 34. He was described in 1885 as 'one of the best bowlers in the west of England, a fast run getter, and good all-round player'. In 1888 he played for Devon. In one game for Tavistock he took 6 wickets, all clean bowled, with consecutive balls. Sammy was a young, dashing, popular cricketer, with a lot of natural talent, who led by example and by radiating his infectious enthusiasm for the game. He also had a sense of humour. Not many could have carried off what he achieved when, attending a temperance meeting in 1876, he persuaded his earnest audience that his own experience as a 'partial abstainer' had made life more difficult for him than it would have been if he had been a teetotaller.

Two other men who each held the captaincy briefly during the early 1880s were the brothers Spencer, sons of the veteran headmaster of the Tavistock Grammar School. Kingsley, the elder brother, held both holy orders and a doctorate. He was to run the old grammar school in Russell Street after his father's retirement. He played for eleven years, had a good technique as a batsman, but was thought, in spite of having a strong drive on both sides of the wicket, to have never delivered, in terms of long innings, what his talents promised. His good deep fielding and safe catching helped to improve a department which had attracted much criticism. Herbert was a lawyer. His 375 runs made at an average of 26.1 when batting at Number 3 in the 1885 season brought this tribute from the secretary, J. J. Camozzi:

> 'He is the safest and best bat in the team, standing the brunt of the bowling and generally making good scores. He is also a change bowler, very difficult to play'.

He was captain the following year when he made the highest innings of the season by a Tavistock player of 93 not out. Apart from a very brief period when, in mid-season 1884, J.G. Wolferstan, another half of a cricketing pair, took over from Kingsley Spencer, the only other captain in the period up to 1888 was E.W. Chilcott. The Hammick brothers, who had the right pedigree for the job, had by then moved on and away. One was commanding H.M.S. *Invincible*. The other, a captain in the 43rd Regiment, was serving in India.

Edward Chilcott had begun his playing career in 1882 at the age of nineteen. He was then an undergraduate at Cambridge, where he was a Rugby Blue. His father had established a law firm at Tavistock, and Edward entered it, taking over its leadership when his father retired in the 1890s. At the same time he inherited his father's second role of clerk to the local magistrates. Edward was to be, for many years, up to his death in 1931, a significant public figure, prominent in Conservative politics, and for ten years a member of the Urban District Council. The family home, Chollacott Lane House, was a stone's throw from both The Ring and the golf course, and Edward, who was a natural ball player, spent a good deal of time at both venues, captaining, at different times, both clubs.

As a cricketer he was blessed with a good eye and great agility. Described in 1885 as 'a fast run-getter and a sensational hitter', he, on one occasion during that season, made 9 from one hit. In addition to his batting, he set a good example in the field. This was the department that was to give him most concern during his captaincy, and in which he was to set standards that alarmed some of the more portly and ageing playing members. His practice of jotting down scores and notes after a game provides us with examples of his thinking on this, and on other aspects of the game. On June 24th 1887, after a game against Kelly College, he noted that the headmaster's wife had provided tea, but went on to record that 'the fielding was very bad indeed; several catches were missed, some not properly tried for'. In the same month, following a defeat at the hands of Plymouth College, he acknowledged Mrs Chilcott for laying on the tea, but then recorded a litany of dropped catches, and a complaint against two players who arrived late: 'Prowse and Liddell did not come until we had lost 8 wickets'. The guilty men were usually named.

After his second match in charge, there was a thank you to Mr Northey for giving a tea, but there were knuckle-raps for the butter-fingered: 'Chave, behind the wicket, missed several, Neat missed one, and Harris one'. On June 16th it was Mrs Featherstone's turn to be thanked for tea. This time 'the fielding was abominable, with sixteen or seventeen catches missed, some ridiculously easy ones'. By the time of his fifth match in charge, on July 2nd, the tone was changing a little. The fielding was 'a little better but not much'. Opener J. Bevan 'fielded very badly, but has not played much this year'. There was praise for Chave's 'faultless innings of 41'. But there were still more grumbles about the difficulties that there sometimes are in raising a team. The latter complaint continued to be a theme, even in a season that saw a Second Eleven playing 8 matches.

By mid-season the comments had become more temperate and balanced. This was, presumably, either because there had been an improvement in standards, or because the captain had readjusted his expectations. In any event, by late July Chilcott was not only thanking Mrs Neat for the tea, but was complimenting Prouse on his wicket keeping, and was displaying one of his most endearing characteristics, a capacity for taking his own share of the blame:

> 'being the day after the Kilworthy dance, some of us were not as fresh as usual'.

The fielding generally, he acknowledged, had improved a good deal by the end of the season.

That a captain's lot is not always a happy one was, however, illustrated in the last match of the season, against the South Staffordshire Regiment at The Ring, when the home side was undone by Sergeant Major Else's fast underhands. James Chave kept wicket, performed 'moderately' in the first innings, but 'left the ground before the second innings without saying a word!'

And there were problems of weather and travel. On Tuesday July 26th, there set out at 8.45 a.m. for a fixture at Liskeard 'the best team that I have ever been away with for the club'. A brake and four had been hired from Truscott, one of the local carriers. The horses were poor, the harness broke two or three times on the way, and the driver was drunk. The party, which included a scorer, an umpire, and three or four supporters, arrived at Liskeard at 11.45. It rained all day, and no play was possible. The party left at 4 o'clock, took tea at Callington, and arrived home at 8. It was, recorded the captain, 'a great disappointment'.

Chilcott was a very popular captain, essentially fair-minded and, once he had got into his stride, as ready to praise as to blame. In early 1888 James Chave had been forgiven his indiscretions, was being praised for his batting, and was even said to have kept wicket 'fairly well'. In mid-season, when an away game at Crediton, necessitating an awkward rail journey with a change at Yeoford Junction, was played on a difficult pitch, the fielding lapses were excused on the grounds that the outfield was bumpy. Chave 'kept wicket very well', and the only target for criticism was the captain himself, who 'missed a bad catch at cover'. This was the game in which the underarm bowling employed by G. C. Smith, a member of the home attack, was by now such an unusual feature as to require particular comment. When Smith reappeared against Tavistock a month later, this time playing for Exeter, he took 6 wickets. By the end of the day, Chilcott had learned that Smith had inherited £3000 a year from his grandfather, a clergyman, whose daughter had eloped with the man who became Smith's father. With such gossip did Victorian cricketers entertain each other in the pavilion when the action on the field failed to distract them.

It seemed as if young Chilcott was mellowing. Not so. Bad performances still brought flashes of anger and strong criticism. When against Liskeard on July 19th the Spencer brothers pulled out at the last minute, and Tavistock were walloped by 160 runs, his diary tersely recorded that 'none of our bowlers could bowl a decent ball'. Much more congenial was the last game of the season, at the Royal Naval Engineering College:

'Went to Devonport by the 10.32. Walked to the ground having sent bags by cab. Began about 12 o'clock. The worst wicket I ever played on. Very pleasant fellows to play against. Gave us lunch in the college and beer on the ground. Came back by the 7 train from Devonport'.

An All-Round Recovery

If successive captains played major roles in restoring the fortunes of the Tavistock club in the 1870s and 1880s, then other officials also played their parts. Two former players, John Carpenter and Reginald Gill, the former an M.P. and the latter a J.P. and county councillor, occupied in turn the presidential chair, and although neither played an active part in club affairs they proved to be ideal figure-heads, providing money and connections. Robert Luxton, treasurer throughout the 1870s, was succeeded by James Wolferstan. When James emigrated to New Zealand in 1885 he took with him a bat presented to him by his fellow-players. The treasurer's seat was now occupied by his brother Harold, who in turn handed on to John Jarrett Daw. Daw was a businessman and one of the last holders of the ancient title of portreeve, then used to denote Tavistock's civic head.

The key post of secretary was, after Henry Trigg, filled temporarily by George Rench, a bank clerk, who moved away from the area quickly and suddenly leaving substantial personal debts, a circumstance that he blamed on his frequent changes of home. He was replaced, in turn, by six playing members. Three of these had also been captain, Wolferstan, Hill, and Spencer. The others were George Chapman, Tom Doidge, and Joseph Camozzi. Chapman, a well-connected official in the Bedford Estate Office, was to find his niche as the enthusiastic captain of the Second Eleven over a long period. As a player his natural abilities were modest. As a leader he had both presence and skill, and was able to relate to both the seasoned cricketer and the raw youth, the two elements that featured with equal value in any successful Second Eleven.

Doidge was a hatter with a shop opposite the parish church. He does not appear to have made his playing debut until 1874, when he was thirty-three, but thereafter he played regularly into the new century and into his sixties. He was described in 1885, when he was in his mid-forties, as 'the smartest field in the team', and as 'a safe catch'. With the bat, he established a reputation as a fierce hitter, 'good', it was said, 'if not elegant'. In a home game against Plymouth in 1876 it was said that 'by his hard hitting he gave his opponents much leather hunting among the furze, outside the chains and posts'. The 'all run' rule, of which this is a reminder, makes some of his feats with the bat in his later years even more remarkable. But it was as a bowler that Tom Doidge made his mark on the fortunes of the club. He bowled fast, was able to get the ball to rise from a length, and was lethal on an uneven pitch. In 1876 he twice took 4 wickets with successive balls. Ten years later his haul for the season was 65 wickets at an average of 7.1. With Sammy Featherstone at the other end, Tavistock had for a number of years as good an opening pair of bowlers as any in the county.

Joseph Camozzi was one half of Cundell and Camozzi, the Duke Street grocers who specialised in tea, wine, and spirits. A player of modest abilities, his commitment to the club was whole-hearted, and as both player and administrator he worked long and hard in its interest. To him, more than anyone else, goes the credit for the expansion of the fixture list and for the successful re-launching of the Second Eleven in 1884. This latter venture reflected a new atmosphere of confidence. Some doubted the capacity of the club to sustain two teams. The optimists, led by Camozzi, felt that they had won a significant victory when, on Wednesday August 20th, both elevens turned out on the same day. Not only that, but while the seconds were beating Lifton at The Ring, the firsts were returning with the laurels from Okehampton.

In 1879 the club's A.G.M. had to be adjourned when only one playing member turned up. It was the year in which Captain Hill returned after a two-year absence to take over as both secretary and captain. Over the course of the next decade the organisation was improved considerably. The committee was expanded and given more to do.

In 1885 there were 141 subscribers, whose contributions provided the club with an income of £50. Much of the balance in these years went towards ground improvements. From 1879 a groundsman was employed. At the end of that season a good deal of re-turfing was carried out, only for the turf to be torn up by vandals. The work continued, however, and by 1880 much of the playing area had been re-laid. Further work was undertaken in 1881, following a summer in which the *Tavistock Gazette* lamented that the club, by losing 5 of its 12 games, had 'come off rather worse than usual'. Confident that 1882 would be a better season, the paper pointed to the improvement that could be expected when players were able to practice on 'their excellent ground', which had been 'newly laid out'. Other improvements followed.

In 1885 a new, more effective roller appeared, bought locally, and at cost price, from Joe Mathews, a former player who was a partner in one of the local iron foundries. In 1887 the pavilion roof was damaged in a gale, and it was some time before the Bedford Office carried out the repairs. The beginning of the 1888 season saw, therefore, a tent. Captain Chilcott reported after the first game: 'We had a tent up, but had no tea', and, after the second: 'We were going to give tea but the tent was blown down'. Meanwhile the club, presumably on the instructions of its landlord, had the pavilion insured for £150 for a period of five years.

One popular form of fund-raising in the 1880s was the Club Ball. The one held on Wednesday January 28th 1885 was typical of such occasions. Over the previous two days much effort had gone into decorating the Town Hall, which featured many motifs and banners with cricketing themes. Some 150 attended, and, with the help of Mr Martin's string band, 'dancing was kept up with much spirit until 4 a.m.'

As in the first few years of its life, the club continued in the 1870s and 1880s to attract the active support of young men who, it was already clear, were destined to be significant figures in the life of the local community. In the latter years of the century there were no more substantial members of the town establishment than Edward Chilcott, solicitor, Edward Rundle, Duke's steward, Edward Yelland, businessman and councillor, and William Winney, headmaster and chairman of the council. They all played for Tavistock in the 1880s. And they all thereafter helped the club in a variety of practical ways. Edward Yelland, for instance, having followed the fortunes of the club down to his death in 1940, left it £50 in his will. Support in numbers from local families also continued an established tradition. Three Timaeuses, three Wests, and two Wolferstans, played at the same time. But the outstanding dynasty were the Spencers. Four sons of the Russell Street headmaster played between 1872 and 1888. In addition to Herbert and Kingsley, there were L.G. and Wilfred, both good all-round cricketers as well as useful footballers. It was an unusual Tavistock team that turned out in the 1870s or 1880s without at least one Spencer in the line-up. There were games in the mid-1880s when three of them played together, often scoring at least half the team's runs between them, and then taking their share of the wickets. They were a remarkable brood, and their father, who came to occupy a unique role as an elder statesman in the town, was very proud of them.

There were a handful of individuals who played during the Spencer era who would have qualified for long-service medals in terms of the length of their playing record, including a Bailey and a Batten, a Bundock and a Chapman. At the other extreme were those who came, saw, conquered, and left. What happened to F.S. Stokes, who played his first game against Plymouth in 1873, scored 41 and took 7 wickets, and then vanished without trace? And there were many others whose names appear fleetingly. Some of them were guesting in a way that was generally acceptable to most of the cricketing fraternity but gave rise to occasional inter-club spats. When R.E. Clitheroe played his one game at The Ring in 1875 and made 41, the club was at pains to pre-empt criticism by announcing that:

> 'he is on a visit to friends near Tavistock, but he is the only one in the side not regularly belonging to the Tavistock club'.

The range of occupations of a typical small-club side in the nineteenth century has given delight to more than one romantic cricket writer. The flannelled heroes of mid-Victorian Tavistock included Barrett the draper and Doidge the hatter, Mallett the painter and Nicholls the mine inspector, Luxton the solicitor and Liddell the doctor. Pulpit, parade ground, and teacher's desk, each provided its quota. Between 1868 and 1888, sixteen clergymen played for the club, the Reverends Beatty, Drake, Drewe, Durham, Featherstone, Ingram, Kingston, Luscombe, Neligan, Richards, Schuster, Scobell, Sleeman, Tancock, Walker, and Wills. Included in the list were young parsons, nonconformist ministers, and school chaplains, but the largest group were the fresh young curates, still in their early twenties but graduates of public school and university cricket, who had been appointed by well-disposed vicars with an eye to their potential for making runs as well as for writing sermons. Of the five serving officers who played, three, Duncan, Fisher, and Hill, were army captains, and two, Neat and Taylor, were naval lieutenants. Three of the six schoolmasters, Agnew May, John Tomlinson, and John Neligan, were masters at Kelly College, a school that, from its foundation in 1877, quickly established a cricket tradition, and formed a very close, and mutually helpful, relationship with the town club. Messrs Thornton and Winney ran small private schools in the town, and F.W. Bere taught at Plymouth College.

The experiment, conducted in 1859 and again in 1866, of employing a professional, had not, it was thought at the time, been a very encouraging one. It was not repeated until 1882. In that year, C.H. Cort appeared, playing his first game on June 17th. He was to serve for four seasons at The Ring, providing coaching and ground work in addition to playing. The club paid him £25 a season. In return for a subscription of one guinea over and above the normal club subscription of five shillings, members could have the pro bowl at them in the nets. Non-subscribers could enjoy the privilege for twenty minutes if they paid threepence. Employed as an all-rounder, Cort knew that his main duty on the field was to take wickets. The committee, believing the old cricketing adage that bowlers win matches, appreciated the runs that he made, but paid him to carry the burden of the bowling. In his first season he produced 68 runs in 10 innings, but took an average of 4.7 wickets per innings. In 1883 he made 109 runs at an average of 17, and took 49 wickets in 11 innings. The 1884 season saw him making 408 runs in 16 innings at an average of 26, and with a top score of 125, while he took 79 wickets at an average of 6. He bowled, in that season, 281 overs, as many as the other six leading bowlers put together, and 91 of them were maidens. His last season, in 1885, saw him make 103 against Liskeard, and come third in the batting averages with an average of 26. His 43 wickets cost 9 runs each.

It was not, perhaps, surprising that in September 1885 the club should provide him with a benefit. This took the form of proceeds from a specially arranged dance in the Town Hall. The club had reason to be grateful to him, and they showed it. While he was the most effective all-round cricketer in the side, he remained a journeyman among gentlemen. Amid the flurry of initials, he remained, simply, 'Cort'.

Old Rivalries

Some of the problems that the club had to confront in the early years remained unresolved as the century wore on. The experience of Mr Clitheroe and his holiday with friends highlighted the fact that there was no requirement of residential qualification, and that this situation contained the potential for continuing aggravation. Then there were the difficulties, and the bad feeling, arising from slack arrangements over hours of play. Three consecutive games in 1875, governed in theory by the same playing conditions, got under way at, respectively, 11 o'clock, 1 o'clock, and 'about the middle of the day'. A long delay would, as likely as not, be used as ammunition by one side which, at the end of the day, might feel aggrieved at the result. And, of course, Sod's Law decreed that such occasions were more frequent in fixtures involving

Okehampton or Launceston or Plymouth. Not that it had to be the clock that sparked off controversy when old rivals met. The *Tavistock Gazette* reported a home match against Okehampton in July 1883:

> 'Nothing about the game excited much interest, except the ill-behaviour of one of the Okehampton men, who, having imbibed too much stimulating liquor, set himself up as a pugilist. But on the appearance on the scene of a P.C., his valour quickly abated'.

It was only later made clear that the offender had been a spectator, not a player.

In August 1876, in the home game against Launceston, it was the visiting umpire who was at the centre of a storm of controversy. The rumpus came at the end of a game which Tavistock lost. The charge was made that the umpire had given out a Tavistock batsman without there having been an appeal. The laws of the game have always stipulated that 'the umpires shall not order a batsman out unless appealed to by the other side'. One of the Launceston players subsequently wrote to the press that he had, in fact, appealed. He went on to twist the knife, as the issues were widened beyond the immediate question of the umpiring incident:

> 'Allow me to take this opportunity of suggesting to the members of the Tavistock Cricket Club that when they have a match played on their ground again, they should previously take some little trouble to get it into a fit state to play upon.'

The fur flew. One respondent began by questioning the honesty of the Launceston players and their umpire, and went on to argue that the references to The Ring 'came ill from a member of a club whose ground is the worst in Europe.' The writer went on, now getting into his stride, to suggest that the correspondent from Launceston may have forgotten the occasion when one of the Launceston team, playing on his home ground, was patrolling the outfield when he disappeared from view in the jungle that surrounded him, and was not found for three days. And so it went on, to the delight, no doubt, of neutrals, and also to the evident bemusement of those for whom cricket and its mysteries remained as obscure as an oriental religion.

On Saturday August 21st 1880 Plymouth were the visitors at The Ring. They batted first and were all out for 65, at which point lunch was taken. The Tavistock innings proceeded quietly and uneventfully against a Plymouth attack that featured overarm bowling, a style that in 1880 was still unusual, although acceptable and uncontroversial. The target came into view with plenty of wickets in hand. The bowlers became desperate as they saw the game slipping away from them. The *Tavistock Gazette* described what happened next:

> 'In their hopeless despair they subjected the Tavistock batsmen to a series of "throws", which repeatedly elicited from the umpire a cry of "no ball". Strong expressions of vexation emanated from the lips of one of the bowlers as the character of the balls was unhesitatingly pronounced by the umpire, W.

> Williams, but that imperturbable individual kept up the cry of "no ball" at each delivery, and this produced the effect of inducing one of the "throwers" to change his tactics and try an underhand ball, the result being that a good hit was effected and several runs realised'.

As soon as the Tavistock innings closed, for a total of 100, the Plymouth side left the ground rapidly, although it was only five o'clock, and two further hours of cricket could have been played. The spectators were upset. Captain Hill, who had made arrangements for the usual post-match dinner, was indignant. And the *Gazette* was suitably lofty. Its report concluded:

> 'Had the tables been turned and the home eleven conquered, then the latter would no doubt have shown their victors how to bear defeat in a noble, manly, good-humoured spirited'.

Well, perhaps so. It is interesting that the reports that appeared in the two Plymouth newspapers contained no references at all to these goings-on. The *Western Morning News* confined itself to recording the result and the individual scores, and to naming the principal bowlers as Featherstone and Doidge on the one side and Gidley and Ford on the other. The 'guilty men' who had remained anonymous in the *Gazette* version were thus identified. The *Western Daily Mercury* provided an equally brief piece. It did, however, offer the view that 'Gidley and Ford bowled exceedingly well for the visiting team'!

Such incidents as these served to resurrect old grievances and to perpetuate ancient grudges. The behaviour of players, spectators, and commentators, may, on such occasions, have been trivial and childish. There is, however, behind this, something to be learned about the extent to which, particularly in a small community, the cricket club might have served as the focus for local loyalty. In the 1870s the club had to assume the role whether it wished to or not, since it had no rival. The football club did not appear until 1888, the hockey club till 1919, and the rugby club till 1927. There was, moreover, no competition for attention from professional sport in the area. In these circumstances, a visit to The Ring could be more than simply an opportunity to enjoy the fine arts of cricket. Something about the large numbers who took the long walk up to the Down spoke of communal loyalty and local identity. If visiting spectators came armed with similar emotions, we may, perhaps, not be too surprised that occasionally things were taken a bit too far.

Part Two: 1889–1914

The Age of Confidence

An Interlude

At the beginning of 1889, Edward Chilcott, having captained the side for two years, told the committee that he would be standing down. He would be away from the town for much of the year, and, while he hoped to play in a few late-season games, he would have to give up the captaincy. A grateful committee wished him well and presented him with a bat. The A.G.M. in March went along with his proposal that his replacement should be the Rev. Sammy Featherstone. The young Vicar of Whitchurch had played for the club since 1876. He was well qualified for the job, in both social and cricketing terms. This genial and talented all-round player was perfectly happy to take over in a situation which he and everyone else recognised as one in which he was keeping the seat warm for Chilcott for as long as the young lawyer needed to be away on his professional duties.

The A.G.M. that saw the change of captaincy also saw J. J. Camozzi give way to the pressures of business and relinquish the secretaryship. The task was taken on jointly by Tom Doidge, the happy hitting hatter, and Henry Neat, one of two sons of a retired clergyman, who was a regular player in the 80s and 90s. John Jarrett Daw, who was maintaining the helpful tradition of long-serving treasurers, reported that a membership of 116 had helped to generate an income of £68 in a year when expenditure had been £59. There was a feeling of general satisfaction, although there were the, by now, traditional grumbles about practice. It had been written into the rules of the club that Wednesday evenings were the regular practice sessions. There had, however, in the previous season, been occasions when only four or five members turned up. Although, as Chilcott, anxious to defend his players, was quick to point out, there had also been evenings when the attendance had been such that the net had been taken down and a double-wicket game played, with everyone batting for ten minutes. It was also reported, unfortunately without explanation, that there was a discussion 'about driving stakes to keep down the chain around the field'.

The first match of the 1889 season saw a novelty. The laws had just been changed to permit declarations. Tavistock's innings, against Kelly College, was closed at 139 for 5, before the school side was dismissed for 53. There followed a further 11 games over the course of the season, 6 of which were won. Following the success of an August Bank Holiday home game against Crediton in the previous year, the fixture was repeated. A large crowd, entertained by a band throughout the afternoon, enjoyed an interesting twelve-a-side game, but saw the home side go under by 58 runs after Chilcott, making a rare appearance, had been run out when batting with a tail-ender, mercifully unnamed. Over the season, Henry Neat topped the batting lists with an unexceptional average of 19. Doctor Liddell, who had played since 1883 and had scored a century in his second season, turned in useful performances with both bat and ball. And Herbert and Wilfred Spencer featured prominently throughout. As for the new captain, he did not make many runs, but topped the bowling averages, taking 21 wickets at 6 runs apiece in a season in which his appearances turned out to be limited. One reason for this was his selection for Devon against Cornwall, when he responded to the opportunity by taking 9 wickets in the two innings.

At the end of the 1889 season, the club decided to discontinue the practice of hiring a professional. The background here was that after Cort's four seasons in the mid 80s, there had been a gap of two years, before the appointment of Kerry in 1888. Previously a pro at an Oxford college, Kerry rewarded his employers, not only by keeping the ground in very good order, but by taking 62 wickets at an average of 7.7. This followed a rather enigmatic introduction of him by Chilcott at the 1887 dinner, as the deliverer of 'a kind of medium slow ball'. In 1889 he was replaced by Howland, who made a few useful runs, averaging 11, but whose 24 wickets were bought, it was thought, rather expensively at 12½ each. It was decided that the money spent on a pro could, at least for the 1890 season, be better spent. In the event, the money saved went in part to buy a water-tank to fit against the pavilion, and to re-lay 1100 square yards of the field. These two items cost £18 and £12. But pro or no pro, someone, had to be responsible for the general maintenance of the ground. The committee turned again to the man who had done the job in the two years' gap between Cort and Kerry. He was John Glanville Davey.

From its beginnings until well into its second century, the Tavistock club was, successively, closely associated with two families. There were, first of all, the Chaves, Tom and Jim. And then, from the 1880s, there were the Daveys. The founder of the Davey cricketing dynasty was John Glanville, or 'Glan'. A few years younger than Jim Chave, he followed him professionally in becoming a printer. He might have learned more than compositing from his older colleague. His club debut came in July 1885, when he made nought batting at Number 9. He was to develop into an impressive all-rounder, an attractive bat, a dangerous round-arm bowler, and a class slip field. Over a long period of service, he was to perform whole-heartedly on the field, and also to act, at different ends of his career, as groundsman and umpire, and to produce a son and a grandson who would, in turn, grace The Ring, as he himself had done for so long.

At the 1890 A.G.M. Sammy Featherstone was re-appointed as captain, and the club proceeded to a programme of 16 matches, 9 of which were won.

Traditional fixtures against locally based schools and regiments continued to feature in the programme, but there were constant efforts to widen the reach. In 1890 Bude and Saltash were entertained. The brunt of the bowling was borne by Doidge, Davey, and Featherstone, hatter, printer, and parson, with Dr. Liddell chipping in usefully from time to time. Francis Stowe made runs at an average of 17 in what was to be the last of six seasons in which he had batted dependably and fielded smartly. And ex-captain Chilcott again returned in August to make some useful scores at Number 8. Of the newer faces, Rev. Edward Wilson was to make a considerable impression. He had come to Tavistock in 1887 as a twenty-eight year old curate. He made his playing debut for the club in 1890, and took over as secretary in 1891. On the field he was an enthusiastic and competent, rather than a talented, cricketer, but the club has had few more popular officials than the young curate, who served as secretary for four years. The end was a very sad one. In September 1895 a new vicar arrived. The Rev. Le Neveu appears to have taken an immediate dislike to his senior curate, and in February 1896, after accusing him of being disloyal, he sacked him. There was uproar. Wilson's popularity in the town spread beyond St. Eustachius, and beyond The Ring. The Bishop tried to calm the situation by finding him a living near Dartmouth. Young Mr Wilson moved away, to general regret. In April, seven weeks after his departure, he died at the age of thirty-seven.

When the club held its annual, and by now traditional, end-of-season dinner, in November 1890, at the Bedford Hotel, the evening was marked by two striking speeches. One was from the veteran Thomas Youren, who was always called upon on these occasions to offer wisdom and reminiscences. This time, he rather surprised his audience by noting with approval the growing popularity of women's cricket. The other contributor was a newcomer to both club and town. John Divett had played a good deal of cricket before he came to Tavistock as manager of one of the local banks. His appearances on the field were now few, but he was immediately appointed vice-chairman, and it was in this capacity that he offered the thought, on that November evening over a century ago, that:

> 'cricket is an old and noble game, but I regret to say that it is not the noble game it was, and not only cricket but other games in England are not what they used to be'.

The culprits were then identified. Chasing after cups and other tangible rewards had turned players into 'pot hunters', and was threatening the amateur basis of the game. Standards of behaviour among spectators had deteriorated alarmingly; at a recent match at The Ring, he had left in embarrassment after ten minutes because of the obscenities hurled by onlookers at the visiting players. And finally cricket-lovers were being seduced by the attractions of a rival summer activity. He spelt it out. The threat was, of course, from 'that abominable game, lawn tennis'.

John Divett was not, of course, the only person to express the feeling that the great game was in decline. There have been those in every age who have told a story of declining standards, often as a reflection of a wider picture of national decay. More than most activities, perhaps, cricket gives expression to nostalgia. The need to locate a golden age somewhere in the past seems to be an overwhelming one, so that, even when things are going well, there are plenty of voices to remind us that we face problems that were unknown in a purer and simpler age. The 1890s was a period of striking success for the Tavistock Cricket Club, and, in many respects, for the game on the wider stage. Yet the decade began with dire warnings about creeping professionalism, and was to end in controversy over the behaviour of spectators. After a match at The Ring in June 1899, a correspondent to the *Tavistock Gazette* wrote angrily about the conduct of a section of the crowd. Some young men had, it was claimed, behaved in a 'rowdy and brutal way', using bad language and hissing and hooting at certain players. He concluded that:

> 'everyone who delights in the noble game of cricket must regret that the disgraceful conduct which keeps so many away from football matches is being gradually introduced onto the cricket field'.

Some felt that the anonymous complainant had gone too far in 'casting a great reflection on the moral character and conduct of a Tavistock crowd', and, after some heated exchanges, the controversy died down. One thing is certain: in so far as there were some examples of boisterous crowd participation in the 1890s, it was no new phenomenon.

The Chilcott Revival

In 1891 Edward Chilcott resumed the captaincy that he was to retain throughout the rest of the decade. Sammy Featherstone, after two seasons in charge, happily handed back the reins. He was to remain a central figure in the activities of the club, both on and off the field, for some years to come. When the first match of the new Chilcott era, in May 1891, was abandoned in early afternoon as the rains fell, it was to Sammy's home, Whitchurch Vicarage, that two dozen cricketers and two umpires repaired to while away some soggy hours with talk, laughter, and refreshment. The Vicar was still at the height of his cricketing powers. In the same season he played in a two-day game for South Devon against North Devon, taking 3 for 27 and 2 for 34. In the following year he topped the club averages for both batting and bowling, scoring 202 runs at an average of 25 and taking 33 wickets at 8 apiece. He was also a smart slip fielder.

As a club benefactor, his gifts included, in 1892, 'a new telegraph board', and, in 1893, a bat for whoever topped the averages. Parochial duties, and particularly the thoughtlessness of Whitchurch residents in wanting to have themselves married or buried on a Saturday, meant that he could not play as often as he would have wished. But when he finally retired, in 1898, after 22 seasons, he had chalked up, even in the incomplete records that have survived, 551 wickets and 2451 runs. His last match was against the Royal Engineering College on June 8th 1898. He made 1 run, took 2 wickets, and held 1 catch.

Moving from Whitchurch to Pinhoe, he was to be, for the rest of his life, a central figure in the administration of the newly-revived Devon County Club, and was its secretary for four years. He was to die in 1908 at the age of fifty-two, after suffering a stroke while playing golf at Exeter.

Five other survivors from an earlier period continued to play through the 1890s. Jim Chave had first played in 1871. By 1893, as he neared the end of his career, he was doing what all seasoned cricketers ought to do when they reach the age of forty: he concentrated on keeping wicket. Tom Doidge, who was in so many games half of the lethal Doidge-Featherstone attack, bowled away until 1897, by which time, after 24 seasons, and at the age of fifty-six, he had a haul of 671 recorded wickets. He continued to play thereafter, but bowled only on ceremonial occasions. Herbert Spencer, former captain, had made his debut in 1881. He retired in 1889, but made a come-back in 1892 when, in late season, he opened the batting against Bude and made 61. In the next season he showed that he could still turn his arm over by taking 3 wickets with consecutive balls (the term 'hat trick' had already entered the cricket vocabulary). He also, in that year, topped the batting averages, and so won the bat that Mr Featherstone had vainly thought would reward one of the younger players. A lengthy, albeit erratic, career ended in 1896; surviving records show him with 1448 runs and 140 wickets. Dr. Liddell's appearances were even more scattered. Playing no more than three or four matches in an average season, it was 1899, thirteen years after his first performance, before he topped 1000 runs. And then there was John Glanville Davey. He took a little time to establish himself in the side after his debut in 1885. In 1889, for example, he scored five ducks in seven innings, and didn't get a bowl. For some time he seemed to be under the shadow of the likes of Featherstone, Doidge, and Moore, and it was the later 1890s before he began to make a real impact. In the three seasons beginning in 1897 he scored 960 runs and took 74 wickets. He had, at last, arrived to occupy a central role in the club's affairs, on and off the field.

The Nineties

The 1890s were the Chilcott years. The respect and affection felt for the captain by players and supporters was very evident. Towards the end the runs rather dried up and in the last five seasons he added only 636 to the 1482 he had already accumulated. But his leadership qualities remained formidable. He was, of course, to all, Mr Chilcott. The days when a captain and his players would be on christian-name terms lay in the distant future. He was not the greatest batsman the club ever produced – although he was good enough to make 50 in a county trial in 1891 – but he knew the game, understood something about motivation, and never compromised when it came to standards of fair play and sportsmanship. His counterpart in a Second XI that consistently played a dozen or so matches each season through the 1880s and 1890s, and regularly won most of them, was George Chapman, useful bowler and entertaining bat, who filled a vacant spot in the first team from time to time over the years, but was more at home leading his collection of veterans and young hopefuls. Meanwhile, much behind-the-scenes work was done by Tom Doidge, who took over as treasurer from John Daw in 1894, and by Chilcott himself, who stepped into the breach as secretary in 1896 when Curate Wilson made his sad and sudden departure. The figurehead role of president passed in 1892 from the representative of one local dynasty to another; from Reginald Gill, businessman and county councillor, to Reginald Morshead, businessman and county councillor.

There were occasional complaints throughout the 1890s that too many matches were left unfinished. There was the problem of the visiting side sometimes arriving late, a circumstance for which the railway company was usually given the blame. And there was the inclination, particularly on a hot afternoon, for the lunch interval to spread itself beyond its proper limits. With the ten minutes between innings often becoming twenty, and with incoming batsmen frequently taking much longer than the permitted two minutes between wickets, there was, it was widely felt, scope for tightening up.

The playing record during the decade does not, on the other hand, suggest a crisis. For the nine years between 1891 and 1899, records of 144 games survive. Of these, only 21, or 15%, were drawn. Of the remainder, one was tied, 84 were won, and 38 were lost. There were victories in 58% of games, and defeats in only 26%. It was a most impressive record. If the two earlier years of Chilcott's captaincy are added, to give the full eleven years of his reign, the record reads : Played 170; Won 95 (56%); Lost 52 (31%). It was not surprising that his retirement in 1899 should have elicited such fulsome tributes. But captaincy was only one ingredient in the mixture that brought the successes of the 1890s. The playing strength was the result, on the one hand, of having a side with a more settled composition than had been possible in earlier periods, and on the other of producing a balance between experience and youth.

To the men who had cut their cricketing teeth in the 1870s and 1880s, men like Chave, Doidge, Spencer, Liddell, Featherstone, Chilcott, and Davey, were added new faces. Some of these came from predictable sources, like Captain Symonds and the Rev. Phillips. But the biggest influx was that of the young schoolmasters. David, Linnell, May, Penny, Selby, Tomlinson, and Wood, were all masters at Kelly College. Three of them were to occupy, over a long period, key positions in the team. They were, in an age when initials were attached to a name as closely as a cricket cap to a head, W. B. Wood, W. Linnell, and A. O. V. Penny. They made their club debuts in, respectively, 1891, 1893, and 1894.

Walter Birkbeck Wood, described as 'Lengthy and be-goggled', was an all-rounder, whose appointment as vice-captain in 1892 made him, in many eyes, the heir apparent. He scored some useful runs – 298 in 1897 at an average of 25 – but his total of 1350 in nine seasons was modest. His chief value to the side was as a bowler. He bowled, on average, 170 overs, and took 35 wickets, each season, at an average of about 9.

William Linnell was said to be, in his prime, the fastest bowler in Devon. A big, robust, man, he played for the county, taking, in a fixture against Dorset, 8 wickets in an innings, the last 6 for no runs. One reporter called him 'the Tavistock Spofforth'. He made his Tavistock debut in May 1893, and in his second game took 8 for 25. By the end of the season he had taken 42 wickets at 5.8 each. By the end of 1899 his accumulated haul in seven seasons was 386, with averages that never reached double figures. He could lay claim to being the most lethal strike bowler in the club's history. His contribution with the bat was also significant. In 1897 he topped both lists, adding a total of 384 runs, including a 99, to a haul of 66 wickets at 7.1 apiece. When Mr Chilcott introduced young Linnell to fellow-members at the club's dinner in November 1892, he had already made a reputation for himself as a footballer. 'He is', said his captain, 'even more brilliant on the cricket field'. And he was.

The final member of that talented Kelly trio who burst onto the scene in the early 1890s was Alfred Oliver Vincent Penny. It took some time, from a hesitant debut in 1894, for him to establish himself in the side, and for the runs to begin to flow. In 1898 he made the Number One position his own. Like many small opening batsmen he scored a lot of runs behind the wicket, turning the ball down to fine leg or cutting it square through the offside field. In 1899 he was to take over as captain and secretary when Edward Chilcott retired.

Some supporters of the club during the 1890s took the view that the playing strength made it unnecessary to incur the expense of employing a professional. The counter-argument that was usually used was that someone had to be paid to look after the ground, and, this being so, you might as well get someone who could play a bit. The 1880s had seen the employment, successively, of Cort, Kerry, and Howland. In 1890 there was no appointment. But from 1891 to the end of the decade a pro was contracted for each season. Charles Attewill, William Moore, and Thomas Gidlow, whose terms were successively, two, six, and two seasons, were all good all-round cricketers. But, respecting the maxim that bowlers win matches, and reflecting the perceived balance of the side, two of the three were essentially bowlers who chipped in regularly with useful runs. Attewill had an explosive influence when he joined the club at the beginning of the 1891 season. In his first game he bowled 17 overs, 9 of which were maidens, and took 4 wickets for 12 runs. In the following season, in a game against Crediton, he took all 10 wickets. His figures for the two seasons were:

Year	*Overs*	*Maidens*	*Runs*	*Wickets*	*Average*
1891	253	99	332	80	4.1
1892	296	85	516	74	6.9

His captain described him, at the end of the second season, as not only a fine bowler, but 'as good a fellow to play with on the field as ever it has been my luck to meet with'. Three months later the tone was rather different. Attewill had been 'distinctly engaged' for a third season, but had 'thrown over the Tavistock club for a more lucrative engagement'.

A hurried approach to Nottingham, that seed-bed of late-Victorian club professionals, produced W. W. Moore, as two years earlier it had produced

Attewill. Moore came with the credentials of an all-rounder. In the event, his bowling was confined to 50 overs or so a season. His 98 innings, spread over six seasons, produced 2451 runs at an average of 25. There were two centuries, the second one of which, 125 not out in July 1898, began a purple patch that realised an average of 85 over 6 innings. He was a good fielder, a popular colleague, and a man with a friendly disposition. For all of which, together with the groundsman duties, he was paid £35 a season. Since the payment was assessed on a weekly basis, the committee was able to reduce costs by delaying the start of a contract, as they did, for example, in 1895, by not engaging him until the third week of May.

Moore served the club well, up to 1899, when he was replaced by Thomas Gidlow. Gidlow came from Lincolnshire, and was hired for two seasons. During that time he took 95 wickets and made 375 runs at an average of 18. 'Honest, worthy, and trustworthy' he may have been, or at least that is how he was described at the Annual Dinner in 1900, but it did not save him from being jettisoned before the next season. The club was now to take advantage of an arrangement with the Devon County Club, by which clubs within the county that hired pros would be given one-third of the cost to them of the contracts, in return for releasing the pros to play for the county when required. On this basis the Tavistock Club employed a young fast bowler who had played in the Yorkshire League, and who had taken 138 wickets and made 88 runs in the previous season. His name was N. J. Minto.

The 'Minto Agreement' was by no means the first contact that there had been between the local and county clubs. The Devon Cricket Club had been founded in 1861. In its early days such Tavistock figures as Messrs Carpenter and Tancock had played a part in its affairs, and in 1889 Sammy Featherstone became the first Tavistock player to represent the county on the field, a selection that entitled him to receive half-a-crown (12½p) in travelling expenses. He and Chilcott both sat on the D.C.C. Committee, and when in 1899 the club was reconstituted on a firmer base, Tavistock was represented at the key meeting, not only by Featherstone, but by William Linnell, and by Linnell's boss, the Kelly Headmaster, William David. An annual subscription of one guinea (£1.05p) thereafter entitled the town club to the benefits of affiliation, of which the Minto deal was an early example. There followed the offer of a county fixture in 1901.

The impossibility of controlling access to The Ring led to the hiring of the Kelly College ground for a two-day game against the M.C.C. in August. A total of 1391 attended, contributing by their sixpences to gate receipts of £34.15s.6d (£34.77½p) Members of the local club, naturally proud that the town was hosting its first county fixture, played a major part in the organisation, which included a dance in the Town Hall on the intervening evening. The match was drawn. The result was the same when the fixture was repeated twelve months later, the M.C.C. being captained on this occasion by the 43 year old Arthur Conan Doyle, who had just been knighted. Unfortunately it rained for the whole two days, and not a ball was bowled. In 1903 they tried again. This time the weather relented, and the M.C.C. won by an innings, Conan Doyle again captaining the side, making 8 runs batting at Number 6, and bowling 4 overs in Devon's first innings to take 0 for 15. The Tavistock Club contributed two players to the county side on this occasion, one of whom was Linnell. Further matches were to be held in the years before the First World War.

The last years of the century saw a few innovations. Declarations had come, and, while a side batting second retained the right to bat on after securing victory, it became more frequent to forego that right. This civilised and merciful convention provided the added benefit of extra time for post-match refreshment.There were some novel additions to the fixture list. On August 1st 1891 there was a home game against Hornsey. On July 31st 1892 the opposition was Ravensbourne. In the middle of August 1893 there were fixtures, within one week, against Oxford Nostiks and Enfield Wanderers. So began a long tradition at The Ring of entertaining touring sides. Many a team of undergraduates, of tired schoolmasters from the home counties, or of young bankers and solicitors representing the Old Boys of their school, have spent a part of their summer holiday on Whitchurch Down, and have taken back memories of captivating views, of intoxicating breezes, and of long evenings at the Bedford or the Queen's Head.

Another tradition that was launched in 1890 was the two-day fixture at Bude, which, with the addition of a game at Holsworthy before or after, could become a Northern Tour, sometimes in Bank Holiday Week. The August games against Bude, home and away, became very popular, attracting large crowds. So did the novelty games which also became features of most programmes, such as the matches against elevens made up of local clergy (inevitably dubbed Saints V Sinners) or games against teams of veterans, the definition of the latter term varying according to the difficulty or otherwise of turning out a full team of oldsters. These were novelties.

Much, however, remained the same. For example, in every age cricketers, who for the most part are amongst the most amiable of people, manage to find some cause for complaint. Three examples, all chosen from the 1891 season, illustrate this continuing undercurrent of grumbling.

On July 4th the club lost to Plymouth College. Captain Chilcott, sidelined by injury, watched the performance, and later noted in his diary:

> 'Tavistock a poor team today. Fine day. We won toss. Attewill bowled well, but single-handed. No lunch'.

A week later the team travelled to Crediton, and won by 150 runs. This time the captain's criticism was aimed elsewhere:

> 'Ground a very bad one. One and a half miles from the town uphill. Very doubtful about going there again'.

For a club whose home was The Ring to complain of a ground because it was distant and uphill would surely have caused most people to mutter about pots and kettles. And then, later the same month, following a victory over Plymouth, there was one of those occasional laments about unfair practices.

This time it appeared in a press report:

> 'During the Tavistock innings an all-along-the-ground daisy-cutting kind of bowling was adopted, which is no more cricket to a real cricketer than shooting a hare in the seat'.

The etiquette that prevailed in the hare-shooting field was, presumably, more widely understood a hundred years ago than it is today.

Optimism and Fellowship

Every season the Tavistock Club fixture list contained a disproportionately high number of home games. The main reason for this, apart from the obvious one that entertainment was given to touring sides and to clubs without homes of their own, was that the Tavistock ground had acquired a reputation among members and supporters of neighbouring clubs. Whitchurch Down was a nice place to spend a sunny Saturday afternoon. And the club continued to attend to the need to carry out improvements, as and when they could.

In 1892 there was the arrival of Mr Featherstone's telegraph board. In the same year a ton of sand and a large quantity of soot, donated by local firms, was administered to the ground, and a local doctor provided protective sheets. In 1897 a lot of heavy rolling took place, using a machine loaned by the neighbouring golf club. Also, in the middle of the decade, the Duke of Bedford had a dressing-room built on to the back of the pavilion, which had the effect of doubling the size of the building. In 1897 Chilcott could tell the Annual Dinner with some pride that 'our ground and pavilion are in very good order and repair'. The optimism was reflected in the size of the membership, which increased from 116 in 1889 to 150 in 1898, and to over 200 by the turn of the century.

The dinner held each autumn was a tradition that went back to the origins of the club. Here was the occasion, usually in the Bedford or the Queen's Head, to celebrate another season, to record the club's gratitude to its friends, and to bring together players old and young. Nostalgia was never far below the surface. The 1875 gathering, for example, was reminded that 'the members present are a year older than they were this time last year'. This stunning observation was met, we are told, 'with immediate acceptance and sympathy'. Between such offerings songs were sung 'some being humorous, some sentimental, and some that were neither the one nor the other'. When the ritual speeches had been made and the required toasts drunk, the company would settle back to listen to the likes of old Tom Youren. Galloping through his seventies as the century came to an end, Tom gave, every year, his views on the great game. In 1893 he was bemoaning the fact that the test matches against the visiting Australians had been played under the new boundary rule, while at The Ring the practice of having to run everything, which was what God had intended, was, mercifully, being maintained. It was surely not cricket, he insisted, to 'make a fine hit without running it out, and to stand with undimmed eye and unshaken nerve, waiting as cool as a cucumber to receive the next ball'. In the previous year he was ranging more widely, finding in cricket

> 'the qualities of pluck, endurance, forbearance, and temper, which were characteristic of Englishmen throughout the world'.

That, of course, led easily to Drake, with Tom showing no concern that the great hero might have promoted the popularity of a rival ball game. And then on, just as smoothly, to the Duke of Wellington. The Bedford Dining Room became the battlefield of Waterloo. The speech ended:

> 'At a critical moment, when the fate of Europe trembled in the balance, by a magnificent rush the duke overthrew the Imperial Guard of France and stopped the career of that desperate warrior Napoleon Bonaparte. I have great pleasure in proposing the health of the chairman'.

Speeches and toasts would go on for some hours, but the evening would contain other delights. In 1892 the *Tavistock Gazette*, having quoted at some length from the twelve principal speeches and the eight toasts, concluded its report: 'Mr W. B. Wood proposed "The Ladies" and the Rev. M. H. M. Byrne responded. Songs were sung at intervals by the Rev. S. W. Featherstone, the Rev. E. C. C. Wilson, and Messrs W. H. B. Barnett, T. Doidge, H. J. Liddell, and J. Squire. Mr J. Tomlinson accompanied on the piano. Lieutenant Spooner gave a recitation'. And, it may be safely assumed, there was no mention of two dozen young ladies travelling down from Northern Scotland.

New Names for a New Age

Edward Chilcott's retirement from the captaincy did not mean the end of either his playing career or his administrative work for the club. He continued to turn out for a number of games each season, batting low down the order but making useful runs. He also found himself being called upon for representative and committee duties. But the captaincy was, at the beginning of the 1900 season, handed on to Alfred Penny. The torch that had been passed from the parson to the lawyer was now to go to the schoolmaster. Penny launched his reign by making 31 and by sharing an opening partnership of 70 that set Tavistock well on the way to a 6 wicket victory against Argyle. By the end of the season the record ran: Played 22, Won 11, Drawn 7, Lost 4.

William Linnell continued to show his value to the side by taking 71 wickets, more than twice the haul of anyone else, at 10.9 each, and scoring 366 runs at an average of 18.3. The new captain out-scored everyone, reaching a total of 498, and finishing second in the batting lists to a local doctor, John Newton Martin. Born at St. Austell in 1867, Martin had first played for Tavistock in 1899, averaging 72 in 4 innings. In 1900 he played seven times, and scored 175. The third season, 1901, brought 540 runs from nine innings, including two centuries against Holsworthy. This was the summer in which he first played for Devon. He went on to captain the county side in the following two seasons, and this commitment meant that he was not able to play for Tavistock. Returning to The Ring in 1905, he celebrated his come-back with an 80 not out, to secure a victory against the Devon Regiment. John Martin has a special distinction among those who have represented the local club. In 1891, before his Tavistock days, he had been selected to play in a first-class match for the MCC. It proved to be a one-off, and he emerged with 30 runs for once out in the two innings. That one game bestowed on him the honour of having played first-class cricket. He was the first member of the Tavistock Cricket Club who can be definitely identified as having done so. Others were to share the distinction in later years. John Martin died at Torquay in 1942 at the age of seventy-five.

Another performer to entertain the turn-of-the-century crowds at The Ring was F.D. Conry, who averaged 42 in his first season in 1899. In July 1900 he scored 101 not out in a home game against Albion, 'evoking the warm appreciation of the spectators by his brilliant leg hits and drives beyond the boundaries'. In the same season he played for Devon. Thirty-five years on he was still enjoying his local cricket, and making runs for Bridestowe. In his early career he was better known as a footballer than a cricketer, and had at one point been offered professional terms by Bristol City. His formative cricketing years had been spent in South Africa. He had returned to the mother country before the outbreak of the Boer War. This war, which broke out in 1899, deprived the Tavistock club of the services of its treasurer, Edward Kay, who joined the army and went off to fight for Queen and Empire. This action may have saved the Empire, but it led to a short-fall in the finances of the Tavistock Cricket Club. Fortunately Tom Doidge was persuaded to resume the post of treasurer that he had only recently given up. In his sixtieth year, and in the twenty-seventh year of his playing career, the merry hatter was to continue his involvement with the club for some years ahead. At the age of sixty-one he led a self-styled 'Old Crocks XI' against the Club First XI, and took 9 wickets. A month before, he had batted at Number 11 against Holsworthy and made 25. He was still turning his arm over, and clouting the ball over the chains, in his mid 60s.

The secretaryship passed in 1900, along with the captaincy, from Chilcott to Penny. 'AOV' therefore counted, among his duties, the arrangement of a fixture list. In the pre-telephone age this usually involved a long programme of correspondence, with proposals, amendments, counter-proposals, and plenty of scope for frustration. There was, however, by 1900, a pattern which had evolved over recent seasons, and a list of regular and reliable opponents, and this made the task of Penny and his successors somewhat less arduous. The 1900 list involved 15 games against local town clubs, 12 of which were by then considered 'traditional fixtures'. These were the home-and-away meetings with Argyle, Albion, Plymouth, Launceston, Bude, and Holsworthy. The three additions were two games against Ashbury and one against Ford Parish. The two games against students, from Plymouth College and the Royal Engineering College, were also regular events. This left four matches against services sides; while this part of the programme would always include the navy and the marines, army opposition would vary somewhat from year to year

The oldest surviving picture of a Second Eleven.

This is the side that Tom Doidge put together towards the end of the 1906 season to honour a fixture for which the First Eleven Captain had been unable to raise a team.
Standing: Bill Monk, Bill Snell, George Chapman, Frederick Nowell, Reg Chapman, J. J. Camozzi (umpire). *Sitting:* Tom Doidge, Bill Johns, Glanville Davey, Henry Cole, Harry Kerslake.
Front: Reg Johns.
Glanville Davey, founder of the best-known local cricket dynasty, was married on the following day.

Some of the heroes of a golden age.

ABOVE: E. W. Chilcott

BELOW: The stone memorial, above a seat halfway up Down Road, lists three of his qualities. His cricketing prowess comes first.

Clockwise from top left: S.W. Featherstone, W. Linnell, A.O.V. Penny, W. B. Wood.

MEMBER'S CARD.

FIXTURES. Season 1914.

Date	Opponents		Scores—For	Agst.	Ind.	Date	Opponents		Scores—For	Agst
May 9	United Services	A.				July 13, 14	Enfield Wanderers	H.		
13	Royal Scots	H.				15	R. N. Barracks	A.		
16	Callington	A.				16	Holsworthy	H.		
20						18	Royal Garrison Artillery	H.		
23	Gordon Highlanders	H.				23	Dunheved College	H.		
27	R.M.L.I. (N.C.O.S and M.)	H.				25	Yelverton	H.		
30	Plymouth Schoolmasters	A.				29	O. P. & M.s	A.		
June 1	Artificers H.M.S. Indus	H.				31, Aug. 1	Devon Dumplings	H.		
3	Royal Scots	H.				6	Holsworthy	A.		
4	Kelly College	A.				8				
6	Calnngton	H.				12, 13	West Monmouth Wanderers	H.		
10						15				
13	United Services	A.				19	Okehampton	A.		
17	Okehampton	H.				22	Plymouth Cpn. Officers	H.		
18	Launceston	H.				24, 25	Somerset Stragglers	H.		
20	Dunheved College	A.				27	Launceston	A.		
24						29	Royal Garrison Artillery	A.		
27	Plymouth Cpn. Officers	A.								
July 4	Yelverton	A.								
8	Middlesex Regiment	H.								
11	Plymouth Schoolmasters	H.								

H—*signifies Home Matches.* A—*signifies Away Matches.*

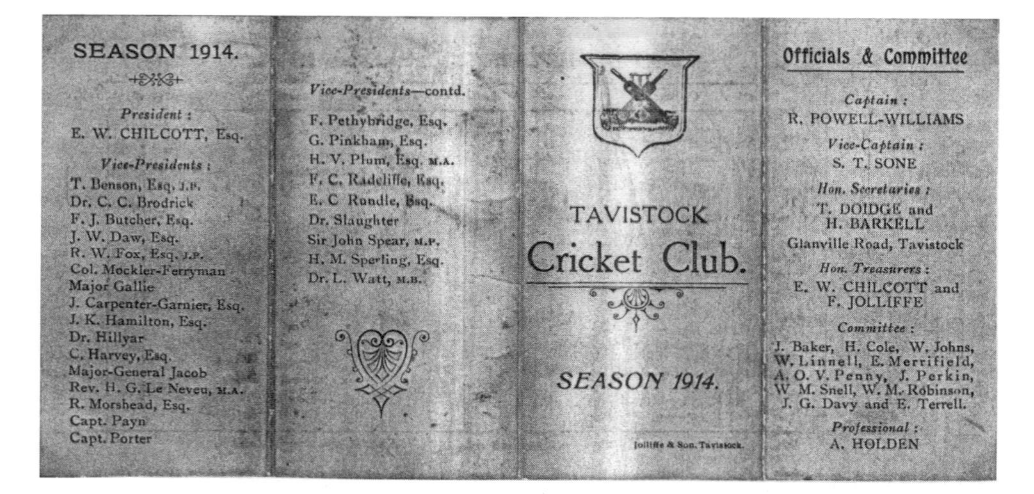

The fixtures for the 1914 season, listed on the annual membership card. A handful of matches at the end of the season were cancelled following the outbreak of war.

according to changes in regimental garrison duties.

Cricket administration is, at every level, subject to a range of uncertainties and imponderables. The weather is one such. In 1900 there were many more, such as problems of rapid communication and the vagaries of the railway timetable. One consequence of this was the persistence of a somewhat vague and imprecise attitude and approach, as if club officials were deliberately building into their planning some insurance against acts of either God or the G.W.R. An announcement from The Ring on May 11th 1900 gives the flavour:

> 'The club will play the first match of the season tomorrow on Whitchurch Down, when Argyle will be met. The match will probably start at about two o'clock'.

One of the reasons for the success of the club in the turn-of-the-century years was the continuing health of the Second Eleven. Under George Chapman's long and enthusiastic leadership ten or a dozen games were played each season, against other club second teams or village sides or school elevens. Interest was high, and invariably more matches were won than lost. Chapman's teams always included the two elements that any decent Second Eleven needs in order to be effective. On the one hand there were the veterans who, like the captain himself, had never quite made it, or who, like Tom Doidge, had once played regular first-team cricket over many years before age caught up with them. Alongside this experience were the lads in their mid-teens, strong, naturally talented, and learning all the time.

The Second Eleven over the years became an essential contributor to the well-being of the club, and helped to enhance its reputation. This reputation, in the town and beyond, was a very positive one, resting, as it did, mainly on the playing strength that the club was able to muster. There was, however, another major source of the positive image. This was the ground. Players and spectators knew that in 1900 some work still needed to be done at The Ring, particularly to level out what was a considerable drop from one end of the ground to the other. But, on the other hand, there was agreement about not only the charm of the setting, but also the quality and reliability of the wickets. The Ring was a high-scoring ground, mainly because it seemed possible, throughout the season, to produce a series of hard, true, flat, fast wickets, which rewarded those batsmen who had a sound technique and punished the bowler who offered anything less than total commitment and concentration.

The last twenty years or so before the outbreak of the First World War saw a considerable number of changes in the ranks of the club's officers. The treasurer's post brought the greatest degree of continuity. Tom Doidge, who took over at short notice when Edward Kay went off to fight the Boers, came to share the duties with Edward Chilcott, and between 1901 and 1925 the arrangement of shared responsibility was formalised by the appointment of joint treasurers. Chilcott was invariably one. For much of the period Frank Jolliffe was the other.

The other convention that originated with Chilcott was that of requiring the captain to double as secretary. This practice had some obvious advantages, and was adopted between 1896 and 1908. After it was abandoned there were five changes of secretary in five years. As for the presidency, the era of the great landed dynasts, Carpenter, Gill, and Morshead, came to an end in 1899. Thereafter, Thomas Smythe was a doctor, William David a headmaster, and Frederick Porter an army officer, while Francis Freeman and Frank Campbell were gentlemen, residing, respectively, at Abbotsfield and Mount Tavy. They each had some money and some local influence, and, most significantly of all, were the kind of people who could be relied upon to project an image of the club that was appropriate and acceptable.

A sad omission from the scattered records of the club in the nineteenth century is information about umpires. There is some reason to believe that in the early days the duties were carried out by playing members of the club who had not been selected to play on that particular day. The two who stood in the Tavistock V Keyham game in June 1858 were Messrs Doidge and Ball, and could well have been the G. Doidge and the A. Ball who are known to have played for the club in the same season. Similarly the umpire involved in the notorious 'throwing' incident at The Ring in August 1880 was W. Williams, who was almost certainly the William Williams who was then in the middle of his career as a Tavistock player. He certainly knew that the laws were very clear, then as now, on the difference between bowling and throwing. In the early years it would probably have been a fruitless search to have looked beyond the ranks of current players to find someone who knew the laws of the game sufficiently well to take on the responsibilities of umpiring. In the last quarter of the century this problem was eased by the emergence of a reservoir of knowledge and experience in the form of old players, who were happy to maintain a close contact with a game that they were no longer able to play, but about which they had a good deal of understanding. Unfortunately no name appears until 1900, when a Mr Harwood was doing the job regularly. He may well have been the J. Harwood who played a game or two in 1888. And he may have been the man who inspired one faithful spectator at The Ring to celebrate the first August Bank Holiday of a new century by composing a few lines:

'The Umpire is dominant always,
He answereth many appeals,
Though ruddy his face, yet his raiment
Is lily from head to the heels.
The ball that is dead on the wicket
Thou shalt not obstruct with thy knee,
If so, then the bowler appealeth
And another shall come after thee.
If a ball after rapping thy fingers
Is caught, while the enemies shout,
Prepare for a dignified exit,
My friend thou art certainly out'.

The Penny Years

In 1901 the club enjoyed another highly successful season. Of the 22 matches played by the First XI, 16 were won, 3 drawn, and 3 lost. One of the 3 losses was in a two-day game at Holsworthy, when the home side scored 410 and bowled Tavistock out for 146. Following on, the visitors made 322 in their second innings, with J. N. Martin scoring 162. Holsworthy were thus made to bat again, although they knocked off the runs required to win by 9 wickets. The 939 runs scored in the game was the highest aggregate in the half-century of the club's history to that date. Doctor Martin's innings helped him towards a season's average of 60. He was headed by A. P. Roe, one of a pair of brothers who had just made their club debuts and who were to prove to be prolific run-makers over the next few seasons. 'AP' played only two games in 1901, scoring 21 in one and 137 not out in the other, so achieving an average of 158.

His brother, H. J. Roe, had an unproductive season, but was to make up for it in subsequent years, particularly in 1905, when his performance featured an innings of 167. Another effective cricketer to establish himself in the side at this time was Charlie Wickenden, an all-rounder, who was the cricket professional at Kelly College. He played alongside the three Kelly masters who continued to constitute the core of the side, Penny, Linnell, and Wood. And he shared the work-horse all-rounder duties with N. J. Minto, the club professional, the payment of whose wages had been the subject of the agreement with the Devon County Club. Minto certainly did what he was asked to do. He played in 18 games, and scored 572 runs at an average of 38.1, with a highest score of 87. An accurate and pacy bowler, he also took 58 wickets. In his second game he scored 86 not out and took 6 wickets. At the end of the season he left, presumably for a more lucrative contract elsewhere. He had been one of four Tavistock players to be selected for the county in that first Edwardian summer. S. N. Mackenzie, a stylish and prolific run-getter, was another. The others were Martin and Linnell, both of whom were to be chosen again in 1902.

For the 1902 season, Minto was replaced by Fred Philpott, who, while not being in the Minto class, was to score useful runs and to take 40 wickets, including 9 for 40 in one innings. After the impressive records of the previous three years, the new campaign was welcomed with some enthusiasm. The *Tavistock Gazette* even managed, in spite of cold, wet May Saturdays, to burst into verse:

> 'The wickets are fixed – each hero now is seen
> Leaping the chain and bounding o'er the green,
> In decent white, most gracefully arrayed,
> Each strong built limb in all its pride displayed'.

In the event, the 'strong built limbs' spent more time than they would have wished in the pavilion, as the season proved to be a rain-affected one to the extent that 9 of the 22 fixtures were drawn. Of the completed games, 11 were won and 2 lost. A highlight was an innings victory over Bude at The Ring, when the visitors were shot out for 20 and 50, William Linnell making the first inroads by taking 4 wickets in 4 balls in his first over. The chief novelty of the season was the first attempt to organise a Cricket Week. The Kelly College ground was borrowed for what turned out to be a cricket half-week in later August. Starting on the Wednesday with a game against a scratch side of veterans led by Tom Doidge, who enjoyed the occasion by taking 9 Tavistock wickets, there followed a tight game against The Marines on the Thursday, and another close match on the Friday against a Touring XI glorying in the name of the Hampshire Hogs.

The 1903 season followed a familiar course, in that 13 of the 20 games played were won, and only 3 lost. Again, the professional played a significant part in both batting and bowling. At the beginning of the season, Alfred Brown, a wicket keeper-batsman from Derbyshire, was appointed, but, for some reason, he did not materialise, and the club, at the last minute, engaged William Robinson, the fifth pro in six years. It was a lucky choice. Robinson took 62 wickets in 16 innings, including 7 for 37 against Plymouth. In the following season he was to take 78 wickets at 8.7 each, as well as to score 361 runs in 24 innings. In 1905, by which time he had put down sufficient roots to set up a boot-making business at 28 King Street, he took 52 wickets and scored 342 runs.

It seemed that some continuity of professional help was being achieved and this was welcomed in playing terms, and also in relation to the question of ground maintenance and pitch preparation. Not that the problem of frequent changes had been the fault of the club officials; pros were free agents when they had served their one-season contracts and a better offer would be tempting. And there were many clubs larger and wealthier than Tavistock, both in Devon and beyond, that could offer inducements. Robinson seemed to be different. And the evidence for that seemed to be the boot business in King Street.

As to the rest of the side, the 1903 season saw few changes. There seemed to be a sudden influx of officers, with Captains Fowler and Porter being joined by Colonels Crowther and Ward-Young. Colonel Alexander Stuart Ward-Young had retired from active service. In his earlier life he had played a good deal of cricket at a high standard. When he died in 1934 he was, at his own insistence, buried at Horrabridge in his cricket blazer.

There were the customary occasional appearances from busy doctors and curates. A reminder of how common a feature of local cricket this was, came in August, when Holsworthy won the annual two-day encounter with Tavistock after an unbroken stand of 200 between the Rev. Lake and Dr Grey. But Tavistock was seen, during that period, as, more than anything else, the club with the three evergreen schoolmasters. Wood and Penny continued to churn out the runs season after season. And William Linnell continued to build up a record that was to make him second to none in the club annals.

Two games in that 1903 season illustrated his unique value to the side. On May 30th, Plymouth were entertained at The Ring. Tavistock batted first, and Penny was able to declare on 221 for 5, with Linnell not out 137. Plymouth were then dismissed for 98, Linnell taking 4 wickets. A month later the visitors were the Royal Naval College. Linnell again took 4 wickets, but the College reached 253. The Tavistock reply was 116, with Linnell going in at Number 3 and ending up with 50 not out. With performances like this from its evergreen all-rounder, supported by useful regular contributions from the other veterans Wood and Penny, with the Roe brothers taking it in turn to play big aggressive knocks, and with Bill Robinson earning his wages, it was not surprising that a mood of optimism, perhaps of complacency, prevailed.

The 1904 season opened with another string of good results, and after 8 games the side was unbeaten. Then, on July 6th, the bubble burst, when Holsworthy went home from The Ring with a 106 run victory. From that point things began to go wrong. By the end of the season 9 games had been lost and 8 won out of a total of 21. It had been the first time since 1887 that a season had seen more defeats than victories. No one blamed the batting for this sharp and unexpected decline, and, indeed, with A.O.V. Penny, F. A. Roe, J. A. Baker, and W. Linnell all averaging between 39 and 29 there was no drying-up of the run supply. Some people felt that the bowling was a bit thin, and, with Linnell perhaps not as sharp and lethal as he had been in his prime, that Robinson lacked support. But criticism tended more to highlight the poor standard of fielding that became very evident in the later stages of the season. Two explanations were offered for this. One was that Penny lacked the sergeant-major qualities that are sometimes needed in team leadership. The other was that the side was an ageing one. Something was to be done on both fronts.

The 1905 season was to be the last under Penny's captaincy. The playing balance-sheet saw the team back in the black, with 13 wins and 7 defeats in 27 matches. Some much-needed new blood was introduced. J. Williams, a pace bowler from Lamerton, burst onto the scene by taking 8 for 25 against the Somerset Light Infantry. In spite of this he could not command a regular place while Linnell and Robinson continued to gather harvests.

Two young men who were later to become well-known figures in other fields made their debuts in 1905. Charles Brittan was to become the best-known local artist of the twentieth century. Charles Brodrick, already in his forties, was not yet half-way through a long career as the town's best-remembered general practitioner. It was also a year when Louis Tamworth, in his third season, not only established his place in the side but became the acknowledged heir apparent to Penny. Two performances in mid-summer confirmed his credentials as both opening bat and occasional wicket taker. Against the Devon Regiment he took 4 wickets, and then made 50 to set up a 6 wicket victory, and against Plymouth College he shared a half-century opening stand with H. J. Roe and then took 6 wickets including the first three batsmen. By contrast, little was seen in these years of 'Glan' Davey, whose long career had peaked around 1900, but who, in the four seasons from 1902, played in only 5 games and bowled only a handful of overs.

One intriguing question from 1905 remains. On Thursday August 17th the club had an away fixture at the Royal Naval Barracks. Penny won the toss, and sent in as Number 1, not himself, but a Captain Bosanquet, playing his first, and it appears his only, game for Tavistock. He was out for nought, but the side totalled 230, and then dismissed RNB for 133, with Bosanquet taking 6 for 66. The interest lies in the fact that in the same year another Bosanquet, B.J.T., was in the middle of a first-class career that included Oxford, Middlesex, and England. 'BJT' has a unique niche in cricket history as the inventor of the googly. Evidence may well prove a close family link between the great man and the captain who once played for Tavistock. It would be nice, if fanciful, to speculate that as a result of the sharing of a family secret, googlies were bowled at the barracks ground on that Thursday afternoon, and that the bemused hosts fell as helpless victims. That one of the wickets was caught and bowled, and one stumped, lends some support to a theory that is otherwise, sadly, without basis.

A Little Local Difficulty

A.O.V. Penny gave up the captaincy after six years at the end of the 1905 season. He continued to play, though not as regularly, and he tended now to bat in the middle order. Being relieved of the cares of leadership did little for his performance; had it not been for a mid-season 49 not out his average in 1906 would have been single-figured. His successor, Louis Tamworth, did well with both bat and ball, but he soon began to show signs of the strains of office.

The 1906 season started reasonably enough, but ran into a trough half-way through, and the side recorded its last victory on July 6th. In the last two months it became increasingly difficult to raise a team. On August 8th the club put out, for a home fixture against Yelverton, a side in which six were making their debuts. They scored 6 runs between them, and the visitors gained an embarrassingly overwhelming win. Worse was to come. The last three games, including the by-now traditional northern tour of Holsworthy and Bude, were cancelled when Tamworth announced that he could not raise a team. The indignation felt in some quarters was reflected in the initiative taken by Tom Doidge, who, noting that the Holsworthy fixture was part of a benefit effort for the latter's professional, raised, without too much effort, a local eleven of mainly second team stalwarts, in order to honour the fixture.

The season had, indeed, fallen apart. At its end, Tavistock had won 4 and lost 9 of the 19 fixtures. Some of the difficulties had arisen because of the departure of some established players. Charles Wickenden, the Kelly College pro, moved on. Walter Wood, one of the trio of schoolmasters who had for two decades provided the nucleus of the team, went into virtual retirement, having served the club, since 1891, to the extent of over 2000 runs and over 400 wickets. Perhaps of even more significance was the fact that William Linnell had the kind of modest season that led commentators to suggest that he was over the hill. It did not prevent him from being selected for the county match against Cornwall, held on the Kelly College ground in mid-July. In this game the local hero, batting at Number 8, was out for a duck, but he bowled

11 overs and took 4 for 31, including 2 wickets with the first 2 balls he bowled. The game was drawn, and the cricket was, on the whole, uninspiring, but the county club was satisfied with the organisation, and about 500 spectators paid sixpence a head to view the proceedings.

In an otherwise disappointing season, the performance of young Thomas, the new professional, proved to be the highlight of the 1906 season. A graduate of the Lord's ground staff, he had been coach at Harrow School before accepting the Tavistock appointment. After 11 innings he was averaging 76.2. Along with the rest of the side he suffered a second-half decline, and was not to be re-engaged. His appointment had been a mystery to some. He was a very promising bat, with an impressive range of strokes, but the need at The Ring was for a penetrative bowler. The faithful Robinson remained in the wings, playing a number of games as an amateur, and, with the fading Linnell, carrying the burden of the attack.

Two particular fixtures, both played at The Ring in June, provided the principal talking-points of the 1906 season. On June 9 against the Rifle Brigade the home side scored 334, including a double-century stand for the second wicket, and thereby set a record for the highest score hitherto recorded on the ground. Eleven days later a game against Gunnislake ended in confusion and controversy, when the two scorers failed to agree on the final score. Tavistock, batting first, had made 198 for 6 when Tamworth made what many thought was an over-generous declaration. For Gunnislake, E.C. Cornish then made what the visitors' book recorded as 117 and the hosts' scorer insisted was 113. The Gunnislake version had the visitors winning by 1 run, the Tavistock book recording a home victory by 3 runs. It was the only game in the history of the club which ended with no agreed result.

It was clear, as the club prepared for the 1907 season, that the bowling needed to be strengthened. The problem was made even more acute by William Linnell's decision that his bowling days were over. He was to be selected in the new season for his batting only, and was to show, by averaging 26, that he was still very much worth his place. Batsmen of his age and experience were considerably heartened by the recent introduction of boundary hits, in which fours and sixes had dispensed with the requirement hitherto obtaining that everything had to be run. The bowling vacuum was to be filled partly by getting Robinson to bowl 139 overs, but even more by employing a specialist 'trundler' (a term extensively used during that period to describe any form of bowling).

The new professional was called Bower. Over the season he bowled 329 overs and took 85 wickets for 961 runs. His contribution made all the difference. At the end of the year the club had won 9 and lost only 4 of its 20 games. Problems clearly remained. J. N. Martin, who had been such a prolific run-scorer over eight seasons left the area, Young players like W. Snell, who took 4 for 4 in his first game in 1906, only played a handful of games in the next two years, and other young talent seemed to be ignored. There was also the strange case of 'Glan' Davey, who continued season after season to be picked only occasionally, but to contribute significantly with either runs or wickets when he got the opportunity. It did seem that there was a greater disposition to provide guest opportunities for transient subalterns and majors than to nurture and develop the home-grown talent on which the longer-term success of the club depended. And with that policy skipper Tamworth must have been associated.

At the end of 1907 he disappeared from the local cricket scene, and from the area. In the following two seasons he was to captain the Devon county side. He was succeeded by a newcomer to, not only the club, but the town. Sidney Sone had become master of the Tavistock workhouse in 1906. He joined the club, and played 9 games in 1907, averaging 47 with the bat and bowling 76 overs to take 13 wickets. At the end of the season he was elected captain.

The Age of the Newcomer

During the two years of his captaincy, 1908 and 1909, Sone showed himself to be a competent all-rounder, batting in the middle of the order to average 11.4, and turning in useful bowling performances, including three occasions in 1908 when he took 6 wickets in an innings. After 1909 he continued to play, down to 1914, as vice-captain, a consistent and dependable performer with both bat and ball who was prepared to bat anywhere in the order and who remained an effective change bowler. But it is one thing to be a good, knowledgeable cricketer, and another to be a successful captain, and in 1909, in spite of a playing record over the two years that brought 26 victories in 45 games, he handed over the leadership to another newcomer to the area, Rowland Powell-Williams, who had settled at Middlemoor.

Here was a man with a considerable cricketing pedigree. Born at Stratford-on-Avon in 1872 and schooled in Birmingham, he had played five times for Warwickshire in the 1897 and 1898 seasons. He was then Rowland Williams; the decision to add the Powell bit was not taken until 1900. He had subsequently played in two further first-class matches, for London County in 1902 and for the Gentlemen of England in 1905. An aggregate of 105 runs in his seven first-class games had left him with an average of 9.5 and a highest score of 38. When he joined the Tavistock club in 1907 he was the second player in the club's history to have had a taste of the first-class game. He played in one match in that season, and then burst onto the scene in 1908, when he batted twelve times, was not out twice, and amassed 606 runs at an average of 60.6 and a top score of 139. Without quite reaching these heights again, he continued to score heavily down to 1914, and to establish a reputation as one of the most confident, consistent, free-hitting, and powerful batsmen ever to play for the club. It was partly through his own individual efforts that the club was so successful during the five years of his captaincy. His reign, which, like so much else, ended in 1914, was in later years to be treated with some overblown, if understandable, nostalgia. The man himself became revered as one of the club's old testament giants. There was hope that he would make an appearance at the centenary celebrations in 1949, but by then he was frail and confined to his Yelverton nursing home. He died in December 1951.

The Powell-Williams years, the last seasons before the Great War, saw the retirement of two of the stalwarts of the Tavistock club, the two remaining members of the Kelly College trio who had played such a major part in the successes of the 1890s. Both gave up regular playing in 1907, although both were lured back to play the occasional game thereafter. Alfred Penny had, in a career stretching back to 1894, scored some 4000 runs and had captained the side for six seasons. William Linnell, who had first played in 1893, had scored over 5000 runs and taken something like 800 wickets, to establish himself, in a twenty-year career, as, surely, the best all-rounder the club has ever had. In May 1909 he found himself doing what he had done countless times over the previous sixteen summers, when he scored 36 against a Services side and then reduced them to rubble with figures of 7 for 11. In terms of pure longevity he did, of course, have to leave centre-stage to Tom Doidge, who turned out twice for the side at the age of sixty-eight. Not quite so old, but a veteran in terms of service, was Glanville Davey, whose thirty-year playing career enjoyed an Indian Summer in 1912.

If Powell-Williams took major responsibility for what happened on the field during these years, much of the work behind the scenes was carried on by the secretaries, veteran players Tom Doidge and Harry Barkell, and by Frank Jolliffe and Edward Chilcott, who shared the treasurer's chores. Apart from the routine club tasks, they were involved in the organisation of three more minor counties fixtures held on the Kelly College ground, against Cornwall in 1910 and again in 1911, and against Berkshire in 1913. The club officials, while happy to be involved in these and other ways in the affairs of the county club, were cautious about its plan to introduce a senior county league. The proposal, made in 1911, was somewhat ahead of its time, and was shelved when only six senior clubs offered a positive response. It is not clear why the one-guinea subscription, faithfully paid each year to the county club up to 1909, was withheld for three years from 1910.

The overall playing record in the Sone and Powell-Williams years was impressive. It read:

Year	*Played*	*Won*	*Drawn*	*Lost*
1908	22	12	1	9
1909	23	14	5	4
1910	27	18	3	6
1911	21	13	2	6
1912	22	17	1	4
1913	24	20	1	3
1914	18	10	2	6

There were occasional humiliations. On August 18th 1908 a large crowd at The Ring turned up to watch a match against Plymouth Argyle. The visitors declared on 226 for 5. The home side, whose cause was not helped by two absentees, were then dismissed for 25. Two months earlier they had been skittled out for 23 by Plymouth, in a match in which Plymouth took revenge for having been beaten at The Ring at the beginning of the season by 185 runs.

On June 5th 1909 the club recorded its lowest-ever total when, in an away game against Callington, they were all out for 4. The *Tavistock Gazette* ran a two-sentence report of the game. It read:

> 'Callington V Tavistock – played at Callington on Saturday and won by the homesters by an innings and 64 runs. Robinson took 9 wickets for 30 runs for Tavistock'.

Thus, with the help of selective reporting from a supportive local press, minor setbacks were overcome and the thinking remained positive. And the record did speak for itself.

Those who followed closely the fortunes of the club were, however, forced to admit that a good deal of the success was due to the efforts of a succession of professionals. The role of Bill Robinson was, in this respect, unique. He played for the club for twelve seasons, from 1903 to 1914. For seven of these years he was the official club pro; for the remainder he played as an amateur, finding that his cricketing exploits helped his King Street business, which had now developed into sportswear. Batting at Number 3 and opening the bowling, he seemed to be always in the game, and he was unstinting in his commitment and irrepressible in his enthusiasm, whether he was being paid for his efforts or not.

Representative honours came his way in 1910, when he played eight times for Devon, finishing the season at the top of the bowling averages in a season when another Tavistock player, F. Hargrave Carroll, topped the batting list. Mr Carroll's disguise was both thin and unintentional. He had adopted his mother's maiden name in order to qualify for an inheritance. His style of play, no less than his physical appearance, revealed his identity. He was originally Jack Featherstone, the eldest son of the Reverend Sammy, of blessed memory.

Some members and supporters did see a danger in becoming over-dependent on professionals. Such anxieties tended to be swept away in the atmosphere of celebration that was generated by the successes of players like Robinson. One week in June 1910, not by any means untypical, illustrated his value to the side. He scored 86 and took 6 wickets against Newton, top-scored on a visit to Holsworthy, and made 52 and took 6 wickets when Okehampton came to The Ring.

The debt that the club owed him, in terms of results, was owed also to the other hired pros, Thomas and Bower in 1906 and 1907, Chambers in 1912, and Holden in 1913 and 1914. Chambers scored 350 runs and took 43 wickets. Arthur Holden scored, in 1913, 515 runs at an average of 32.2 and took 78 wickets at 6.6 each. In 1914 he made another 424 runs at an average of 28.3 and took another 78 wickets. Only occasionally did the pro either not turn out or under-perform, and on such occasions the effect was to expose vulnerability. For example, on August 3rd 1912, playing at Yelverton, Chambers made a duck and took only one wicket. The home side cruised to an easy six-wicket victory.

Such examples of failure may have been uncommon, but they were not lost on the captain, who began to advise of the risks of over-reliance on the efforts of the professional. He also showed increasing concern about the wider problem, as he saw it, of the side becoming unbalanced. An emphasis on experience at the expense of youth and raw talent was, Powell-Williams now decided, threatening the future of the club. Tavistock was gaining the reputation of being a 'team of grandfathers'. And when the grandfathers were crocked, or were taking their grandchildren to the seaside, it was difficult to raise a team. In June 1914 an appeal was published in the *Tavistock Gazette* above the signature of the captain. It was aimed at the young men of the district, and was a plea for support. Two events had triggered off this initiative. One was the reappearance, after a fourteen-year gap, of an old favourite at The Ring. F. D. Conry's swashbuckling return provided entertainment and was the occasion for much nostalgia, but equally it raised questions as to where the club was going if it turned for new blood to forty-year-olds. The other development was a noticeable decline in the standard of fielding which drew criticism even in the sympathetic columns of the *Gazette*. 'Poor' and 'Disgraceful' were descriptions that were used of the ground fielding, and the general lack of athleticism was seen to be a reflection of the average age of the side. Hence the public appeal to the youth of the area. If only Powell-Williams had been able to foresee the events of the next two months. This was the summer of 1914. Within weeks those same young men were again being urged into action. But the call this time was of a different, and of an altogether more momentous, kind.

Part Three: 1915–1939

The Age of Stability

Suspension and Reconstitution

Britain went to war on August 4th 1914. The cricket season was, for the Tavistock Club, coming towards its end, with only seven fixtures remaining. In the event, only two of them were played. The season ended prematurely, but in a reassuringly familiar way, with Holden and Robinson sharing the wickets as the opposition was dismissed for 25 and 29. There was, inevitably, some uncertainty about the future. As young men, in increasing numbers, responded to the call to enlist, doubts began to be felt about whether cricket, at any level, would maintain its established patterns. But there were far more serious matters to be concerned about. And when thoughts were allowed to drift back to summer scenes on village greens there was always the encouraging expectation that the war would either be over soon, or would at least not intrude too far into the arrangements or requirements of civilian life. Those who were present on August 19th 1914 to see Tavistock beat Okehampton by 127 runs can scarcely have imagined that the pause, before anything like normal service could be resumed, would be six years. But so it was to be.

It is not clear whether much, if any, cricket was played at The Ring during the four full summers of the war. No official fixtures were organised, as the club suspended all activity 'for the duration'. The only record of a game to have survived refers to a contest held on June 19th 1917 between W. M. Robinson's Eleven, which included a handful of members of the club, and the Royal Engineers. It would not be surprising, with so many troops billeted nearby, if other matches were organised on a similar basis, to keep the soldiers entertained, fit, and out of mischief. But it was not until the armistice of November 1918 that thoughts could again be turned to the affairs of the club. Even then, there were more immediate preoccupations, and before the focus of a punch-drunk community could be satisfactorily concentrated, it was the middle of 1919. Time only to celebrate with a short, hastily-compiled, list of local friendlies against the likes of Lamerton and Mary Tavy. The re-launch would have to await the early summer of 1920.

The first A.G.M. since 1914 was held in the Guildhall on May 3rd 1920. Ten members attended. They were able to call on the experience of the likes of

Harry Barkell, Edward Chilcott, Frank Jolliffe, and Frank Campbell, who resumed their pre-war roles. Twenty worthies were appointed vice-presidents. A small committee was established to supervise the day-to-day running of the club. Subscription rates were fixed at ten shillings (50p) for those over twenty-one, and five shillings (25p) for minors. As for a captain and vice-captain, it was natural to turn to men who had established themselves in the years before the war. Bill Snell had made his club debut in 1906. Although initially seen as principally a bowler, he had quickly showed that he could bat a bit, impressing one observer with 'his slashing cuts, powerful drives, and effective pulling'. He could also keep wicket. This all-round ability, his playing experience, and the fact that he was a captain in the army, were all factors that contributed to the decision to give him the captaincy in 1920. He was to do the job for eight successive seasons. During this period he was to prove himself the most consistent bat in the side, scoring a total of 1679 runs, bowling the occasional stint, keeping a bit when required, and showing in the field his party piece, the underarm flick.

His first vice-captain, in the classical bits-and-pieces mould of the journeyman club cricketer, was Sidney Sone, whose career at The Ring coincided with his twenty years as master of the workhouse. He had captained the side in 1908 and 1909, and was to play on until 1925. Under this leadership a slim and rather undemanding fixture list was negotiated in the first post-war season, with seven victories in eight matches. Snell, as befitted his military background, imposed a fairly strict regime, with selection for a game on a Saturday depending on attendance at nets on Monday and Tuesday. The team was also expected to turn up on Friday evening for a session combining fielding practice and pitch preparation. The captain tended to treat his players as rather raw recruits, which in a sense most of them were. Only a handful of pre-war veterans extended their playing days into the 1920s. There was S. L. Terrell and Edward Jasper, and A. J. Ellis, who, when turned out for the first time in thirteen years, made 49. But apart from Snell and Sone, the only surviver of the old days who could be classified as a heavyweight was Arthur Holden. He had been a Hampshire trialist before making his debut at The Ring in 1908 as a pace bowler. For two seasons he was the club pro, following retirement from a soccer career that had taken him from Plymouth Argyle to Chelsea via Portsmouth. After the war he launched a newsagent's business in King Street, and also took a job as a cricket coach at Kelly College. He continued to play at The Ring intermittently throughout the 1920s, enjoying himself particularly in 1921, when a 42 wicket haul included a 10 for 63, and in 1927 when, turning to his batting for late-career light relief, he scored 335 in 10 innings, including a 100 not out.

A New Generation

For the first few seasons following its reconstitution after the war, the club relied heavily on the efforts, on and off the field, of three men. Bill Snell was one. The others were Gordon Parry and Frank Millman. Parry began, in

1920, an association with the club that was to last for many years. As a player, he was a stylish and consistent batsman, a useful fast-medium change bowler, and a specialist slip field. Always near the centre of affairs, he was, at various times, captain, vice-captain, and secretary. Over the years his name became synonymous with that of the club, and he retained throughout a youthful enthusiasm and an infectious keenness. His most successful playing season was 1922, when he scored 540 runs at an average of 30, and took 84 of the 194 wickets that fell to Tavistock bowlers in the season. This included 8 for 26 against the Royal William Yard and 9 for 32 against the Royal Naval Barracks. In 1923 he recorded twice as many wickets as runs in the first half of the season, but recovered to hit a maiden century. In the following year, he took 5 or more wickets on 6 of his 10 outings. These included a game against Plymouth Corporation Officers in which he held the batting together with an undefeated 68 and then took all the 6 opposition wickets to fall. Throughout the years as vice-captain, from 1922 to 1927, he was seen as primarily a bowler. When he took over the captaincy from Snell in 1928 the balance changed, and he became increasingly the cornerstone of the batting, while his bowling became an occasional emergency service.

By this time the third of the trio of key inter-war stalwarts had established a permanent place in the side. Frank Millman played first in 1923, but it was not until 1927 that he achieved a double-figure average. Each season saw an increase in his aggregate, and in 1929 his average topped 17. The best was yet to come. He was a cautious player, solid rather than stylish, who was particularly strong on the on side, and whose specialities were the hook and the glance.

Among the other performers to gladden the hearts of spectators at The Ring in the 1920s was Theo Rowe, who ended his Tavistock career with a brief spell as vice-captain before moving to Plymouth in 1929. A fine, free-hitting batsman, his *annus mirabilis* was 1926, when he averaged 34 and hit two centuries. Only a knee injury prevented a repeat performance in the next season. To the great delight of his former colleagues, when he played for the first time for Plymouth against his old club, he was out for a duck.

And then there was C. L. Strachan, described by one admirer as 'a plucky lynx-like little fellow with the heart of a lion and the muscles of a giant'. He was an entertaining, if erratic run-maker, who also bowled a bit and was a member of that special breed of cricketers referred to as 'occasional wicket keepers'. Immortality came to him in the early evening of Saturday June 26th 1926. St. Devereau were the guests at The Ring. The game, as was so often the case, started rather late, and by the time the visitors had been dismissed for 158 only seventy minutes of playing time remained. Strachan, who had taken 3 wickets for 26, went in first. He lost his partner, Gordon Parry's brother Rex, with just a few on the board, and then enjoyed a fruitful partnership with Bill Snell, before the captain was bowled with 60 still needed in 20 minutes. Strachan now rode his luck, and everything went right. He hit 3 sixes and 13 fours, and, with five minutes to spare, the target was reached, Strachan finishing on 95 not out. 'Never', said a spectator, 'Have I seen so much enthusiasm at a cricket match on the Tavistock ground'. Sod's Law, operating in cricket as in less significant areas of life, saw to it that the hero of the hour was, in his next match, removed for 5 by a schoolboy in a match against Kelly College.

One of the features of the composition of the club before the war had been the large number of soldiers and teachers, more specifically of officers and public school masters, who were involved. The pattern continued in the 1920s. There were Captains Cannell and Curtoys, and Majors Brown, Brodrick, Troup, and Ellis, as well as Lieutenant Spencer and Commander Wise. Other occasional weekend duties often got in the way of the cricket, and meant that they were occasional performers, and the same tended to be true of the half-dozen Kelly College masters who replaced the retired generation of Wood, Linnell, and Penny. Frank Cannell was a useful pace bowler, and Stephen Murphy a good and enthusiastic wicket keeper. E. M. Edwards batted aggressively, and D. M. Godfrey chipped in with helpful knocks and a few wickets.

The appearances of H. V. Plum were limited by his duties as headmaster, but when he did turn out he batted, as his status presumably required, at Number 1. The last of this breed, J. Hulley, did not make his debut until 1930, but in the seven seasons that followed he proved to be a sound bat and an effective left-arm medium-pacer. In the 1931 season, while limited to six appearances, he topped the batting averages and came second in the bowling list. After him, this particular source of talent for the club tended to dry up. A similar, and equally sad, development from the club's point of view, was the decline in the supply of young clergymen. Only the Rev. Veale in the early 1920s, and the Rev. Bevan Barton, the Congregational Minister, in the last years of the decade, represented the cloth during the inter-war years.

Of those who, in the 1920s, crossed the firmament, made an impact, left a memory, and then moved on, two were called Hamilton. Sir Robert Hamilton played only a dozen or so games altogether. In May 1926, in his first match for three years and his penultimate game for the club, he scored 52 out of a total of 118, and took 6 Royal Engineering College wickets for 52. Sandy Hamilton, who may, of course, have been a son, or a brother, topped the bowling averages in 1927, but played thereafter for Seale Hayne College.

Those who were remembered really for one game included F. E. Bennett, a Callington man, who in the first over of his first innings hit 13 and E. E. Cornish from Luckett, who in his first appearance took 7 for 45. L. Stoney, a young clerk, took 3 for 5 in his first outing, and 4 wickets in each of the next two; he then disappeared without trace.

Walter Troup, a retired army officer, appeared in 1922 to play 6 games at the age of fifty-three. He had had a distinguished career as a county cricketer, playing 80 times for Gloucestershire between 1887 and 1911, and captaining that county in succession to W. G. Grace. His handful of matches towards the end of the summer of 1922 realised 113 runs with a top score of 46 and an average of 18.8. His son also played in the same season. Frank Colin Troup had, like his father, been born in India, and, also like his father, had represented Gloucestershire, though only in 3 matches. He was twenty-six years old when he played his one season for Tavistock. At the end of 1922 he emigrated to Australia, and there, within a year, he was killed in a motor accident. As a county player he had not been in the same class as his father, but was one of those all-round performers who inhabit the border areas between first-class and club cricket. In his 9 innings for Tavistock he scored 379 runs, with a highest score of 130, and he topped the club averages for the summer with 54.1. He also bowled 63 overs of spin, a rarish commodity at The Ring, and took 19 wickets at 8.8 each.

Another spinner who only played in one season was Ernie Terrell, who, in 1929, when still a schoolboy, took 36 wickets at 8 apiece, and also averaged 23 with the bat. The appearance of two other very occasional performers evoked memories of an earlier age. Lieutenant E.S.V. Spencer was the son of Herbert, a former captain. And E. Mockler-Ferryman, who played in 1921 and hit 89 against Plymouth Y.M.C.A., was the brother of a young man who had opened the batting in the 1913 season, and who had been killed in the war.

A New Pattern of Fixtures

The 1920s was a decade of some considerable change in the playing strength of the club. It was, in these circumstances, even more helpful to have two of the key administrative posts in the hands of committed officials, one of whom had done the job for some years before the war. Frank Jolliffe was the experienced treasurer. Gordon Parry was the secretary and general factotum. The continuing interest of Edward Chilcott, wise and benign, was harnessed by creating for him the post of chairman, which meant principally running the A.G.M., but which left the club free to offer the presidency to a series of deserving, or influential, figures, without imposing any duties on them. The list of presidents from 1921 to 1928 included Dr. Charles Brodrick, Major Frederick Porter, Dr. Leslie Watt, and Messrs Theo Rowe and Alfred Penny. Two general practitioners, a soldier, a bank manager, and a schoolmaster, provided the club with an appropriate image of soundness and respectability. They had all played for Tavistock at some time, except for Dr. Watt, who had, at least, provided two sons for the team. Mr Porter had gained promotion since his playing days, which seemed appropriate.

One of the first responsibilities of the administrators after 1920 was to re-build a fixture list to match the pre-war pattern, when more than twenty games had been played in an average season. There were 8 matches in 1920, but 20 in 1921, and thereafter, for the rest of the decade, the average number was 20, almost all played on Saturday afternoons, with the very occasional evening game against such as Gunnislake or Milton Abbot.

The token annual fixture against a local village was always played at The Ring, as were 62% of Tavistock's games during the 1920s. Featuring regularly in the lists were Holsworthy, Okehampton, Callington, Plymstock, Yelverton, and Liskeard. Kelly College and the Dartmoor Prison Officers were perennial opponents. But the bulk of fixtures were with Plymouth-based sides of students, soldiers, sailors, civil servants, and others, some of them homeless and therefore grateful not only for a fixture but for a venue.

Games against the Plymouth club proved to be rather one-sided. Between 1921 and 1926 there were 10 matches between the clubs. Plymouth won them all, by 10 wickets in one case and in the others by margins ranging from 50 to 189 runs. As a result, in 1927, one of the two games was against the Plymouth Second XI. Between that season and 1932, 8 games involved the Second XI and 6 were played against the First XI. The Tavistock record was, in the first group, Won 3, Lost 3, and Drawn 2 ; and in the second group, Won 1, Lost 4, and Drawn 1. From 1933 to 1935 the traditional pattern was resumed, with two bank holiday games being played each year, and a special game on Jubilee Day in 1935. Thereafter, for some reason, there were no fixtures between the clubs before the outbreak of the war.

Pre-war programmes had included the reception of touring sides, and this feature was resumed in 1926, when Cheltenham were entertained. Southsea were the visitors in 1928. In 1929 a side from New College Oxford made the first of a series of annual visits. Throughout the 1930s there were, each season, at least one, usually two, fixtures against clubs who had organised western tours as part of their overall programmes, or ad hoc groups of cricketers who wanted a playing holiday in a delightful part of the country. In other respects the fixture pattern in the 1930s remained similar to that of the 1920s, with a fixture against St. Luke's College Exeter being the only significant permanent innovation. The playing record during the 1930s was impressive, with 60% of matches being won, compared with 52% in the 1920s. The records of the two decades were :

Period	*Played*	*Won*	*Drawn*	*Lost*	*Tied*
1920-1929	185	97	19	68	1
1930-1939	209	125	31	52	1
Combined	394	222	50	120	2

There were, of course, fluctuations of fortune from season to season. In 1920, 7 of the 8 games were won. In 1921 the victories were 7 out of 20. In 1922 a full season brought only 2 defeats, in the 2 matches against Plymouth. In 1925 there were 5 successes in 15 matches. The 1926 season saw a 62% success rate. The following summer brought a figure of 20%. There were plenty of explanations for these variations, but the erratic availability of key players was certainly a factor. So was the decision not to employ a professional. The responsibility for maintaining some continuity of performance fell on a small group of players and administrators, like Parry and Millman, who in the earlier years were somewhat lacking in experience. By the 1930s they had come of age. The club had also, by the 1930s, produced a nucleus of performers who provided strength and consistency. The improvement in the playing record was the result, first of all, of a settled pace attack which displayed both containing and penetrative powers. There were a lot of victories in low-scoring matches. It was not until the last half of the decade that the batting recovered some of the solidity, and the occasional flourish, of earlier years. Even then, some brittleness remained. The team that in June 1937 scored 206 for 5, including an opening stand of 120, against Holsworthy, were humiliated by Callington four weeks later, when they were shot out for 28.

Five Stalwarts

Gordon Parry had, by 1930, come to occupy the pivotal position in the club's affairs that he was to retain for so many years. He had already done a stint as secretary. One of the innovations for which he had been responsible had been the siting of a notice-board in West Street where details of fixtures and teams were regularly displayed. He seemed to have the time to devote to administrative chores, like fixture compilation, pre-match arrangements, and publicity, and to taking care of the ground and pavilion. The impression was that cricket had few rivals for his attentions. The son of a Unitarian Minister who had died in 1924, he had had a sound education, but appeared to have no steady professional commitment until he joined Bishop and Turnbull as company secretary in the 1940s. He was a bachelor, who lived with his widowed mother, a lady who for some years organised the major operation of match teas. Outside the family of the cricket club he was seen as something of a loner. At The Ring he was at home.

On the field, he was captain from 1928 to 1931, and vice-captain thereafter for the rest of the pre-war period. As the years went by, less and less was seen of the whirlwind action that had brought him harvests of wickets in the early 1920s. He continued to be a safe slip fielder, and a permanent fixture as opening bat. There was the occasional interruption to his career, by illness in 1925 and again in 1930, and by landing a job as a cricket coach at a college in Sussex in 1935, but overall he continued to play, year after year, the role of sheet-anchor batsman. At the end of 1939, his twentieth season, he had amassed a total of 4430 runs and taken 388 wickets. If the club had offered what became fashionable in sporting clubs in a later age, a 'clubman of the year' award, Parry would have walked off with it in most seasons.

And in the years when he did not win it, it would have gone to Frank Millman. Millman was a quiet, modest character, who lived in College Avenue and worked in the Labour Exchange in Drake Road. He took over the secretarial duties in 1928 and carried them on until the war. On the field, his most productive seasons were in the mid 1930s, when he was averaging about 20 and featuring in second or third place in the tables. By 1939 his career aggregate over seventeen seasons had reached 4284. The 1935 season brought the high point of his career, when, in an away game against Holsworthy, he made 112 not out, out of a total of 215. The same year also produced one of his most embarrassing moments. It came during the Jubilee Day game against Plymouth on May 6th. Chasing a Plymouth total of 172 for 5 declared, the home side sank to 10 for 3 before recovering to 73 before the fourth wicket fell. This brought in Bill Fellowes. Millman, 25 not out and at the non-striker's end, called out his advice: 'Be careful Bill'. Fellowes saw out the rest of the over. Millman then faced up, pushed the first ball straight to a close fielder, called for a run, and was run out by ten yards. After that the innings subsided to a total of 86. Frank, the most likeable of men, was not the toast of the club that night.

On June 13th 1924 the *Tavistock Gazette* carried the following story:

> 'Playing in the Meadows for R Oates's Eleven against the West End Cricket Club, Eric Davey, son of Mr Glanville Davey of Bannawell Street, one of the cleverest all-round cricketers that Tavistock has ever produced, had the remarkable bowling analysis of 14 wickets for 12 runs. In the first innings he had 8 for 2, and in the second innings 6 for 10. He has a beautiful action, and keeps a perfect length. More should be heard of this capable young cricketer, who is evidently bent on following in his father's footsteps.'

Young Eric was then sixteen, the only son of the legendary 'Glan', who had by now graduated from player to umpire. The following year saw Eric's club debut, in the penultimate game of the season, when, batting at Number 11, he took part in a last-wicket stand of 80 that doubled the Tavistock score and won the match. In 1927 he played in 5 games, scoring 56 runs and taking 7 wickets. It was the 1928 season that launched his phenomenal career. He played 20 games, scored 284 runs, and took 66 wickets at an average of 10.5, following this up in 1929 with 326 runs and 59 wickets at 9.0 each. The 1930 season saw him in his pomp, scoring nearly twice as many runs, and taking more than twice as many wickets, as anyone else. In 1931 he took 66 wickets at an average of 5.3, and in 1932, when he had the captaincy, he bowled 247 overs, topped the bowling averages by a wide margin, and was fourth in the batting list. Those years, when he was in his early twenties, saw him performing as a genuine all-rounder. As a batsman he had strength, confidence, and a keen eye.

In the middle of the 1933 season he not only made his maiden century, but made the runs in 45 minutes in an innings that included 4 sixes and 14 fours. In that season he scored 519 runs at an average of 25.9. But he always saw himself as a bowler who could incidentally make useful quick runs. And he certainly was a thoroughbred bowler. His action, it was said, was reminiscent of that of his father, with the same rather crouching delivery. He bowled medium fast, had the stamina to sustain a long spell, was capable of moving the ball into the bat, and showed, above all, control of line and length. A bowler who can offer high rates of both wicket-taking and economy is a priceless asset. When Davey took his 99 wickets at 4.1 each in 1933, and his 97 at 7.9 apiece in 1934, equally impressive was his capacity to bowl between 300 and 400 overs in each of those seasons with an economy rate that scarcely exceeded 2 runs per over.

The 1935 record was the most impressive of all. He bowled 364 overs, of which 120 were maidens, and conceded 696 runs in taking 100 wickets. Of his 100 victims, 75 were clean bowled. In one week in the early part of the season he took, in two games, 13 wickets for 34 runs, all of them bowled. His feat in achieving the century of wickets, having missed the target by 1 and by 3 in the previous two summers, was duly recognised by the club in a special ceremony at which Dr. Leslie Watt, patron and former president, presented him with a ball inscribed with the details of a record that had never been achieved by any previous Tavistock player.

Davey became, in that season, the first member of the club to be selected for Devon since William Linnell. Unfortunately the game, against Cornwall, was washed out, and in the return match the selectors, in the way these things are sometimes done, overlooked him. He continued, throughout the 1930s, to bowl 300 overs or so of tight accurate seamers per season, and to make useful runs, about 250 of them in the average summer. At the 1937 A.G.M., the chairman, driven to try to find something new to say about him, complimented him on his fielding, pointing out that he also topped the list of catchers. The interruptions to the flow were few and brief. A special bellringing festival, perhaps, that might call him away. Or a honeymoon, causing him to miss, not one, but two games. By 1939, after thirteen years with the club, he had scored 2853 runs and taken 760 wickets, while his shovel-like hands had scooped hundreds of slip catches.

Opening bowlers, as everyone knows, hunt best in pairs. In the 1930s the Larwood and Voce of The Ring were Eric Davey and Maurice Avery. They had been born in the same year, 1908, and made their club debuts in the same season, 1925. They were both to be thirty-one when the war came to interrupt their cricket careers at a point when they were both in their prime.

Maurice Avery was a native of Dawlish, who had been educated at Truro, and had followed his father into a career in the Prudential Assurance Company. His job took him to Okehampton and to Minehead, for both of which clubs he played for a time before he and his wife Dot settled in Plymouth in 1949. But for 62 years he remained a member of the Tavistock club, and his commitment to it over the years, in varying capacities, was very strong. He was seen in his early years, in the mid-1920s, as a promising bowler who could bat a bit. He enjoyed batting, but had no pretensions to being other than a free-scoring tailender. He had a good eye, could hit cleanly, and was just the man to exploit a tired attack towards the end of an innings. By 1939 he had amassed a career total of 2032 runs, with a highest score of 72 not out. But it was his bowling that caught the eye, particularly when he was operating in tandem with Davey.

The home game against the Royal Naval Engineering College, played on May 19th 1928, was not seen at the time as having any particular significance. But years later it could be seen as having marked the beginning of an era. It was the first occasion on which Davey and Avery cleaned up between them. It was to happen on many occasions over the next ten years. In 1936 they took between them 136 of the 184 wickets to fall to Tavistock bowlers, a large proportion of them being clean bowled. Most spectacular was the early-season annihilation of Callington, who were bowled out for 18, with Davey taking 6 for 13 and Avery 3 for 5. In the following season the terrible twins were responsible for 152 of a total of 203 dismissals.

Tavistock Cricket Club

after a lapse of 5 years a general meeting was held at the Guildhall on Tuesday May 3rd. 1920.

Present E.W. Chilcott (Chairman) Mess. A.W. Perry, Barkell A.B. Trelour W.H. Rose F.S. Cannell W. Johns B. Doidge, G. Smith H.O. Edwards.

Resolved that Mr. Johns add credit balance of new account to old account at Mess. Fox Fowler & Co.s Bank.

The following officers were elected. President & Vice Presidents as on other side. Captain - W.W. Snell.

Vice Captain. W. Sone.

Hon. Sec. W. Barkell. G.A. Hutchin[illegible] Hon Sec appointed May 12 1920

Hon. Treas. W.F. Joliffe

The following were elected on Committee.

W. E.W. Chilcott, W. Johns, W. Perry - W. Redstone & W. Edwards (with power to add to their number.

Subscription. Playing members over 21. 10/ } subscriptions to be paid before playing

" " under 21. 5/.

The secretary was empowered to order sufficient playing material to start the season.

Edw W Chilcott 31.3.21.

Mr. Perry V. 01. T.

The record of the 1920 A.G.M. when the club was revived after the Great War.

19th August 1922
Standing: S. H. Murphy, N. C. Metherell, C. C. Morrison, E.St.V. Spencer, S. Richards, S.T. Sone, G. Chapman (umpire). *Seated:* G. H. Parry, W. M. Snell (captain), A. L. B. Watt. *Front Row:* J. B. Newsome, A. S. Newsome.
The game against the Constructive Draughtsmen was won by 113 runs, J.B. Newsome scoring 117, including 5 sixes and 16 fours, and Parry taking 6 for 41.

4th May 1929
Standing: Mr Glubb (supporter), Ernie Terrell, Eric Davey, Bill Tucker, Rex Parry, Bray Treloar, Mr Maunder (umpire), Mr Clemo (scorer). *Seated:* Alfred Treloar, Gordon Parry (captain), Dr. Watt (president), Tom Niven, Frank Millman. *Front Row:* Frank Bond, Kenneth Terrell.
A grey early-season scene before a rain-affected game against Buckfastleigh.

20th August 1932.
Standing: Mr Maunder (umpire), Gordon Parry, Jim Beale, Bill Tucker, John Hulley, Frank Millman, Frank Bond, Mr Martin (scorer), Rex Parry. *Seated:* Doug May, Eric Davey (captain), Fred Barkell, Maurice Avery. The game, a late season fixture against a club on tour from Kent, resulted in a narrow defeat. Hulley and Bond took eight of the wickets, and Davey top-scored with 48.

19th June 1937.
Standing: Bill Martin (scorer), Bill Rankin, Fred Barkell, Gordon Parry, Bill Colling, Len Avery, Glanville Davey (umpire). *Seated:* Frank Millman, Eric Davey (captain), Bill Fellowes, Doug May.
Front Row: Frank Bond, Maurice Avery.
Holsworthy were the visitors to The Ring. They were dismissed for 104, Davey taking six wickets and Avery four. Parry and Colling then scored 120 for the first wicket. The other seven players enjoyed the game.

The Ring in 1915.
Arthur Holden, the former club professional, ran a newsagent's business through which he sold his postcards of local scenes, like this one above.

End of an era. August Bank Holiday Monday 1939. Tavistock lose an exciting match to an Invitation Eleven by two runs.
Standing: Umpire Tucker, F. W. Steed, T. White, Roy Acton, Eric Davey, Bill Tucker, Frank Howe, Bill Martin. *Seated:* Frank Bond, Frank Millman, Bill Colling, Nick Kelly, Les Baker.
Within a month, war had been declared. Les Baker was to be killed on active duty.

Statistically Avery, whose efforts would, in another context, have been seen as outstanding, had to take second place, and it was not until the 1939 season that, playing in more games, he was able to claim more victims than his partner. By the end of that season he had accumulated a total of 406 wickets.

The triumphs of Davey and Avery were, to some degree, to eclipse the staunch efforts of other quick bowlers. There was, for example, Frank Bond, who, between 1926 and 1937 played, season after season, a key role as either opening bowler or first change. He had been quickly recognised as 'a promising lad' when he made his first appearance for the club in 1926. He was blooded, in a late season game when one or two regular players were on holiday, and, in the traditional way, an opportunity was taken to test some raw youth. Given four or five overs, the young man acquitted himself well, taking 3 for 13. Thereafter, through until 1937, his left-arm quickies would bring him harvests of 40 wickets or so a season. His most productive summer was that of 1929, when he topped the averages with 59 wickets at 6.2 each. This included a midsummer bonanza of 8 for 7 when a team of local government officers were shot out for 30 at The Ring.

Like nearly all the members of the team in that period, Bond lived and worked in the town, in his case at Exeter Street and the G.W.R. station respectively. This was, more than was the case in earlier and later periods, a local club. The benefits of this came at two levels. In a practical sense it made for easier administration and communication if someone, on his bike, could get round most of the players' homes in half-an-hour with a message about a practice session or a rearranged fixture. And secondly, less easy to define but no less potent, there was a sense of identity which is more difficult to sustain when there is a heavy dependence on mercenaries, professionals, and guests.

Captains, Critics, and Others

When Bill Snell retired from the captaincy after the 1927 season, Gordon Parry was the natural replacement. He led the side through three full seasons. During that period, 63 games were played, and the balance of victories and defeats was 32 to 25. It was hardly a discreditable record, but by the end of the 1930 season there were murmurings of discontent. Parry was a rather shy and private man with a somewhat low-key style of leadership. This did not appeal to all the players. Two in particular began to voice private criticism. One was Bill Fellowes, an enthusiastic all-round cricketer and a forceful bat, who had first appeared in 1926 but had firmly established himself in the side in 1929 as a wicketkeeper-batsman. Born in Yorkshire, but translated to Tavistock when his father moved south to take over the running of the Town Mill at Parkwood, he was also, in the late 1920s, launching a career in professional football that was to take him from Plymouth Argyle via Clapton Orient to Luton Town. He was reckoned to be a young who would speak his mind.

The other voice of criticism was that of L. H. Woollett. He joined the staff of the Grammar School in 1929 as sportsmaster, the first such appointment. His success in enhancing the cricket tradition of the school may be seen in a record where, in three years under his leadership, 32 matches were played and 31 won. He played his first season for the club in 1930, showing his all-round ability by gaining second and third places in the batting and bowling averages. He was, some thought, a young man in a hurry.

The 1931 season began with Parry's reappointment at the Spring A.G.M. The first game of the season, a match against Milton Abbot seen as an undemanding pre-season run-out, ended in ignominious defeat. The following Saturday brought another defeat, this time at the hands of the Keyham Engineering Students. It was, perhaps, overlooked that in each of these games the Tavistock captain had top-scored. The next two fixtures were, frustratingly, washed out. A narrow victory on Whit Monday was followed by a near-debacle against Holsworthy, when honour was saved only by the tail managing to give three figures to an innings that had stood at 17 for 6. Over the next month victories over modest opposition and defeat at the hands of Yelverton failed to lift the gloom. Parry himself entered a trough that brought him successive scores of 6, 1, 19, 2, 3, 5, and 9. In the first week in July the critics went public. Parry immediately resigned, readily agreeing to play on under a new captain. Eric Davey was thereupon appointed, and took over for the game against Buckfastleigh on July 11th. Fellowes and Woollett were requested by the club committee to send an apology for their actions. They declined. Neither was selected again for the rest of the season. Woollett was never to play for the club again. Fellowes came back in 1933 after a two-year exile. Parry played out the rest of the season as vice-captain, though he could not recover his batting form, and ended the season with an aggregate of 119 and an average of 8. It had been a sad season. Perhaps things might have turned out differently had the club been able to turn to Edward Chilcott, as they had done on so many occasions over the years. But the Grand Old Man was in decline and not available for advice. He was to die at the end of the year.

Eric Davey captained the side, with Parry as his vice-captain, through the rest of the 1931 season, and through 1932. He then happily passed the job on to J.E.T. Beale, who was to be in charge for four seasons. Jim Beale was a recent arrival in the town, having moved from Taunton to manage the local branch of Lloyds Bank. He had been born in Bournemouth in 1894, and was a seasoned cricketer when he played his first summer at The Ring in 1932. He retained a youthful enthusiasm for the game, and conveyed it to the rest of the side in a manner unique to wicketkeepers. His individual contributions with the bat were not substantial, but that was partly the result of his putting himself in at Number 11. His contribution to team spirit was significant, and in playing terms this showed itself in the most obvious way, in the standard of fielding.

The results speak for themselves. In his four years, 94 games were played, 61 were won, 16 were drawn, and 17 were lost. In 1936 he moved on to Fowey. He was to return to the area in retirement and to die at his home at Dousland in 1964 at the age of seventy. His departure was followed by a second interregnum year of Davey leadership, before, in 1938, S.W. Colling became the club's last pre-war captain.

Bill Colling was, some have said, the most cultured bat in the club's history. He had been a member of Woollett's triumphant Grammar School team, and had then played for St. Luke's College while training to be a teacher. In the mid 1930s he came back to Tavistock and joined the staff of the Plymouth Road Junior School. He first played for the club in 1935, but burst onto the scene in 1936 with an aggregate of 527 runs and an average of 37.7. In successive games in July he scored 70, 73, 75, 1, and 68. Appointed vice-captain in 1937, he scored a further 456 runs and topped the averages again. In his two years as captain he was marginally less prolific, although he achieved in 1939 the century – 108 not out – that had hitherto eluded him. By the end of that season he had scored, in his five years with the club, a total of 1894 runs. An opening bat in a classic mould, he managed to give an unhurried air to his batting, a hallmark, surely, of real class. He also excelled on the football field, and was to establish himself as a figure as substantial at Langsford Park as he was at The Ring. Like so many talented sportsmen of his generation, the war was to remove a big slice from the middle of his sporting career. For that generation, even for those who were to be able to resume their playing career after the war, there would always be an element of might-have-been.

Other individuals who made their mark in the inter-war years, and who entertained the large crowds that gathered at The Ring on Saturday afternoons, included Bill Tucker, a long-handled lower-order batsman who contributed useful scores in season after season, and had the distinction, in 1939, of being second in the averages to Bill Colling. Then there was Tom Niven, who only played for four seasons, but had topped 1000 runs before the second one was over. And C. J. Horne, a left arm slow bowler who added variety to the attack in the mid 1930s, when Davey and Avery left him anyone to bowl at. And, in the fallen idol class, came Nelson Hall, who bowled his medium-pace seamers to very good effect between 1932 and 1936. In 1934 he took 57 wickets at 8.8 apiece. In the next two years his contributions became rather overshadowed by those of Davey and Avery, but he still managed to turn in performances like 7 for 39 in 23 overs against Yelverton and 4 for 7 in 5 overs against Holsworthy.

In November 1936 he was charged with obtaining money by false pretences. He confessed to collecting sums of money, ostensibly for the cricket and football clubs, from a number of people, principally elderly and gullible neighbours of his in Watts Road. He was bound over for three years.

The king of Tavistock cricket in the 1930s was Eric Davey, and Eric had, of course, been brought into the club under the tutelage of his father. One of the appealing aspects of club cricket, particularly in a small town, has always been the family connections that have served as sinews for the club. There were a number of examples, between the wars, of brothers playing at the same time: the Mackenzies, the Millers, and the Morrisons in 1921, and the Newsomes in 1922. In 1923 there were the Minhinnicks, the Phillipses, and the Watts, in 1933 the Gibsons, and in 1936 the Biddells. Three Ward brothers, Rex, Humphrey, and John, played between 1923 and 1925. Maurice Avery's brother Len turned out a lot between 1929 and 1937, and Rex Parry, brother of Gordon, batted effectively through nine seasons from 1926. Charles

Millman joined the club in the same year as his brother Frank.

As for fathers and sons, the careers of Bill Fellowes and his father Jim overlapped. In 1937 Nick Kelly burst onto the scene, scoring a lot of runs over the season including a 99 not out. Perhaps he brooded on this latter mishap through the whole of the 1937-38 winter. In the first game of the new season, on April 30th, he scored 104 not out; by September he had topped the averages throughout the summer. His father, who also played in 1937, was F. L., or Squire, Kelly, of Kelly.

And then there were the Treloars. A. B. Treloar, the paterfamilias, was the headmaster of the Dolvin Road School. He played during the period between 1920 and 1932, turning out in about a third of the fixtures, batting low down and keeping wicket when required. Three of his sons played for the club, Bray, Douglas, and Harry. The one whose participation and service was to last the whole of his lifetime was Douglas. He made his debut in 1932 at the age of sixteen, but it was 1938 before he began doing what, after the war, he was to do with rare consistency, season after season. He started taking wickets. He was another of those players whose careers had to be put on ice in 1939 'for the duration', but who still had a lot of cricket left when normal service was resumed. Bill Colling was another. Others included Roy Acton, an eighteen-year-old wicketkeeper-batsman, Bill Barnes, an all-rounder of considerable potential, and Doug May, an opening bat with a two-eyed stance and a resolute defence, who, on one occasion, while wickets fell around him, batted through 38 overs to hold an innings together, and to finish on 34 not out, garnered from 25 scoring strokes.

Family connections and loyalties constituted one of the routes by which young men came into the club. Local village clubs offered another possible source. Maurice Clemo, Bill Guest, and Edward Cornish came to The Ring via Gulworthy, Milton Abbot, and Luckett respectively. Some lads cut their teeth in school cricket, and had been encouraged, perhaps by supportive sports masters like L. H. Woollett, to graduate early to the town club. These included sixth-formers L. Lee at the Grammar School, E. E. Down at Kelly College, and E. J. Terrell at Plymouth College.

In the 1920s there did exist what was in effect a nursery for the senior club. This was the Tavistock Athletic Cricket Club. Among those who gained an apprenticeship in this particular cricket academy were Eric Davey and Jimmy Fellowes, although the latter, a spin bowler, was already middle-aged. There were also 'Riggy' Eva and Jack Craze. 'Blossom' Cole, who was left with a limp following a soccer accident, was a strong on-side batsman. Charlie Harry, a slow and cautious bat, delighted his friends with a leg glide known as 'Char's rabbit stroke', but also infuriated them with his dangerous habit of throwing the ball sky-high when he had made a slip catch. Billy Redstone's batting reflected his extrovert character; he was above all carefree and erratic. And then there was Fred Barkell, greatly talented, impetuous, and fallible. A typical Barkell innings would produce 30 runs in 20 minutes, 24 of them in boundaries, and would be ended by a catch to wicket keeper or slips as he chased a ball two feet outside his off stump. To watch Fred bat for half an hour was a treat which made the long climb to The Ring worthwhile, but too often, of course, he fell on his sword. At his best he was, to use the term then applied as the one of highest commendation, Jessopian.

A number of the Athletic players were also accomplished and enthusiastic footballers. Billy Redstone, 'Riggy' Eva, Fred Barkell, and Jack Craze were as well known for their exploits for the town soccer club as for their deeds at The Ring. The same was true of Bert Southcott. And there were the two men who played the winter game at the professional level. Arthur Holden had played league soccer before the war. Bill Fellowes played in the 1930s, seeking relaxation and enjoyment at The Ring in the ten weeks break that top footballers are allowed. To the 1937 A.G.M. Fellowes sent a telegram of apology for non-attendance, and giving as the reason his duties as captain of Luton Town.

Officers, Rules, and the Laws

The presidency of the club had rotated regularly in the years after the war. In the 1930s this pattern changed, in reflection of a wider trend towards greater continuity in administration as well as in playing terms. The post was held from 1930 to 1937 by A.K.G. Johnstone, lawyer, town celebrity, and pre-war player. He was followed by Squire Kelly. Secretarial duties meanwhile passed quietly in 1928 from Gordon Parry to Frank Millman, where they remained until the war. Millman was a conscientious and long-suffering official, as secretaries have to be. He was once referred to, in the kind of prose characteristic of sports journalists of the age, as 'the club's hard-working quill-driller'. Frank Jolliffe, the long-serving treasurer, left the town in 1930. His duties fell to George Bricknell.

Of the occupants of two other key posts, little is known. Umpires and scorers are, of course, modest and self-effacing men, determinedly refusing publicity. Glanville Davey was the regular umpire in the 1920s. In the 1930s there were two names. Mr Maunder was a prison officer, Mr R.G. Chapman was chief clerk at the Bedford Estate Office. The veteran scorer, W.F. Clemo, died in 1930 and was replaced by Bill Martin, who was to do the job for many years.

Someone in the administration has, of course, to try to ensure that eleven men turn up at the right place at the right time to honour a fixture. This was a more difficult exercise than it was to become in the age of the universal motor car and the telephone. The number of occasions when arrangements came unstuck were remarkably few. It happened on May 20th 1929, when the side could only launch its scheduled expedition to Holsworthy by the last-minute inclusion of six rookies, who, in the event, were to contribute just 9 runs between them in what was to be a two-run defeat.

On June 4th 1932 a visiting team from Plymouth experienced a similar hiccup, this time arriving at The Ring with six players. Five Tavistock players who were there that afternoon, and who had not been selected to play, agreed to turn out for the visitors. No one suggested that they did anything other than give of their best. They were, however, unable to contribute more than 5 runs to a modest total. These were the exceptional games, which people remembered for their exceptional features. There were other reasons for remembering particular afternoons.

On July 16th 1927, in an away game against the Royal Naval Engineering College, Tavistock scored 183, and left their opponents only one hour to reply. It might have been thought that the only response could have been to play for a draw, but the result was a home victory by 6 wickets. The run-chase, particularly if it brings a home victory, is, of course, one of the most exciting features of cricket. So is the dramatic collapse. On July 7th 1934 Tavistock batted first against Plymstock, and scored 176. When, after 40 minutes batting, the visitors had reached 39 for 2, the contest appeared to be well balanced. In the next four overs Davey and Hall took 4 wickets each, and the final total was 40 all out.

A tie is a very unusual result in cricket, and only two were recorded in the inter-war period. On June 6th 1927 Tavistock made 152 in a game at Holsworthy, largely through Gordon Parry holding the innings together with a patient 45. Parry remained the hero during the Holsworthy reply, having the last man caught behind with the scores level. Three years later Tavistock and Yelverton ended a thrilling match by scoring 110 each, some of the crowd showing their appreciation by contributing a collection of twenty-seven shillings (£1.35p), while others complained loudly of two debatable lbw decisions that had checked the Yelverton innings. These were the close games, the tight finishes, that had both crowd and players on their toes. There was one such on a July afternoon in 1926 when a visiting Plymouth team were beaten by 1 run. Two weeks later a Tavistock side almost identical in composition played again at The Ring against one of its regular visitors. This time the margin of victory was 292 runs. Satisfying, of course, but not the sort of stuff to create a deathly hush in Chollacott Close.

Results were not the only features of games that were remembered and talked about long after the events. There were the occasions when unexpected interventions changed the course of the proceedings. This could be the weather, like the snow storm that briefly held up play against the Royal Naval Barracks in 1935. Or it might just as easily have been Bill Tucker's motor bike. This piece of machinery almost changed the fortunes of one game in May 1930. It was an away match. The opponents were Holsworthy. This fixture, over the years, provided a surprisingly large number of good stories. On this particular day the visitors arrived one short, and fortunately won the toss. After half an hour they were 16 for 5. There was then a recovery to 42 for 5, and a further slump to 55 for 9. By this time Bill Tucker had arrived on the motor bike, in time to inspire a last-wicket stand which raised the total to 94. The heroics of man and machine were not quite enough. Holsworthy won by 1 wicket.

There were, in the 1930s, two significant amendments to the laws of the game. In each case the club agreed to requests to incorporate the changes before they received the full authority of the omnipotent M.C.C. In March

1930 it was agreed, in anticipation of a law change of the following year, to increase the size of the wickets in respect of both height and width by one inch, bringing them to a height of 28 inches and a width of 9 inches. Then, in 1936, came contentious proposals to amend the lbw law, to encompass the possibility of a dismissal in the case of a ball pitching outside off stump. Strong reservations were expressed at the A.G.M. about this radical proposal. The general feeling of the meeting was hostile to change. Frank Millman resignedly noted: 'It was decided to comply with the M.C.C.'s request to adopt the new rule'. It received Mount Sinai authority in the following year.

These major departures apart, the controversies of the 1930s were concerned with playing conditions rather than rules and time remained the biggest problem. The modern conventions of one-day cricket, in which the governing limitation is a specified number of overs, was unknown in the pre-war game. In those days the outcomes were decided by the operation of the eternal trinity of runs, wickets, and time. The clock was the over-reaching arbiter. Evening games, which were very few, ended at 9 p.m. The standard Saturday fixture was scheduled to start at 2.30, with an agreement that stumps would be drawn at 7.30. The tea interval, normally taken between innings, was supposed to occupy only twenty minutes. Such civilised arrangements were subjected to pressure when, as was often the case, there was a late start. The 7.30 curfew remained a constant and well-understood feature, so well established that it was usually felt to be unnecessary to confirm it before each game. Only occasionally did this lead to uncertainty, or worse.

In an away game against a naval team in August 1932, Tavistock appeared to be cruising to a comfortable victory as they aimed to overhaul a modest total of 113. At 90 for 3, and with the clock showing 6.45, a rumour swept the visiting dressing-room that there was to be a 7 o'clock finish. Heads went up in the air, blades flashed across the line, and by the time that 7.30 was confirmed as the correct closure-time the board was showing 99 for 8. The hosts ran out winners by 12 runs. The explanation for these events may have been quite innocent. Certainly no suspicion was aroused when, on another occasion, controversy clouded a finish. This was the occasion of a home match against Callington in 1937, when one of the umpires called off the players, to discover, too late, that his watch was eight minutes fast. The position of the game at the time was that Tavistock needed 24 runs to win and had 4 wickets in hand. Eight minutes would have generated 2, possibly 3, overs. Any one of four results could have ensued. The umpire was not the most popular figure in the bars of the town that evening as differing scenarios were offered. The Tavistock players had no doubt about what would have happened: Fred Barkell was batting, and had already made 33.

Developments at The Ring

The care of the ground was, in the years immediately following the war, largely in the hands of the club's small inner cabinet, and most of the work was done by Snell and Parry. They had the help, for some time, of a suitable mower loaned by Henry Soltau, a well-disposed brewer who lived in nearby Down Road. The preparation of wickets was the most time-consuming task, and in the mid-1920s the club was finding it necessary to offer a small honorarium – £1 a season – to a Mr Woodrow as recognition of his efforts in that direction. By 1933 the recipient of this payment, to be made in two instalments of ten shillings each, was a Mr Morrish. Pitch preparation was, of course, a specialist task.

Not so the job of picking up litter after a game. A readiness to take a share in such chores has always been, reasonably, a test of a man's commitment to the club. The players were expected to participate in such necessary exercises, particularly the ones that were created by substantial gatherings of spectators, and the crowds were, on average, large. It was not unusual for a holiday-time fixture to attract an attendance of 200 or 300. Some spectators were encouraged to the Down by the provision of a special bus that left Bedford Square at 2.30 each match day. A number of attempts were made to have more seating provided, but this had not materialised by 1939.

The threat of wilful damage to ground and buildings remained an ever-present concern, given the relative isolation of the site, but in only one instance was the club driven to take a strong response. This was in 1929, when, following a spate of vandalism, notices of impending legal action were inserted in the press, rewards for information were offered, and higher insurance premiums became payable. Improvements were made. In 1930 a new store shed was installed at a cost of £23. In 1935 there was a fleeting hope that the town's permanent jubilee memorial would take the form of a major redevelopment of The Ring. The rather insignificant little riverside archway leading into The Meadows emerged instead.

The club was, at least, sustained through such disappointments by the pegging of its annual rent at the level of a manageable five shillings and sixpence (27½p). There was, it is true, a further burden of five shillings a year in the form of water rates. This became payable in 1923, when £36 was spent on improvements that resulted in bringing water into the pavilion, and closing the outside entrance to the privy and opening one inside. A small space was also enclosed to provide a kitchen. The kitchen contained a fireplace which gave problems when the wind was in the wrong direction. It was later replaced by a calor gas stove, which was, in 1953, to be the cause of a fire. This was the first of two expensive additions made to the pavilion during the inter-war period. The second was in 1937, when £40 was spent on a drainage scheme, a project that required a further £24 of expenditure in the following year.

The need for the provision of a kitchen, which was met in 1923, was pressed hard by the secretary, Gordon Parry, who, in turn, was under pressure from his mother. Mrs Parry, the widow of a unitarian minister and the mother of Gordon and Rex, had organised match teas since her two sons had joined the club in 1920. Through until 1927 regular and fulsome thanks were offered at club meetings to Mrs Parry and her lady helpers for their care and hard work. And then, in 1928, there is talk of the need to 'improve' the tea arrangements, and Theo Rowe, vice-captain and presumably well-placed to make such an appeal, is required to seek the assistance of lady supporters.

The ladies continue to receive ritual thanks, without names, down to 1932, by which time Mrs Johnstone, the wife of the president, has clearly emerged as the organiser. It was, it seems, increasingly difficult to carry out the operation with the voluntary help of mothers, wives and girl friends. Hence the decision to employ lady helpers and to pay them four shillings (20p) a match.

Teas were the only sustenance that a host club was expected to provide in an afternoon-evening game. Only one instance is recorded during this period of lunches being provided at The Ring. This was in 1926, when Holsworthy were entertained. Since the visitors had left home at mid-morning, it was decided to arrange for Herbert Brown, the Brook Street dairy proprietor, to lay on the necessary refreshment. 'An excellent luncheon', we are told, 'was provided in the pavilion'. Excellent, no doubt, and very welcome after a tedious journey from Holsworthy, but costly perhaps. The idea appears not to have been repeated.

Running the Club

The period between the wars was not one in which the club developed its social activities. There is no reference to an annual dinner, a major feature of the calendar in an earlier period, except in 1935. In December of that year a dinner was held at the Union Hotel. The fact that a slight loss was made on the event may explain why it did not re-emerge as a regular occasion. There were two other types of money-raising social activities, both of them introduced in 1923. The occasional dance could be expected to raise up to £10. The jumble sale was a more frequent exercise, having the additional benefit of involving few expenses. By such occasional injections of income the club was helped towards keeping its finances sound.

There were other one-off windfalls, like the £10 from the Royal Marines in 1923 for the use of the ground, and the £50 bequest in 1940 under the will of Edward Yelland, retired draper, ex-councillor, and former player. This latter gift enabled the treasurer to show, for the first time in the club's history, a three-figure balance. Up to then successive A.G.M.s had shown the accounts to be in the black by amounts varying from £1 to £36, the balance in an average year being of the order of £15. Fund-raising apart, there were two principal sources of income. One was subscriptions, which in a good year could realise over £40, and which rarely fell below £20; the other was the regular collection at the ground on match days. The first such was taken on August 6th 1921 in a match against Plymouth, and raised £1.2s (£1.10p). Thereafter, each season, a total of between £6 and £16 came to the club via the tins that rattled round the boundary of The Ring, particularly when the home side was doing well. In 1930 a Mr Glubb was being recognised for his help in organising the collections with an honorarium of ten shillings (50p). In 1937 Messrs A. Jago and A. D. Lowe were being thanked for similar services.

With these steady sources providing an adequate income, there was no need for too much frenzied fund-raising. Expenses were modest. There was no professional. Some improvements to ground and pavilion could be afforded. And there remained in the kitty each year a few pounds which could be used to pay both the wages of a groundsman and a modest scale of travelling expenses for away games. The former principle, which began with the £1 honoraria offered to Messrs Woodrow and Morrish, was extended to the point at which £4 or £5 a year was being expended on payments to the groundsman. In addition, from 1935, a Mr Geake was employed on match days to do odd jobs around the ground and pavilion, and there were also the tea ladies, who were paid four shillings (20p) a match. Travelling expenses were introduced in 1936, and in the first season £9.16s (£9.80p) was paid out under this item. The impression of the careful husbanding of limited resources is a strong one, and George Bricknell was clearly an effective treasurer. The decision not to employ a professional obviously helped. The club was also fortunate in having a benevolent landlord, and in benefiting from a lease under which the rent remained, throughout the period, on a steady and affordable five shillings and sixpence a year.

Technically, the running of the club was in the hands of a committee elected by the A.G.M. In practice, as is the case in so many comparable organisations, the day-to-day operation of the enterprise was in the hands of a small 'kitchen cabinet', maybe two or three people who were able to devote an abnormal amount of time and attention to the affairs of the business, and who were ready in an informal way, through their experience and their contacts, to offer solutions to problems that cropped up, even if this meant short-cutting the strictly constitutional procedures. The formal committee met, perhaps not more than once or twice a year, usually to prepare the ground for, or to deal with the consequences of, an A.G.M. A crisis like the Hall scandal would require a special meeting. But a routine gathering might find itself a little short of matters of substance. One wonders, for example, what was happening between 8 and 10 on the evening of March 24th 1936 at the Cattle Market Hotel. According to the minute-book, 'Present were Messrs Parry, Davey, Mitchell, Jago, Lowe, and Millman. It was decided on the proposition of Mr Parry to hold a jumble sale on Saturday the 4th of April at 3.30 in the Market Hall'.

A significant innovation in the mid 1930s was the decision to involve non-playing supporters of the club in the administration by inviting them to join specialist sub-committees. Bill Martin, the scorer, thus became a member of the Selection Committee. The so-called Gear Committee, responsible for the bag, was appropriately left in the hands of two senior players. The two other sub-committees, concerned with the ground and with the teas, were happy to engage the interest and goodwill of non-playing members.

One dimension of the club's interests that had featured quite prominently in earlier years lay dormant in these inter-war years, and that was the relationship with the county club. Whether it was because neither side seemed to have much interest in organising a fixture at Tavistock, or because of the feeling that Tavistock players were constantly overlooked by the Exeter-based selection machinery, there was not much communication between the two. The annual guinea subscription had lapsed after 1910. It was paid in 1931 in response to a special appeal from the county, but that appears to have been a one-off gesture. A former Tavistock captain, Louis Tamworth, who was president of the Devon club from 1919 to 921, and thereafter figures prominent in local cricket circles in both the past and the present, had, like Alfred Penny and Frank Cannell, held committee seats. But these men did not serve as representatives of the Tavistock club, and their work, estimable as no doubt it was, did not serve to bring the two clubs closer together.

The formal curtain-raising prelude to each playing season was the Annual General Meeting held at the end of March or the beginning of April. The 1920 meeting that formally announced the club's post-war resurrection, was held in the Guildhall. An attendance of ten suggested that in future years the adjacent magistrates' room would offer adequate accommodation. The next twelve meetings were held in this ante-room, which could comfortably house both the six who turned up in 1924 and the sixteen who attended in 1925. When, in the early 1930s, the numbers went up to the upper teens, it was decided to seek an alternative room. From 1933 the A.G.M. was held in the chamber of the Urban District Council in Drake Road.

The business of such meetings was inevitably routine. There was the presentation of the accounts. The appointments for the forthcoming year were usually predetermined. The review of the previous season was important for public relations purposes, but contained nothing of which the playing members were not already aware. There were the occasional extra items, like the decision in 1935 to offer a celebratory bat and ball each year to those who topped the respective averages, and the gestures of Mr Johnstone and Dr Watt, who undertook to pay for such tokens.

Just occasionally, but not often, there was a scandal, or a potential contest, to generate some extra interest. But generally it was routine, albeit necessary, business, with the added advantage of providing an opportunity to remind the Tavistock public that another season of cricket was about to begin.

The message that came out of the 1940 meeting was rather different. Squire Kelly presided over a small gathering on April 1st, and, in the absence of a number of other leading players, was elected captain. The 1939 season had closed prematurely, although the last match, on August 19th, might be thought to have had an appropriate end, with rain stopping play as Plymouth Post Office reached 13 for 1 in reply to Tavistock's 144. There was, in the last days of the phoney war, no feeling that the club need go out of business, or suspend all activity. There was, after all, money to be accounted for, and that included this year a bequest. There was Edward Yelland's passing to be appropriately marked, as well as that of a great figure of the pre-1914 side, Tom Doidge. There was the real prospect that some cricket could be played in the forthcoming summer, and that meant keeping The Ring in shape and exploring possibilities for fixtures. There was much that could be done, but great uncertainty about what the future might bring. For the time being, the message could only be that if Hitler thought he could stop us playing cricket, then he had better think again.

Part Four: 1940–1959

The Age of Achievement

War

Fifteen club members were present when the Annual Meeting was held in the Council Offices in Drake Road at 7.30 p.m. on Monday April 1st 1940. There were, inevitably, some notable absentees: the war was by now in its eighth month. Squire Kelly took the chair, and, now well into his sixties, soon found that to his figurehead role of president had been added the far-from-token office of captain. Frank Millman was asked to combine the duties of secretary and vice captain, while C. B. Lacey became the new treasurer. Young Roy Acton was given the task of arranging as many fixtures as possible for the forthcoming season, a difficult assignment in a situation where most of the traditional opponents had already indicated that they were suspending activities. There was no suggestion at the meeting that the Tavistock club should follow this course. There was, instead, some discussion on decorating the inside of the pavilion and on the need to buy new seats for spectators. It was not until the last item, a decision to send a letter of sympathy to the Callington Club following the loss, on active service, of one of its best-known players, that the national emergency was formally acknowledged.

These were the last days of the phoney war. There was, no doubt, some speculation, as that meeting broke up and the members adjourned for a drink, about what the next few weeks might bring. Was Mr Chamberlain right in telling us that Hitler had 'missed the bus'? We were soon to know. The minutes of that meeting, carefully recorded by Frank Millman, were to be confirmed as a true and accurate record on Tuesday March 19th 1946. A lot of cricket was to be played locally during those intervening six years but formally, and in administrative terms, the club moved into a state of suspended animation.

It was an obvious result of the situation created by the long years of war, in which any arrangements that could be made to play any cricket were inevitably fluid and ad hoc. Fixtures depended on the availability of three major components: an opposition, a pitch, and eleven players. The last requirement could only be met by inviting guest players to supplement the core of club members. Hence the large number of unfamiliar names that feature on the scorecards of wartime games. Some names appear only once: a soldier temporarily billeted nearby perhaps, or a member of a neighbouring club home on short-term leave and keen for a game of cricket. They were all welcome. Without them the club could not have played on, as it did, throughout the war years. As to the second requirement for continuity, the preparation of wickets, there was once again heavy dependance on Frank Millman and Gordon Parry, together with a Mr Timaeus, who was so keen to assist in the care of the ground that he became almost a permanent fixture at The Ring for some years.

In the extraordinary twilight world of the early summer of 1940, cricket resumed at The Ring. On May 4th St. Luke's College were the visitors. The composition of the home side was typical of much that was to follow. There were two firmly-established club figures in Frank Millman and Doug Treloar, and three younger players, Nick Kelly, Bill Barnes, and Roy Acton, who had been on the point of establishing themselves in the side when the war had begun. Kelly was the son of the patriarchal squire. Barnes was a young schoolmaster. And Roy Acton, whose father was the caretaker of the Town Hall, was to enjoy an illustrious post-war career in the police service. The rest of the side did not contain any known cricketers. They tended to fall into three categories. There were the boys, still at school in some cases, or awaiting call up. There were the men in early-middle age, involved maybe in reserved occupations, who had a taste for the game but had never made it at the required level. And there were the older men, who had perhaps played a bit af cricket in their younger days, had long since given up thought of serious competitive activity, but relished the prospect of a Saturday or two of exercise and companionship where their individual performances would not be too carefully scrutinised. Their participation might depend on their capacity to fit into those pairs of mothballed cream flannels that they had worn so self-consciously thirty years before. Later, a fourth element was to be added, as guest-players, military and otherwise, became an increasingly common feature. Such was to be the typical chemistry of a home side playing at The Ring during the five seasons beginning with the summer of 1940.

The allsorts who turned out against St. Luke's College went under to the students by 79 runs, but not before Treloar and Barnes had bowled well and pocketed 4 wickets each. One week later, on May 11th, President Kelly produced an eleven to challenge the home side. Since the events of the previous day, the German invasion of the Low Countries and the replacement of Chamberlain by Churchill, were those over which the Tavistock Cricket Club had no control, the game went ahead. The squire's team, which included a second sixty-four-year-old in addition to himself, made 108, but lost by 60 runs.

The following week the visit of the Royal Naval Hospital brought a drawn game and the second successive half-century for Nick Kelly. Thereafter, records of only two other games in that summer have survived, both of them played in June. A journey to Liskeard resulted in a defeat, while a home match against the Anglo-Saxon Petroleum Company turned into a high-scoring victory, with Roy Acton and Bill Tucker both featuring prominently. It is not clear whether any cricket was played after June 29th. Perhaps the consequences of the deteriorating war situation (France surrendered on June 22nd) brought the season to a premature end. Or perhaps the odd game was played and has gone unrecorded.

The pattern of the 1941 season appears to be that of 1940 in reverse. No evidence survives of cricket in the first half of the season, and the first fixture seems to have been on June 28th. Thus, unless records have been lost, there was a twelve month gap between the last game of 1940 and the first of 1941. Once into their stride, local players went some way to making up for lost time by playing twelve matches before the season ended on September 6th. Eight of these games were played on Saturdays, one on a Bank Holiday Monday, and the remaining three were mid-week fixtures. Five of the games were against army elevens. In the nature of things, against such unknown opposition, the outcome was always unpredictable. Scratch service sides might include anyone.

On August 2nd an army eleven scored 203 for 9 declared at The Ring, to win by 83 runs. Top-scoring for them was Bainbridge, who made 137 not out. He was a Yorkshire Second Eleven player. A month later Tavistock suffered another defeat at the hands of a team that included Leonard Parkinson, a leg-spinner who had played 88 times for Lancashire in first-class matches over five seasons. Games against Old Plymouthians, village sides, and invitation elevens, which made up the remainder of the fixture list, presented the home players with rather more predictable fare. Overall, five matches were won, six lost, and one drawn. The club benefited from the arrival on the scene of W. T. Bolt, a bank clerk, who scored heavily and consistently, and even more from the return of Davey, Avery, and Parry. Though they did not play in all games, the reappearance of this trio of stalwarts gave the side a more familiar look. Eric Davey in particular picked up where he had left off, harvesting both runs and wickets with prodigious consistency. There was also a cameo 35 from Bill Colling in a one-off innings played during a short leave. With Millman, Tucker, Treloar, and Kelly playing regularly, there was the occasional afternoon at The Ring when a spectator, awaking from a snooze, might have felt that he was back in 1938.

The 1942 season was in some ways a triumph, in terms both of organisation and of results. The playing staff was depleted by the temporary loss of Maurice Avery and Doug Treloar, and by the departure of Roy Acton. And the two Bills, Colling and Fellowes, continued to be sorely missed. And yet a programme of twenty games was carried through without a single cancellation. Significantly, only eight members were able to play in ten or more of the games, and no one managed more than fifteen. Parry, Millman, Davey, and Tucker, seen as the nucleus of the side, chalked up thirty-six games between them.

A lot of the credit for a remarkably busy and successful season (the twenty games produced fifteen victories) went to three veterans: Squire Kelly, the evergreen captain, Jim Fellowes, now aged fifty-eight, and a new figure, H.G. Bonhote Wilson. Wilson, as well as turning out twelve times, filled a gap by throwing himself into the task of arranging fixtures. At the end of the year he was able to claim that:

> 'it might be that some of us are the halt, the maimed, and the blind, so far as cricket is concerned, but we did something in providing games for service teams'.

The remark is a significant one in that it represents a local reflection of a wider national approach to the question of sport in wartime. During the First World War there had been a good deal of unease at the prospect of organised sport continuing during the conflict. It was as if such frivolities were seen as distractions from the war effort or as some kind of insult to the boys at the front. This widespread view had its local echoes. The Second War brought a different, more positive, response. Mr Wilson was reflecting the national mood when he claimed that by staying in business, though admittedly not business as usual, the Tavistock Cricket Club was making a contribution to the war effort.

Two young players caught the eye in the 1942 season. A young bank clerk called Hoare, who was later to join the R.A F., played some good innings and took third place in the batting averages. And Alec Pethick burst onto the scene. Here was a cricketer of considerable natural talent. He played in thirteen games in that first season, scoring 249 runs at an average of 18.4. He also took 35 wickets at 6.2 apiece. Against one army side he took 4 wickets in 4 balls, and ended with 8 for 25. A family illness brought a premature end to his season, but in spite of that he scored more runs than any other player, and took second place in both the batting and the bowling lists. The top rung of each of these ladders continued, for the time being, to be occupied by the sturdy feet of Eric Davey.

In April 1943 a resident of Whitchurch, taking an afternoon stroll across the Down, observed 'Mr Timaeus busily engaged preparing the pitch at The Ring'. Did this, he enquired in the columns of the *Tavistock Gazette*, mean that there would be another season of cricket? If so, it would presumably be played by the flotsam that the war had left behind, the collection of 'old men and a few boys'. Millman, wearing his secretarial hat, replied somewhat gloomily. The prospects were not good. Only a few players were available and they included men who, like himself, could not be relied upon because they were occupied in important work.

H. G. B. Wilson, writing from Crelake Park as the fixtures secretary, offered a more hopeful prospect, suggesting that the playing strength could be at least equal to that of the 1942 season. His optimism seemed well founded when quite a few players turned out for a 'pick up game' on April 24th, to be followed, one week later, by the trouncing of an army eleven in the first match of the season. In this game Frank Millman shared an unbroken stand of 155 with R. Lovell, playing his first game.

Lovell was obviously a keen young cricketer. He had walked to the ground from Princetown before celebrating with 87 not out, an innings that included five sixes. With Pethick and Hoare he was to dominate the Tavistock batting for much of the season, while Pethick and Davey shared the bulk of the wickets. Fellowes, Millman, Parry, and Kelly, who could now muster over 200 years between them, continued to offer support with bat, ball, advice, and, generally, good humour. Jimmy Fellowes in particular was enjoying the Indian Summer of a career in which he was able to show that a 59-year-old could sustain a longish spell of accurate spin bowling, and turn in figures, in consecutive weeks, of 7 for 27 and 5 for 47. Of the thirteen games for which details survive, six were won, three drawn, and four lost. The pattern of fixtures remained very similar to those of the preceding two summers, with one exception. On July 17th the opposition was provided by the Royal Australian Air Force. How nice it would be to discover that the visiting team had featured the likes of Pilot Officer Keith Miller!

As with previous wartime seasons, cricket arrived at The Ring rather late in the summer of 1944. General uncertainty, and the prospect that an imminent invasion of Europe could radically alter plans and preparations, led to fixture arrangements that tended to be both delayed and hand-to-mouth. The first game was on May 28th. By September, 17 matches had been played, of which 12 were won, 4 were lost, and 1 was tied. Contests tended to be low-scoring affairs, a condition brought about partly by the difficulty of preparing pitches and partly by the lack of batting practice facilities. Alec Pethick was again the principal scorer, with 404 runs at an average of 31. This young Gulworthy-based sportsman, a forestry worker with strong arms, shoulders, and back, had the power to blast away the top opposition batting, as well as the stamina to bowl through an innings. On one of the many occasions when a delivery hit the stumps, a bail flew 28 yards. Not surprisingly Squire Kelly, who liked to keep wicket, would position himself about that distance behind the stumps when Pethick was operating.

The other mainstay of the attack was Jim Fellowes, who took 72 wickets at 5.5 each. Alec, it could be said, softened them up; Jim bamboozled them. Also lending weight in that 1944 summer were D. J. Evans, Ken Lightfoot, Jack Bolt, and Ralph Bennett. The latter kept wicket very well, when the squire could be persuaded to let him have a go. As the core of available regulars became smaller, the reliance on visiting players increased. One of the most welcome of these was Frank Bond, who played a couple of games while visiting his parents in the town. Behind one particular match there lies a story which cannot yet be told. Against Kelly College, Tavistock opened their innings, according to the details released to the press, with that well-known pair A. Pethick and A. Hitler. A really big story, to do with British Intelligence, lies behind this. The cricket historian must, however, confine himself to the game. Hitler was out for 4, but Tavistock won the game by 2 runs.

Peace

The summer of 1944 was a time for holding your breath and hoping. One year on, and the hopes had been realised. The war had not ended in May 1945, but the fighting in Europe was over, and the lads were beginning to come home. One aspect of the national mood of relief that followed VE Day was a concern to re-establish, as quickly as possible, some of the reassuringly familiar patterns and rhythms of English life. This was echoed in local communities up and down the land. Cricket played a part in this. And the resurgence of the game, at all levels, for both players and spectators, in the immediate post-war years, was very noticeable. The Tavistock club played its first 1945 fixture within four days of the German surrender. There could have been no more reassuring indication of the return to normality than occurred on that Saturday afternoon at The Ring, when Squire Kelly won the toss, and out to the middle, to begin the Tavistock innings, strode Gordon Parry and Bill Colling.

Apart from the welcome reappearance of some old favourites, there was a comforting familiarity about some parts of the 1945 programme, although some of the club sides that had provided opposition before the war were to take another year to get themselves back into action. Sixteen games were sandwiched, somewhat breathlessly as it seems, between VE and VJ Days. Thirteen were won, two lost, and one drawn. There were strong performances from such stalwarts as Davey and Pethick, while the middle of the season was given added colour by guest appearances from a Lieutenant William Barber, who opened the batting and also took some wickets with his left-arm spin.

Barber was, in fact, a Middlesex second eleven player, who in 1946 was to join the select ranks of first-class players by representing the Combined Services. Just as welcome, but for different reasons, was Harold Youlden, back from a prisoner-of-war camp. His first match, against the Plymouth Corporation Officers in August, was memorable also for a remarkable last-wicket stand. Tavistock turned up one short for this away fixture, and at 86 for 9 it looked as if they were going to have to settle for a disappointingly low total. Help was at hand in the shape of a spectator, a sailor called Quarrington, who joined Eric Davey, then 24 not out. Half an hour later the welcome stranger was 14 not out, while Davey had added 60 to his score. An unbroken stand of 76 made possible a declaration at 162 for 9. It was, perhaps, the most perfectly timed declaration in the club's entire history. Their opponents were all out for 71, the last wicket falling three minutes before stumps were to be drawn.

Two weeks before these stirring events occurred, The Ring had received its most distinguished visitor. Frank Woolley, who was then fifty-nine years old, had, in a first-class career spanning thirty-two years, played 764 times for Kent and 64 times for England. He certainly has to be near the top of any list of the game's greatest all-rounders. In July 1945 he was holidaying in a farmhouse near Kelly and visiting his old friend A.T. Goss, who had recently moved to Tavistock to set up a sweet factory on Parkwood Road. Mr Goss was keen on cricket and had become involved with the local club by taking on some umpiring duties. On July 28th there was a home game against a Plymouth police eleven, and Mr Goss collected his illustrious friend and brought him to The Ring in his motor car.

Interestingly, such a mode of travelling to the ground was still sufficiently unusual as to warrant particular comment. Woolley umpired. Whether it was he who lifted the finger in response to lbw appeals against three home batsmen, one of them Lieutenant Barber, is not recorded. He was certainly complimentary about the bowling, particularly of Davey, who took 6 for 32 including a hat trick, and Pethick, who mopped up the tail with 3 wickets for no runs. A low-scoring game ended in a narrow Tavistock victory.

Mr Woolley appeared to enjoy his afternoon, and, like so many less famous visitors before and since, was much taken by the charm of the ground and its setting. Bill Tucker also remembers the great man turning up on practice nights to stand behind the nets and offer his advice. Considering the position that Woolley occupied in the pantheon of English cricketers, the effect of the visits on the local players may well be imagined. Nothing could have provided a more fitting prelude to the new era on which they were just embarking.

Before the year was out, two deaths had occurred to temper, to some degree, the atmosphere of joy and relief. The first was that of Glan Davey, player, umpire, and founder of a dynasty, who died in the same month that his son performed his hat trick under the knowing gaze of Frank Woolley. The other death was that of Francis Leigh Kelly. Within weeks of playing his last game, the squire had vanished from the scene. He had, throughout the war, captained the side, and helped to provide some stability during a difficult period. A maverick figure, and in playing terms at his age a natural number eleven, his legacy to the club was secure. Along with a handful of others he was responsible for the fact that, unlike so many clubs, Tavistock had managed to play through. It was all thoroughly English. The ageing squire, prevented from active service, could at least contribute to keeping the home fires burning by helping to preserve an activity that was more English than anything else that could be imagined.

In the six wartime summers there were 83 games of which we have records. Of these, 53 were won, 6 drawn, 1 tied, and 23 lost. In view of the unpredictable standard of some of the opposition, too much should not be read into such figures. The really significant thing is that a lot of cricket was played. As a result, some veterans were able to give to their careers a pleasurable, because unexpected, last chapter. At the same time some new players were provided with opportunities for being blooded. The losers were, of course, those for whom war service took what would have been the period of the flowering of their cricketing careers. And every club in England could furnish examples to set alongside the great national figures who had similarly suffered, like Wally Hammond, Len Hutton, and Dennis Compton. There were also those who were not to return. Young Les Baker was described in 1939 as a useful change bowler and a nippy and agile fielder. He was killed while serving in the R.A.F.

An Impression of Familiarity

For better or worse, the post-war side, as it paraded during the 1946 season, had a distinctly pre-war appearance. Those who played in at least three-quarters of the fixtures included Bill Colling, Gordon Parry, Frank Millman, Eric Davey, Jim Fellowes, Doug May, and Bill Barnes. Along with Doug

Treloar and Frank Bond, they constituted a core of experience. To these products of the 1920s and 1930s were added a small number who had established themselves during the war years: Frank Howe, Gerry Masters, George Waye, Ralph Bennett, and, pre-eminently, Alec Pethick.

The picture on the playing side was reflected in the administration. Frank Millman resumed the secretaryship that had first fallen to him in 1928. Claud Lacey remained as treasurer. Bill Colling once again led the side, with Gordon Parry, the inevitable bridesmaid, as his vice-captain. The indefatigable trio of Parry, Millman, and Timaeus worked on the ground. The latter figure, such a familiar feature of the local landscape in the 1940s as he cycled regularly from his home in the Institution through the town and up to The Ring, had played some cricket in his younger days. He was now free with time that was devoted, exclusively it seemed, to acting like a parent both to the ground, which received motherly attention, and to young players like Alec Pethick who were offered fatherly advice on technique and strategy.

Meanwhile Bill Martin began to enjoy a third decade as the regular scorer. A veteran of the First War, he lived in Parkwood Road, ran a bakery, and was a pillar of the Russell Street Methodist Church. A teetotaller, he found himself often, after an away game, sitting in solitary state, or accompanied by an under-age player or supporter, outside some distant pub, while the team refreshed itself for the return journey.

The welcome addition to the club establishment had been A.T. Goss. He was, for a number of years, to support the club in three roles. As president he was figurehead and benefactor. As a car owner he could help in practical ways like providing transport for players and baggage. The third duty, as umpire, kept him close to the action, but also led, at times, to some controversy. There was, for instance, some feeling among the Callington players, who, in a mid-season game at The Ring, failed by 20 runs to reach the victory target of 94, that they had fallen victim, not only to Alec Pethick's bowling (he took 7 for 28) but to Mr Goss's finger.

It is not surprising that a number of members of the club and local supporters should have felt, in the immediate post-war atmosphere, a sense of reassurance that the landscape was occupied by so many familiar figures. There was, on the other hand, some concern that enough was not being done to introduce new talent or encourage youngsters to become involved. One member, Bill Metters, expressed this unease at the 1947 A.G.M. He felt that the club was exclusive and unwelcoming, and that little effort was made to appeal to the promising working-class lad. This attitude, he claimed, was reinforced by the deterrent effects of high subscription levels (ten shillings for those over 21 and five shillings for minors) and of travel costs. This had resulted in the club becoming the preserve of 'the black coated man'. The case for the defence was presented by Messrs Colling and Parry in a way that appears to have satisfied Mr Metters. Although the charges were moderated, the underlying message was heard and understood. The halving of the subscription rate for under-18s was an immediate result. Renewed urgency was also given to the attempt to establish a second eleven. Efforts to incorporate this as part of the wider reconstitution had not been successful. Instead, a programme of five evening games had been arranged, in which, as Parry put it, teams were 'composed of about 50% of regulars, and 50% of the second eleven which never quite came into being'. This pattern was to continue for some years. In spite of regular calls for the institution of a properly constituted second team, and the obvious need for such a provision if the club was to grow and develop, the project remained for a number of years in the 'not quite came into being' category.

The late 1940s and early 1950s saw the playing fortunes of the club dominated by seven experienced players: Avery, Davey, and Treloar in the bowling; Millman, Parry, and Colling in the batting; and Pethick the all-rounder. Jim Fellowes and Frank Bond hung up their boots, while Bill Barnes moved on. Meanwhile each season brought a handful of newcomers. George Waye, described by one enthusiastic spectator as 'a Jessopian hitter', burst onto the scene in 1947 with an innings of 97 against Saltash that included seven sixes. In the same year Jack Rogers played his first game for the club. A Callington man, he was to play for Cornwall in 1949. Scoring a not-out century in one of his first games for Tavistock, he scored 1000 runs in 1948, his second season, and continued to play regularly in the 1950s, producing harvests of runs and occasionally keeping wicket. Other debutants in 1947 and 1948 were R. Pate and B. Hill, youngsters who together helped to redress, to some degree, the imbalance of an ageing team. Brian Hill was a fourteen-year-old Dolvin Road schoolboy when he played his first game. He was to develop, among other skills, an impressively strong arm, and his returns from the deep field became a particular feature of Tavistock's out-cricket. D. Pearse, the son of G. G. Pearse, lawyer and city father, also began to play regularly in 1948.

The 1949 season saw the first appearances of four men who were to prove to be productive players. J. D. Wedd, the headmaster of Mount House School, scored 61 not out, out of a total of 113, in his first game, and thereafter turned out regularly for three seasons. Commander W. M. Elderton topped the batting averages in the first of his two seasons, the highlight being an 85 not out, out of a total of 139 for 7. At the end of the 1950 season he was posted away. David Gordon, Ceylon born and Whitchurch reared, played for three seasons, sharing the summers with undergraduate studies at Oxford. In August 1949 he caught the eye of the county selectors and was picked to play against Dorset.

Also in 1949 Walter Spry played his first game for Tavistock. This left-handed bat, whose roots were in Lamerton, was to have a long career with the club. A relief station-master with the old G.W.R., he had graduated from village cricket, and was to become a loyal servant of the club as both player and administrator. He showed particular distinction also in his leading of the community singing aboard the coach on return journeys from away matches. An unconnected foible, for which presumably he had a good reason, was his practice of playing the occasional match under an alias. There was a problem in that he found it difficult to remember which initial he had intended to use.

Thus it is that the scorebooks of the early 1950s record the occasional exploits of someone called Price, who is often W, sometimes R, and occasionally T.

Of the other newcomers of that period, Ken Jarman began his career in 1950. P. Bloy played in 1950 and 1951. Based at Okehampton, he had settled into the side as a dependable run maker when he was ordained and moved to a living in the north. Another cleric, the Rev. Basil Guy, the Vicar of Tavistock who was later to be Bishop of Gloucester, played in 1950. Robert Featherstonhaugh, wicketkeeper-batsman, launched a three-year career in the same season. The summer of 1951 saw the first appearances of Dennis Paull, who made a big impression when he joined the end-of-season tour of Sussex, and was to become one of the club's most prolific post-war run makers.

The following year an eighteen-year-old lad from Lewdown, soon to do his national service, became an established member of the club. The *Tavistock Times* said of Gerry Parsons:

> 'His beautiful style, a gift inherited from his father Fred, who was a well known local cricketer, caught the eye of Tavistock players and officials, and he was asked to join the team'.

The first eye-catching had occurred in September 1950 when, as a sixteen-year-old lad, he had played against the club for a District XI. In this particular fixture, played either at the dawn or the sunset of a season, a team recruited from local village sides came to The Ring to test the townies. For the home club it proved to be a valuable opportunity to look at, and possibly to recruit, some of the brightest talent on the local village scene. Featured in that 1950 game, for example, were Ken Jarman and George Clements, respectively from Lamerton and Lydford, who were both to become pillars of the Tavistock club. But it was the young man from Lewdown who stole the show, batting at Number 4 and top-scoring with 36. A repeat performance in the same fixture in May 1952 led to a chat with Eric Davey and to an invitation to become a Tavistock player. His first season brought him, in his first ten games, 135 runs at an average of 15, and, in his second ten, 345 runs at an average of 43. His was to be a cricket career based on natural talent and pursued through five decades. Those who played with him knew that his mood was changeable and also that he was more concerned than some others with his personal performances and records. Nothing, however, could detract from the fact that he was a fine all-round cricketer, and one of the best half-dozen batsmen ever to play for Tavistock.

Two other newcomers joined the ranks at about the same time. Michael Kelly was the son of the squire. Eric Jarman, the brother of Ken, played his first game in May 1953. Along with Spry, Paull, Parsons, and his brother Ken, he was to become part of a core of young players ready to replace the nucleus of ageing heroes when they should decide to hang up their boots.

Not that the old guard showed any inclination to take premature retirement. Maurice Avery's bowling continued, on its day, to mow down batting sides like a scythe. In August 1947 he took 9 for 19 against Saltash. In the 1949 season his haul was 79 wickets. And he continued to make useful runs. In a game at Exeter his 46, made in an unbroken last wicket stand of 65 with Jarman, earned the most unlikely of draws. But he was played for his bowling. He and Davey could still perform in tandem to destroy the opposition. At Dartington in July 1951 they bowled between them 31 overs, of which 15 were maidens, at the end of which the home side were all out for 31.

Eric Davey's inimitable crouching style persistently delivered more than 200 overs a season. In 1946 he took 67 wickets at an average of 4.8. In 1949 his 60 wickets cost him 8.3 apiece, but he still topped the averages. And he remained capable of bravura performances with either bat or ball. In August 1952 he took 8 for 26 against Plymouth Y.M.C.A. In June 1949, against the same side, he came in at 37 for 8 chasing a target of 72. Hitting one six and seven fours he brought, not only victory, but victory with style. In the 1946 season his principal feats were achieved in tandem with Alec Pethick, who relished the wet wickets that that summer produced. His 6 for 8 in a mid-season game at Yelverton, which included a hat trick, reduced the home side to 15 all out. Davey took 4 for 7. Between them, the two bowled 430 overs in that season, and took 140 wickets. The combined totals for the rest of the side were 111 overs and 27 wickets.

Pethick was to play in two county trials in 1948. After a blank season in 1949 he played in only seven games in 1950, but in one of them, against a touring side from an Oxford college, he took 9 for 34 and then opened the batting with an innings of 63.

The *Tavistock Times* reporter had never seen anything like it:

> 'We saw a spell of wizardry. Just sheer wizardry. True, the pitch helped his bowling a bit and the wind was in his favour, but taking all that into consideration there was no gainsaying the sheer magic of his work'.

While not playing regularly in the early 1950s, he still produced both consistently impressive figures and frequent virtuoso performances. Two such, in 1953, stand out. Against Plymouth Y.M.C.A. he scored 125 out of 205 for 5 declared. Against Yelverton his innings of 93 in 35 minutes included ten fours and six sixes. The chronic illness of his wife, throughout these years, made demands on him which, in some seasons, limited his appearances. Had he, in the years of his prime, been able to play regularly, he would surely have broken every record in the book. Mr Timaeus, the ever present sage, may be left the final word on the Pethick phenomenon. He knew of a winning strategy, and one day he confided it to the young Clifford Alford. 'All you have to do', he said, 'Is to water one end of the pitch and put Pethick on at the other end'.

The thoroughbred batsman of the period from 1946 to 1953 remained Bill Colling. For both consistency and style he was unmatched. In 1949 he scored 832 runs, with a top score of 112 not out and an average of 26. In 1952 his pairing with Walter Spry produced in June a record opening stand of 163. Two months later they bettered this by putting on 167 before being parted. Colling also enjoyed, during this period, bowling a bit of recreational offspin, but his main concerns, apart from his batting, were with his captaincy.

His last season was 1953. He scored 980 runs. At the end of the summer he moved away, having been appointed to the headship of Lapford County Primary School. His departure came at a time when the two most experienced playing members, Gordon Parry and Frank Millman, were in the 'occasional games only' phase of their career.

But for Doug Treloar there was still a long way to go. His career resumed after the war in rather a low gear, because of the success of the other seam bowlers. By 1949, however, he had become a work-horse of the attack, bowling, in that season, 376 overs and taking 88 wickets. He was always an enthusiastic fielder, and, as he showed on one particular Saturday afternoon in May 1951, he could bring off the spectacular coup. This was, according to some, the catch of the century. A Yelverton batsman called Trahair was on 55 when he tried to hook Davey and instead top-edged him high to fine leg. Treloar took the catch just inside the boundary after running from first slip. No one seems to have asked why Davey, or Colling, had not posted a fine leg.

When peace-time cricket was resumed at The Ring in 1946 it was assumed that Bill Colling, who had led the side in 1938 and 1939, would resume the captaincy, and when this happened it was widely welcomed. His unopposed re-election was confirmed at the A.G.M.s of 1947 and 1948. In 1949, with the club preparing for its centenary season, he offered to stand aside in favour of the Grand Old Man, but Parry declined the honour with characteristic grace and modesty, and Colling remained in office.

In 1951, after seven seasons in charge, he announced his wish to stand down 'for various reasons'. His recommendation to the A.G.M. that he should be succeeded by Maurice Avery was accepted by the meeting, and Avery began a two year spell as captain, with Colling as his vice-captain. In 1953 they switched roles after both had been nominated and a ballot had been held among the twenty-three members present at the meeting. It was to be Colling's last season, and it was also the last occasion on which the office of captain was decided by the A.G.M. A new procedure adopted in 1954 put the decision in the hands of the players, who met before the A.G.M. and then reported their resolution to the wider membership. Avery was the first skipper to be so chosen. Other, purely administrative, offices continued to be filled at the annual meeting.

The three principal posts were to have long-term occupants. Albert Goss was to fill the presidency through until the 1960s; Eric Davey and Bernard Kerswill, who in 1947 took over as secretary and treasurer respectively, were both to remain in office for some years. The stability and continuity that had been features of the club's operations for many years were to continue as major elements in its post-war life.

Old Bowlers and Young Batsmen

In the 1946 season the average total achieved by Tavistock's opponents was 56. The pattern that was to be maintained for the next few years was one of success, based principally on the performances of the bowlers. If man-of-the-match awards had been made, the great majority would, during this period, have gone to bowlers. Tavistock had four bowlers, each of whom was capable, on his day, of dismissing a side virtually single-handed. It was an unusual day when at least one of them was not firing. The figures indicate the degree to which the side depended on their wicket-taking performances.

Percentage of the wickets that fell to bowlers that were taken by:

Season	*Avery*	*Davey*	*Pethick*	*Treloar*	*Others*
1947	29	19	23	15	14
1948	32	19	20	11	18
1949	25	19	0	28	28

Three factors explain the dominant role that the pace attack played in the side's performances in these post-war years. One was the existence of a tradition within the club, going back to its origins, of producing, in each generation, a thoroughbred seam attack. This had a potent influence, transmitted as it was through the veteran players who had personal links with an earlier epoch. Secondly there was the good fortune of being able, for practically every fixture, to pick at least two dependable and experienced opening bowlers. And thirdly there was the weather. With the exception of the blissfully remembered season of 1947, the summers were wet, and the preparation of hard, true surfaces difficult to achieve.

In this respect The Ring, which had more care lavished on it than most local club grounds, fared better than most. There was certainly no suggestion that anyone, other than God, was preparing a wicket for Davey and Avery. But pitches both in home and away games did tend, for the most part, to favour the bowlers, and Tavistock had the men to exploit these advantages. The resultant pattern emerges very clearly in the results.

There was, however, to be a significant change of balance in the early 1950s. The bowlers were growing old together, and their replacements were not in sight. The young recruits with their potential and promise all seemed to be batsmen. Rogers, Paull, and Parsons burst onto the scene. Skipper Colling found himself with at least two sturdy openers in Walter Spry and Alec Pethick who could, with him, lay the foundations of an innings. Batting performances, individual and collective, became, for the first time for many years, the principal features of many games. There were more high-scoring matches. One consequence of this was an increase in the number of drawn games. In the four seasons between 1946 and 1949, 18% of games ended in draws; the equivalent figure for the next four years, from 1950 to 1953, is 40%. The team's playing record for the whole period is :

Season	*Played*	*Won*	*Drawn*	*Lost*	*Tied*
1946	18	13	4	1	0
1947	40	27	8	5	0
1948	40	30	2	8	0
1949	41	20	10	10	1

1950	31	8	14	9	0
1951	34	12	12	10	0
1952	34	12	14	8	0
1953	35	14	13	7	1
Total	273	136	77	58	2

The arrival of some promising new batsmen in the early 1950s tended to obscure the fact that Tavistock had an ageing team. It was unfortunate that the good intentions about a second eleven were not realised. The idea that a programme of half-a-dozen evening fixtures against village sides would be an adequate substitute was misguided. These games were enjoyable, and often closely contested, but the variability of the opposition, and even more the 80 minutes limit on an innings, meant that they were scarcely good testing grounds for young cricketers. The shoot-outs against Gunnislake, Milton Abbot, and Stoke Climsland remained popular events, and occasioned great pleasure when a village side could win against a team that included five or six Tavistock regulars.

The remainder of the fixture list had, by 1950, reverted substantially to the pre-war pattern. There were regular games against the likes of Plympton, Plymouth, Yelverton, Okehampton, Launceston, Callington, Tiverton, Paignton, Dartington, Exeter, and Hatherleigh. Half a dozen or so matches per season were played against Plymouth-based sides like the Naval Engineering College and the Y.M.C.A. St. Luke's College provided regular, and stern, opposition, and there was the occasional game against a regimental team.

An increasing proportion of the list was, however, taken by fixtures against touring sides. The 1950 season, for example, contained six such engagements between mid-July and early-September. And this experience of playing against clubs from other parts of the country led in turn to a resolution that the club could mount its own tour.

In 1948 it happened. Nine members of the club, along with three guests from Callington and one from Bude, spent the second week of August in Sussex, having organised a base in Brighton and a programme of six games. Two of the matches were, in the event, rained off; the other four, against Lewes Priory, Portslade, Brighton Regency, and Barcombe, were all won, three of them decisively. The tour was reckoned a success, in spite of the weather. It was repeated three years later. This time, in 1951, the full schedule of six matches was played. The hospitality was again generous, but the opposition proved to be stiffer and only one of the games was won, with another two being drawn. Neither the purpose nor the value of a tour can be measured by results, and the innovation was greeted as a successful departure that could with benefit be repeated.

The Coming of Sunday Cricket

The most radical change to the structure of the playing season came about in the club's ninety-eighth year. The introduction of Sunday cricket would, it was anticipated, divide the town, stir up sectarian bitterness, and drive away some players and supporters, actual and potential, who took a sternly literal view of the requirements of the fourth commandment. Was there not, at that very time, a fevered battle being fought over the question of the opening of the cinemas in the town on Sundays?

The first Sunday fixture involving the club had been on August 18th 1946, but that had been in the midst of the fleshpots of faraway Bude. The real test came with the committee's decision, in March 1947, to 'arrange Sunday fixtures as deemed desirable, providing Mr Parry receives the assurance that Sunday cricket would in no way injure our lease'. There being no obstacles in that area, Tavistock played Plymouth Queries at The Ring on Sunday July 13th 1947, and a new era opened. The club announced its hope 'in all sincerity, that they have offended the susceptibilities of no one by playing Sunday cricket'. If offence had been taken in certain quarters it remained remarkably muted, for neither within the club nor in the wider community was any significant opposition expressed. That only seven Sunday fixtures were played in the first season was the result, not of a need to meet the concerns of sabbatarian lobbies, but of the fact that only a few other clubs had taken the plunge.

As far as the acceptability of the innovation to the cricketing public of Tavistock was concerned, some measure of its popularity may be gauged from the fact that the two Sunday games in August attracted crowds of between 200 and 300. By the end of the season the officers could feel confident enough to replace their guarded, somewhat apprehensive, statements by a more positive commitment. 'I am sure', said secretary Davey, 'that all the committee are happy to have been associated with the innovation'. Sighs of relief all round.

Sunday cricket brought in the spectators. There was a further reason for satisfaction on the part of those who had supported the initiative. A handful of players, who belonged to neighbouring clubs where there was a more cautious approach to the question, began to make enquiries. These circumstances brought to the club such players as R. Forbes and W. Lee, who both enjoyed two successful seasons. But the biggest catch was Jack Rogers, the Callington batsman who became one of Tavistock's most distinguished batsmen and captains.

It was a Sunday match at The Ring in 1949 that brought forth from a *Tavistock Times* reporter a piece of prose that now reads like the drawing of an idyllic picture of cricket in post-war England, when the sun always shone, and Edrich and Compton were always batting. He wrote:

> 'Under a blazing scintillating July sun in a cloudless sky of deep azure blue, 250 spectators, garbed in all colours of the rainbow, sat round and enjoyed not only the cricket shown by the white-flanneled representatives of Tavistock and Bude, but the lovely panoramic view of the west end of the town and the high ground of Heathfield and Gulworthy, with Kit Hill and the long range of the Cornish moors in the distance. Here and there sat little parties devouring with ravenous appetites the edibles they had brought. Men, many with open white shirts, relaxed in a carefree style on the green verdure. And women, looking

radiant and cool in floral dresses, sat gazing with admiring eyes on the bonnie tiny tots gambolling over the turf.'

There were bluebirds over . . .

Marking the Centenary

On Tuesday March 19th 1946 at 7.30 p.m., thirteen members of the club gathered in the Magistrates' Room, an annexe to the courtroom in the Guildhall, to hold the first post-war A.G.M. The minutes of the 1940 A.G.M. were read and approved. Normal business had been resumed. Thereafter, for a number of years, in the same room and during the same mid-March week, the formalities were conducted by an average assembly of eighteen members. Proceedings often began with a moment of silence for those who had passed on during the year. In 1950, for example, there was cause to remember two great figures from the early part of the century, William Linnell and F. Hargrave Carroll. The latter, it was noted admiringly, had died at the billiards table, indeed with the cue in his hand. His father, Sammy Featherstone, had, it was recalled, also departed in style, in the middle of a round of golf.

The fact that the average A.G.M. went on to rubber-stamp decisions that had already been made informally did not detract from the importance of the occasion. The main purposes of the A.G.M. were twofold: to generate some useful publicity as the new season approached, and to attend to the club's finances. A modest, though perfectly healthy, balance was maintained over these years, with the staple sources of income being subscriptions and ground collections. In 1951 the amounts realised from these two sources were £78 and £39 respectively. Harry Spencer, who had organised the collections for many years, died in 1952; he had collected, on an average afternoon, £2 from the spectators, mostly in coppers and threepenny bits. The main items of expenditure each year were repairs and maintenance of the ground, equipment, and travelling expenses. There was the annual subscription to the county club (one guinea in 1946, increased to two guineas in 1948) and the one-off payment to meet a particular situation, such as the decision in 1948 to send five guineas to the Callington Club, who had lost their pavilion in a fire.

On only one occasion did the sums of money involved in running the club reach the dizzy heights of three figures. This followed the decision to push the boat out in 1949 in celebration of the club's centenary. Funds were augmented by a special appeal to the town's tradesmen, which produced £49, and by three dances, which realised £82. Two major projects were planned to mark the great occasion. One was the re-roofing and re-decoration of the pavilion, a renovation programme that was to cost £210. The other was a two-day celebration in mid-August including a match against a Devon County Eleven and a centenary dinner. The match created a good deal of interest, although it proved more one-sided than either neutral observers, or the home crowd of 250, would have wished. The county side was dismissed, in the middle of the first afternoon, for 163, but Tavistock, in reply, posted five ducks, and had subsided, soon after tea, to an all-out total of 36. Stumps were drawn, on Monday evening, with the visitors at 72 for 4 in their second innings. On the second morning they batted on, to be all out for 161, leaving the home side to get 289 to win. They managed 155. Heroes of the Tavistock side were Commander Elderton, who, in spite of facial bruising from an earlier game, kept wicket and top scored, and young David Gordon, whose match analysis of 11 for 104 impressed watching county officials and led to selection for Devon.

The evening between the two days saw the centenary dinner in the Town Hall, for which 'Messrs Perraton catered, and Mr C. Gregory of the Union Hotel supplied excisable and other beverages'. The 120 who attended included local dignitaries, representatives of the county club, and Tavistock players past and present, among them Messrs Snell and Beale, two captains from the inter-war period. Speeches were made and toasts were drunk in champagne. Gordon Parry made one of the most notable contributions to the evening, reflecting on thirty years of association with the club. At one point he said that he had 'sometimes indulged in pipe dreams that our pretty little ground could be improved by shifting back the stones and levelling certain parts'. It was an idea taken up by W. H. Passmore, Devon county secretary, in the next speech. His advice was crisp: 'Put the posts back ten to fifteen yards and get a bulldozer at work, and you can make it one of the sweetest grounds in the country'. Within four years the Parry pipe-dream was to become a reality and the club was to benefit from a really tangible, if slightly belated, memorial of its centenary.

The introduction of Sunday cricket, with the consequent doubling of the size of the fixture list, created headaches for the small band of volunteers, led by Gordon Parry, who, in the absence of a groundsman, tended The Ring. More matches meant more wickets, and the need for a bigger square. But that, in turn, required a bigger playing area, which could only be brought about, as Mr Passmore had suggested, by a bulldozer.

In 1951 an appeal was launched, which raised £127, and a formal application was submitted for permission to enlarge the ground. In October 1952 work began. The principal alteration involved digging into the bank on the eastern side of the ground, opposite the pavilion, to provide an additional playing area some twenty-five yards wide at its maximum point. Additionally, enlargements of seven yards were achieved behind the bowlers' run-up at each end. The plan involved the re-siting of thirty of the granite posts marking the boundary. It also meant that a good deal of re-seeding had to be carried out and the areas concerned protected by electrified fencing. The hope was that it would all be completed by the beginning of the 1953 season. At that year's A.G.M. Gordon Parry said:

> 'I admit that at the present it looks like a nasty scar, and I must apologise to the public for any inconvenience they have been caused. If they will bear with us for a short time I think everyone will be pleased with the finished result'.

Two moments during the 1949 Centenary Match.

ABOVE: The home side takes the field. *From left to right* - D. Treloar, E. Stockbridge, M. C. Avery, D. Gordon, E. Davey, G. H. Parry (captain), J. D. Wedd, S. W. Colling, R. Forbes, W. M. Elderton. Hidden, or late out of the pavilion, is F. Millman.

BELOW: Gordon Parry holds the bat presented to the club by Mrs Goss, the President's wife. Adding his signature is Norman Borrett, former Essex player and a member of the visiting Devon County eleven.

Two occasions when Colonel Wadham (centre back in both pictures) brought an all-star side to The Ring for a late-season festival match.

ABOVE: 1953. The home side is seated. Standing sixth from the left is Harold Gimblett, who scored 81 for the visitors. Third from the left is Bernard Kerswill, the club's treasurer. The umpire is Bertie Goss, the long-serving president.

BELOW: 1955. This time the visitors have the seats. All the front row are county players. *Left to right* - Jack Walsh, Jock Livingstone, Harold Stephenson, Les Jackson, Cliff Gladwin, George Tribe, George Dawkes, Bruce Dooland, John Mortimore.

Two postwar innovations.

ABOVE: 24th August 1947. The team that performed before a crowd of 250 in the third home Sunday game in the club's history.
Standing: Ralph Bennett, Jack Rogers, Frank Millman, Eric Davey, George Waye, Doug Treloar, Albert Goss. *Seated:* Maurice Avery, Bill Colling, Ron Forbes, Gordon Parry. *Front Row:* Clifford Alford, Frank Bond.

BELOW: 10th August 1948. The first match of the club's first tour. Lewes Priory batsman Philpott edges Maurice Avery to gully, where Doug May takes the catch. Eric Davey stands at second slip, while Jack Rogers keeps wicket.

A festival game on a cool September afternoon in 1962 attracts a large crowd.

The bar has been a feature of the pavilion facilities since the early 1960s. Manning it here are three club stalwarts: Len Jackman, Alf Coombe and Peter Redstone.

In the event, the new area was included for the first time on July 18th, when Tavistock made light of the longer boundaries by scoring 171 for 4 declared, and beating Hythe Green by 127 runs.

That season, the coronation summer of 1953, that saw the enlargement of the ground, saw also a near-disaster, when a fire broke out in the pavilion. The first game of the season, against a district eleven, was under way, when, at three o'clock, the gas cylinder in the kitchen caught fire. The fire brigade was quickly on the scene, but the engine was too wide to get through the gate leading from Chollacott Lane. The fire was subdued by a hand extinguisher and a line of hose from a hydrant on the moor. Meanwhile a second appliance arrived via Down Road. Members closed their eyes as, on its way to the pavilion, it crossed the newly-seeded area. The interruption was brief. The game proceeded. Teas were served.

In 1946 the Cricket Club, like other local institutions and organisations, emerged blinking in the light and still suffering the privations of the war years. Rationing restrictions meant that only thirty teas could be served on match days. The fall of 20 wickets for 75 runs at Liskeard was easily explained by the fact that the army had only recently vacated the field.

By 1953 a lot had changed. At the end of that season, 150 cars turned up at The Ring on one Sunday afternoon, as 600 people crowded round the boundary to watch a charity game featuring five Somerset players, Harold Gimblett, Roy Smith, Harold Stephenson, Eric Hill, and Brian Langford. It had not been long since a gaggle of urchins had stared open-mouthed, not at Frank Woolley, but at the motor car that had brought him to the ground. Times were changing. It was, however, reassuring to be reminded that some things did not change. In 1948 a late-season fixture against Okehampton at The Ring was cancelled by the visitors on the day before the match, because several of their players wanted to go to Taunton to watch the Australian tourists, while some others were playing football. Indignation knew no bounds. Whatever else was happening, Tavistock and Okehampton could still snarl at each other, as they had done for centuries, whenever a suitable excuse presented itself.

The Mid Fifties

The departure of Bill Colling at the end of the 1953 season was a major blow. He had first captained the side fifteen years earlier, and under his leadership the team had lost just 48 of the 243 games that had been played. He had been, moreover, a batsman who had brought both consistency and style to the opening of an innings. He was to return for the occasional match, but with his removal to Lapford the side lost its linchpin, and he was sorely missed.

Maurice Avery, who took over as skipper, brought three advantages to the task. He had done the job before, captaining in the 1951 and 1952 seasons. He was an experienced cricketer, and, although he was now forty-six, no one doubted that he was still worth his place in the side as a player. He was also popular with his colleagues. A genial easy-going style and temperament enabled him to relate comfortably to others, whether out in the middle or in the pavilion. It was no surprise that he was the players' choice to replace Colling. He realised, however, that he was being asked to take over at a time of transition, brought about by what he called 'the depletion of our playing strength'.

The two main factors here were retirements on the one hand and the calls of national service on the other. Gordon Parry and Eric Davey, while remaining at the centre of the club's affairs, ended playing careers of unique service and of great distinction. David Gordon and Ken Hayhurst moved away. Missing in 1955 were Dennis Paull and Alec Pethick, and, for much of the season, Gerry Parsons. The main batting responsibilities were carried by the Jarman brothers, Jack Rogers, Brian Hill, and Walter Spry, with the brunt of the bowling being borne by Avery himself and Doug Treloar.

Some new players, like Roger Jephcott and Basil Steer, were blooded, but the only newcomer to play a major part in the proceedings over the course of the season was Brian Gawman, who proved to be an effective all-rounder. So stretched were the resources that Frank Millman was plucked out of near retirement to play four games in 1954, when, batting at Number 9, he averaged 34. In 1955 he turned out six times, bowling a long stint in one game to finish with figures of 6 for 36.

One of the most intriguing proposals for strengthening the playing staff concerned Harold Gimblett. This great Somerset batsman had, amidst much acrimony, ended his twenty-year career with his native county, and was looking for a job. Kelly College was ready to hire him as cricket coach, and the suggestion was made that the school and the club might share his services. This resulted in the club committee making an offer of £50, for which they required the former test player to contract for games on Saturdays, Sundays, and Bank Holidays, together with weekly coaching sessions. In the event the 'tormented genius of cricket', as his biographer describes him, accepted a post at Millfield School. Harold Gimblett was not to add to his single appearance at The Ring in the festival game on September 13th 1953, when the scorebook recorded that he was 'caught Colling, bowled Avery, 81'. Here is a might-have-been. Gimblett was, indeed, a great batsman. He might have become the club's first professional since before the First World War. His life thereafter was to pursue an erratic, and ultimately a tragic, course.

In 1954, out of 37 games, 18 were won and 12 were drawn. In 1955, however, the record showed only 12 victories in 40 matches, with 13 drawn, 14 lost, and 1 tied. Some blamed the standard of the fielding, and indirectly the leadership on the field. The loss of key players was certainly a major factor. It was the seventh game of the season before a victory was registered, and then it was only achieved through the aid of two 'guests', one of whom made 101 not out while the other took 4 wickets. A mid-season game against Plymouth Y.M.C.A. in which Tavistock crashed to a 10 wicket defeat after being bundled out for 28 represented the nadir of their fortunes. Gawman lifted spirits a little the following week by scoring 57 and then taking 4 wickets for 1 run.

One particular event in the mid 1950s created high levels of both interest and controversy. On Sunday September 5th 1954 a festival match at The Ring attracted 400 cars and 3000 spectators. The attraction was the participation of eight county cricketers in Bruce Dooland, Harold Stephenson, Vic Jackson, Cliff Gladwin, Jock Livingstone, George Tribe, Jack Walsh, and George Dawkes. An innovation was a loudspeaker commentary to help spectators to identify the stars. The occasion did not pass without criticism. Councillor W.H. Gulley, methodist, sabbatarian, and leader of the abortive campaign to keep the cinemas closed on Sundays, voiced the disquiet that was clearly felt, but that had been rather muted hitherto. 'Are we', he asked, 'drifting towards a continental Sunday?' Gordon Parry, it was felt, was the right man to give a measured response on behalf of the club, and he obliged by talking about 'the genuine and innocent enjoyment of many good citizens'. The animosities which this issue might have evoked did not develop. Meanwhile Mr Gulley has, as we can now all see, been proved right in his implied prediction.

Jack Rogers, who had played for the club since 1947, and had been vice-captain for the two years that Avery led the side, took over as skipper in 1956. With nine successful playing seasons behind him, this experienced cricketer and proven run getter was an obvious choice. His first season in charge was highly successful, in terms both of personal achievement and team record. He scored 598 runs at an average of 28.5, and managed, throughout the whole season, to lose the toss on only four occasions. Out of 36 games, 21 were won, and only 6 lost. The record for 1957 was less impressive, with 12 wins and 10 defeats in 34 matches.

The big disappointment of this summer was the weather, which interfered with play to the extent of helping to produce 12 drawn games. There was, however, a more fundamental reason for a change in the pattern of results that was to produce, over the three seasons between 1957 and 1959, an almost equal number of victories, defeats, and draws. This was the failure to produce a pair of opening bowlers of wicket-taking potential to replace Avery and Davey. Individual performances of distinction were frequently recorded, but the days of the great double-acts were over, with the result that visiting sides at The Ring, for the first time for many years, could feel that some respite was on offer even if a Doug Treloar or a Roger Jeffcott was firing from one end.

Maurice Avery, having freed himself from the cares of captaincy, decided that he had one more full season in him, and in 1956, at the age of forty-eight, he bowled more overs (302) and took more wickets (71) than anyone else. In the following year he played in only 5 games, bowling in only 3 of them, to finish the season with 6 wickets for 89. His long-time partner Eric Davey played only one game after 1955, as did Frank Millman, who turned to a career as an umpire.

Bill Colling made welcome, but increasingly rare appearances, most of which seemed to produce a headline. In June 1956 he played against Tiverton, occupying his old position as opener. One ball he struck almost to the boundary, and he and Pethick ran two and turned for a third. The return from the deep was inaccurate, and resulted in two overthrows. The retrieving fielder, hoping to recover the situation by putting pressure on the batsmen as they ran the second, threw at the unguarded wicket, and the ball sped past to the boundary. One ball; nine runs. Colling's partner that day, Alec Pethick, having had a blank season in 1955, played for half the summer in 1956, making his presence very much felt by scoring 302 runs and taking 35 wickets. He was, however, missing in 1957, as was Colling, apart from one game, in which he scored 103 not out.

The departure, in the mid-1950s, of some veteran players, was compounded by the loss of Bill Martin, who had been the club's faithful scorer for so many years, and who died in 1954. His successor, the young man who had been his understudy, and who was to serve the club in a variety of functions over more than four decades, was Clifford Alford. Bertie Goss continued as a benign and generous president, although he handed over umpiring duties to Frank Millman, who had the benefit of many years of playing experience.

Some of the gaps, on the playing side, were filled by young, but blooded, players returning from national service. Brian Hill, who had first been selected as a fourteen-year-old schoolboy, was back in 1957. He was a good bat, in spite of showing some inconsistencies in defence technique. Gerry Parsons, after playing only one game in two seasons, returned in 1957 to play a full season, to average 27, and to again show his talent as a fine attacking batsman. Dennis Paull marked his reappearance by scoring 662 runs, bowling 147 overs to take 33 wickets, acting as vice-captain, and setting a high example in the field. And David Toye, while not quite fulfilling the high promise of his pre-service career, turned in a number of useful bowling performances and was a strong all-round player. These men, in their early- or mid-twenties, joined half a dozen well-established team members to form the core of the club's playing strength.

In the latter group were Doug Treloar, now the father of the house in terms of years of service but still a lethal wicket taker, and Walter Spry, who had been almost an ever-present since 1949 and who usually opened the batting. There was Roger Jephcott, an intelligent and economical bowler, and Charlie Lovell, a good clubman who made useful runs and chipped in occasionally with helpful wickets, like the 4 for 4 that did for Plympton in 1957. And there were the Jarman brothers. Ken had the dual reputation of being a hard-working, loyal, and popular clubman, and a solid defensive batsman who could grind down an opposition attack. Eric was, by the middle of the decade, an established opening bat with an attacking instinct, and was being seen by some as the long-term replacement for Bill Colling.

Of the new faces, the two that most impressed observers of the 1957 scene belonged to Tony Bickley and Roger Quick, young cricketers seen to have considerable potential. The exploits of Brian Vaughan in 1956 also caused a stir. A naval officer, he came to the club with a reputation as a fine rugby player, and played 10 games in the season. In one he hit 122 not out in 92 minutes, an innings that included ten fours and five sixes. By the end of the season he had topped both lists, with a batting average of 41 and a bowling average of 8.6.

The greatest disappointment of these years was the failure to establish a second eleven. Hopes and ambitions were regularly expressed, but the realisation seemed as far away as ever. Similarly depressing was the decline of the midweek evening fixture, which had in some eyes provided a reasonable substitute for running a regular second team. There was increasing concern that these games, traditionally against village sides, were not being taken seriously, and that their value in introducing new young talent was being lost. The real problem lay in the need to call on regular weekend players to provide the core of a midweek team. Some of those who were already giving more than thirty weekend days, as well as practice sessions, to cricket, may not have minded giving also a few Wednesday evenings, but wives and girlfriends may, of course, have taken a different view.

There was one other occasional embarrassment. There was a long tradition at The Ring, going back to the nineteenth century, of 'double blues'. An Alec Pethick or a Bill Colling could hold stage at The Ring from May to August and at Langsford Park from October to March. But where were loyalties to lie in April or in September? When a touring side was entertained in September 1956 three players had to be borrowed from Plymouth in order to make up a team. The awkwardness was only partly relieved, if at all, by the performance of one of the guests in taking 4 for 6 and reducing the visitors to 26 all out.

As against these discomforting factors, there were a good many causes for satisfaction. In 1956, following the major improvements to both the playing area and the pavilion that had been carried out in recent years, the future of The Ring as the club's home was made more secure by the signing of a 99-year lease. Financially, the heavy expenditure on the renovations, and before that on the centenary celebrations, had strained resources, but a healthy position was maintained through the care and vigilance of Bernard Kerswill, the treasurer from 1947 to 1959, and as the result of the assistance afforded by well-wishers.

Among the most faithful supporters was Mrs F. S. Milton, who not only opened her home for regular fund-raising whist drives, but presented club members with caps. On the field there was a positive response to the criticisms that had been made of the standard of fielding. The game against Old Colfeians in June 1957, when four of the visitors were run out, was given as evidence of a greater keenness and alertness.

There was also the attractiveness, to both players and spectators, of featuring in the programme of fixtures a sprinkling of games against touring sides (a time-honoured institution) and against invitation elevens (a more recent innovation). The former offered prospects of fresh unknown challenges. The latter, which were often associated with benefit appeals, brought stars to The Ring, even if some of them were slightly faded. On successive Sundays in August 1957 there were home games against Dowgate, a metropolitan club on tour, and a Hampshire Eleven, supporting a county beneficiary. Spectators were able to enjoy performances from Leslie Compton in the first week and Roy Marshall in the second.

Annual General Meetings during the 1950s contained few surprises. Having lost the right to select the captain and vice-captain, the 1959 meeting found itself acting as a mere rubber stamp for a change of treasurer. There was nothing sinister about this. The meeting served necessary purposes, but when it came to making detailed decisions a much more appropriate forum was the committee. This small group, elected annually but altering little in composition, found a regular meeting place at the Cattle Market Inn, though other venues included the British Legion Club and the pavilion. Meetings tended to be on an ad hoc basis, and to concern themselves with one major issue.

Thus at least one regular autumn meeting would involve itself in preparations for the New Year's Party, the centrepiece of the club's social programme in the 1950s. The venue for this knees-up was the Red Barn on Kilworthy Hill, and members were expected to be able to dispose of four tickets each, at five shillings a ticket.

At other times the emphasis might be on ways to increase income, such as was the case in 1956 when the committee decided to supplement the subscriptions from players with match fees, chargeable at sixpence a time. This remained a small, if valuable, element in the budget. There were other items to be exhaustively discussed between pints at the Cattle Market Inn, like securing contract arrangements to supply ice cream on match days or to provide transport for away games (the usual arrangement here was the hiring of Down's twenty-seater).

The committee was understandably very cost conscious. Much time was spent, for instance, in balancing the conflicting needs to save money and to show appreciation to those who helped the club. The tea ladies gave up a lot of their time. Could they be offered free transport to away games? No, this would prove too expensive. Could they be offered free transport to one away game per season of their own choosing? A fair compromise. But should this limitation also apply to Mrs Milton, who after all was not only a tea lady but the organiser of the whist drives? This particular issue, much to the credit of the committee, required a special meeting.

The Late Fifties

Jack Rogers's career in banking took him away in 1957, and his eleven-year spell with the club, which included the two years of captaincy, came to an end. Like a number of his predecessors he was to be a guest in the side on an occasional visit to the town over the next few years, but such appearances were to be rare. To no one's surprise, his vice-captain, Dennis Paull, was promoted. The 1958 A.G.M., the venue of which was switched from the Guildhall to the British Legion Club, also approved the appointment of Eric Jarman as vice-captain. Further efforts were made to give the midweek fixtures a greater measure of weight and significance, and it was hoped that the appointment of Charlie Lovell as the Wednesday captain would further that objective.

The new season began promisingly, with 157 from Eric Jarman's bat contributing to two victories. The Jarman brothers were to open together on a number of occasions, with a good deal of success, notably against H.M.S.

Centaur in June, when Eric made 55 and Ken 116 not out. The batting was, throughout the season, effective, with consistent scoring from Parsons and Paull, and a notable contribution, in his first season, from E. L. McEntyre, a class batsman of some pedigree who had represented Cheshire in the minor counties competition. Others chipped in, so that the batsmen rarely left the bowlers too few runs to bowl at. The problem was that of bowling sides out, particularly during another wet summer. Some enterprising work from the impressive all-rounder McEntyre; a blitz, on his day, from Treloar; a cameo act from Vaughan (taking 7 for 8 in 10 overs in his first game for two years); the promise of Tony Bickley: these together never quite added up to a threatening attack. Significantly, Maurice Avery was drafted in for two games and asked to produce two lengthy stints, in which he took 3 for 25 and 1 for 22. At the end of the summer the record read: Played 35, Won 11, Drawn 13, Lost 11.

The season ended with a remarkable flourish. Dennis Brookes, the popular Northants professional, was taking his benefit, and he brought to Tavistock, on September 7th, what must rank as the most impressive array of cricketing talent ever to gather at The Ring. His side were all county professionals. Eight of them were test players past or present: Jack Robertson and Fred Titmus of Middlesex, Ken Barrington and Tony Lock of Surrey, Keith Andrew and Brookes himself of Northants, Les Jackson from Derbyshire, and Ian Thomson of Sussex. Almost as well known to some of the spectators was Ross Salmon, author and television personality, who had played a handful of games for Tavistock during the season, but who, on this afternoon, provided the commentary.

These end-of-term festival games had proved very popular through the 1950s, bringing to The Ring many spectators who would not otherwise have patronised Tavistock cricket. Both club and cause benefited. The enterprise was made possible by an arrangement with the authorities of the Torquay Cricket Festival. When that festival was cancelled in 1959, the Tavistock public was deprived of what it had come to expect as its annual end-of-summer treat. On average, the profit made on each of these events was of the order of £100. A quarter or a third of this might come to the club. This was not only a welcome boost to the funds, but also some recompense for the hard work that inevitably preceded such an ambitious venture.

Dennis Paull resigned the captaincy at the end of the 1958 season, announcing that he would not be able to play in 1959 because of business commitments. Ken Jarman was approached to take on the job, but declined. The players thereupon decided to entrust the leadership to Len McEntyre, who had made such an impressive mark in his debut season the previous year. It was a surprising choice. McEntyre was obviously a good all-round cricketer, who had shown in his play both ability and responsibility. But it was an appointment that clearly carried some risk. It was one of those situations where, in the absence of a candidate with the ideal combination of popularity, experience, and ability, someone emerges who possesses only one of those characteristics, but who, it is hoped, will develop the other two as he gets into the job. Two other changes were made at the same time. one was the sensible decision to harness some of Gerry Parsons's abundant energy and drive into leading the midweek team, a strategy that was amply justified by events. The other was the appointment of Maurice Avery as treasurer in place of Bernard Kerswill, who retired after filling the post very effectively for twelve years.

The 1959 season saw significant achievements both behind the scenes and in the middle. An extension to the pavilion, bringing enlarged changing-room and kitchen facilities, was put in hand. A proposal to instal a telephone was, however, deferred. On the field there was some strong batting, particularly from Parsons and McEntyre, who occupied the first two places in the averages and who scored 790 and 812 runs respectively. But the overall record reflected again only a modest level of success, with 11 victories and 13 defeats in a total of 37 matches. A settled side had been one of the most obvious features of the club's profile in earlier periods. Indeed there had sometimes been criticism on the grounds that there had been too much continuity of selection. In 1959 the picture was different. Only four players featured in more than 21 of the 37 fixtures. The two most frequent performers, McEntyre and Parsons, who dominated the batting, also carried the burden of the attack, bowling between them 40% of the overs and taking 40% of the wickets. Tony Bickley, the newcomer, and Doug Treloar, the evergreen, bowled well, but only played in 13 and 14 games respectively. Significantly Maurice Avery, at fifty-one, played 7 games and bowled 98 overs.

The first whispers of criticism began to be heard as the season was getting under way. Within eight days, towards the end of May, the side was trounced, successively, by Bovey Tracey, Okehampton, and St. Luke's College. In the first of these Tavistock were skittled out for 23, including six ducks, and were beaten by nine wickets. On the following day, Okehampton came to The Ring and left victors by eight wickets. And then St. Luke's carried out a demolition job that resulted in a ten wicket defeat. There was something of a mid-season recovery, but the malaise was, it was felt, deep-seated. The quality of team spirit, the level of morale, and the style of leadership, all came in for added scrutiny as the season pursued a rather listless course.

In August the *Tavistock Gazette*, normally so restrained and generous when it came to commenting on the club and its doings, printed a stinging attack, in which it was claimed that:

> 'late starts, slack fielding, indifference of the players as to the preparation of the wicket, faulty tactics, and the incorrect employment of the talent available, have combined to put a severe strain on the loyalty of even the staunchest of supporters'.

Some of this was obviously aimed at the captain. McEntyre played in every game, scored more runs and took more wickets than anyone else, and only occasionally lost the toss. (*The Gazette*, in a Parryesque phrase, described him as 'no tyro when it comes to Numismatic Ballistics'.) There was, however, an impression of drift.

There was also a good deal of resentment at his style of leadership, on the grounds that off the field he was too ready to leave to others the mundane tasks that had to be undertaken, while on the field he was rather autocratic and insensitive. To focus all the blame on one man was certainly unfair. To see the problem as having suddenly arisen in one year was also misleading. What was happening, as the decade came to an end, was that the club was paying the price for not having made adequate preparation for what could, and should, have been foreseen years earlier, namely the almost simultaneous retirement of a generation of players. The 1960s might start with four safe pairs of hands guiding the club in administrative and supporting capacities. But there was no comparable depth of experience and knowledge on the field.

Among the concerns identified in the *Gazette* broadside was 'the indifference of the players as to the preparation of the wickets'. Here was a familiar problem. The quality of cricket, perhaps to a greater extent than in any other game, is dependent on the surface on which it is played. Pitch preparation requires knowledge and experience and demands time. The temptation for the ordinary player is to find any excuse to leave the work to others. For many years it had been possible to rely on a handful of wise and willing helpers. The situation would not last for ever. Everyone knew this, but the instinctive tendency was to delay decisions for as long as possible, in the vain hope that solutions would somehow materialise.

In this spirit frequent attempts to have a more organised approach to the care of the ground, to require a greater commitment from members, and to arrange work rotas, did not get very far. Some associated problems shocked contemporary observers. Litter was one such. Surely no previous generation of cricket watchers had been so thoughtless about the mess they left behind them? Vandalism was another. The wanton damage done to the pavilion one night in 1957 – which cost the club £10 – led to the posting of notices warning of prosecutions. It was, sadly, not an isolated example of mindless delinquency in that, or for that matter in any, decade.

The concerns of the late 1950s need to be kept in perspective. The playing record was modest, but only in terms relative to earlier periods. Every club has to endure ups and downs in its playing fortunes. The remarkable feature of the Tavistock story is that even in the troughs the record scarcely ever showed more defeats than victories. But by 1960 it had become fashionable to compare the team unfavourably with sides that had carried the Tavistock colours in earlier periods. Cricket lovers, more than most, are creatures of nostalgia. There are always giants from the past to put alongside the pygmies of the present. Of cricket it may be said, as it was once said of the magazine *Punch*: It isn't what it used to be; but then it never was.

Part Five: 1960–1979

The Age of Expansion

New Blood

The 1960s began with the aftermath of the experiment of Len McEntyre's captaincy, and ended with a two-year reign by Evan Kemp. In between, leadership was in the hands of either Doug Treloar or Eric Jarman, the former for three years and the latter for five seasons in two spells. McEntyre stood down after one season in charge, although he kept in touch by contributing usefully in the half-dozen games that he played in each of the 1960 and 1961 seasons. In the Jarman-Treloar years that followed, the captaincy was held by men who were not only seasoned cricketers but active and popular clubmen.

Then, in 1968, Evan Kemp, one of a number of young schoolmasters who came into the Tavistock side during the decade, became captain. Kemp was a thoughtful cricketer and a talented all-rounder, who was reliable in performance with both bat and ball. He had first played for the club in 1963. It was obvious that one of the main functions of captaincy during these years would be to preside over some essential team rebuilding. And so it proved. The prize was that elusive formula that would provide the right balance between youth and experience. To achieve this, the team required new blood in all departments.

At the beginning of the 1960s the club possessed a nucleus of batting strength. This was spearheaded by Eric Jarman, an established opening bat who continued to play in the forceful mode that was his natural game. His ability to provide early momentum by jump-starting an innings was one of three distinctive contributions that he made to Tavistock cricket during the decade. The second was in his captaincy. He was a popular and positive skipper. Tactically, there was a change of approach between his first period in office, from 1960 to 1961, and his second, from 1965 to 1967. Initially, he had been disposed to vary, and experiment with, both batting orders and bowling options, and to give to all the players equal opportunities to shine. Later, he became more cautious of change, and more ready to back his own judgment on such matters. His third contribution was as a clubman, and here he displayed a commitment and a loyalty of a very high order. Few of the initiatives, and few of the humdrum chores, were done without his active and enthusiastic participation. His older brother Ken also fitted this description, and was particularly involved in all matters related to the ground. He ended his playing days in 1962.

At about the same time Walter Spry, as he entered his fifties, began to reduce his playing commitments. He was to become one of the old heads in the newly-formed second eleven in the middle of the decade. His career ended with a flourish in 1967; having hit a century for the seconds, he was recalled to first team duty, at the age of fifty-six. Two of the other star batsmen of the 1950s had also moved on by then. Dennis Paull played only irregularly in the early 1960s. Gerry Parsons took his leave in 1965. In the three previous summers his run-totals had been, successively, 1191, 1094, and 1169, and his averages had in each case been in the high 40s. On June 15th 1963 he scored 101 not out to enable skipper Treloar to declare on 210 for 1. He then bowled his leg-breaks to such effect that he finished with 5 for 14. Twelve months later he got the nod from the Devon county selectors, and celebrated by scoring 88 and 49 for Tavistock on successive days.

The following spring should have been the crowning moment of his thirteen year career with Tavistock. Doug Treloar had decided to stand down from the captaincy, and most of the players, as they prepared for their pre-A.G.M. gathering, had decided that Parsons was the man to succeed him. He was not at the meeting. A letter from him to Eric Davey revealed that he had accepted a contract with Wadebridge, and would be playing Cornish league cricket. His subsequent career took him to the captaincy of Cornwall, and he added to his other achievements the distinction of having played for both Cornwall and Devon.

Thus, of the six specialist batsmen from the 1950s who played on into the 1960s, four, Spry, Paull, Parsons, and Ken Jarman, had virtually retired from the scene by mid-decade. The two others who survived were Eric Jarman and George Clements. Clements was another of the graduates from village cricket, having begun his playing days at Lydford. He continued, season after season, to be a reliable middle-order bat, and to provide valuable experience in an otherwise quite youthful side.

On August 21st 1960, Tavistock visited Budleigh Salterton. For the home side the second highest scorer was the opening bat Eric Davey. The next season he was a Tavistock player. Between 1961 and 1966 he was a regular, almost ever-present, opener, scoring his 1000 or so runs each summer (1236 in 1964) and playing a sheet-anchor role which provided a perfect foil for the more dashing approach of Eric Jarman or Gerry Parsons. He was a painstaking innings-builder, and on very many occasions he held things together while wickets were falling at the other end. After six highly productive seasons he moved away, pursuing his banking career, but he had by then done an invaluable job during a crucial period.

His presence at The Ring gave rise to only one significant problem. The other Eric Davey was not playing any more, but he was still a very important figure in the club. How would you avoid confusion? Solution to hand! The new arrival hailed from Budleigh Salterton. 'Budleigh' Davey he was to be.

Two other new batsmen also made their entries in the early 1960s. John Gelsthorpe had formerly played for Yelverton. Oxford trained, he was a teacher, rode an old cycle with enthusiasm, and was very quick on the field, whether batting or fielding. Those who batted with him tend, even thirty years later, to become breathless at the recollection of trying to keep up with his pace between the wickets. As far as his Tavistock career was concerned, he hit the ground running, by making 67 in his debut game in 1964. The next year brought in Peter Earl, a batsman who could, on his day, decide a game with a half-hour of blistering attack. In 1968, for example, he began his season by scoring 66 in 39 minutes, and ended it five months later with 57 not out in 37 minutes.

The pattern of the bowling attack mirrored that of the batting in that a nucleus of experience was supplemented by an injection of new blood. Appearances by Tony Bickley (colleagues usually used his second name Piers) were, in the early 1960s, limited by his attendance at Exeter University (he played for the university against Tavistock in 1960 and took 7 for 30). His return, in the second half of each season, was invariably followed by a handful of demolition jobs. In August 1960, for example, he took 6 for 6 as Okehampton were dismissed for 85. Out of a reply of 69 he scored 29 runs, batting at Number 9. There can have been few greater triumphs in a losing cause. Three weeks later, when Plymouth Queries were bundled out for 24, he took 7 for 18. In 1962 he launched what was to be his last season with the club by taking 6 for 17 against the same side.

Roger Jephcott had played since 1955. An accurate and thoughtful bowler, he could, on his day, like Bickley, mow down a batting side with almost ruthless efficiency. The 1961 season was a particularly productive time. It began in April with an 8 for 11 demolition of Dartington Hall, and ended in September with a 9 for 19 destruction of an Exeter touring side. That summer also saw examples of what generations of Tavistock cricket watchers had enjoyed: the spectacle of two strike bowlers operating in tandem, each both hostile and accurate. As Jephcott and Bickley despatched Yelverton for 37, or Crediton (Bill Colling et al) for 40, memories were stirred of the great days of Davey and Avery, while behind some of the older, moistening, eyes, watching from the pavilion, lurked images of even earlier days, perhaps of Robinson and Linnell. The difference this time was that the feast was not to last very long. Bickley's departure in 1962 was followed by Jephcott's one year later. The void that they left was partly filled by the man who was captain at the time, and who was now showing as much enthusiasm for his cricket as he had shown in each of the previous three decades in which he had played for Tavistock.

Doug Treloar was a one-off. As a strike bowler he retained throughout his career the same potentially lethal qualities of pace, length, and sometimes wicked deviation. The action had to be seen to be believed. He bowled off the wrong foot. The bowling arm seemed to appear, arc-like, from behind his head, imparting swing to a ball that then pitched and seamed in the opposite direction. Few batsmen could face such an awkward customer with comfort. During his three years in the captaincy he bowled himself a lot. And he was justified in doing so. In 1962, at the age of forty-six, he took over 100 wickets. This was followed, in the next two seasons, by hauls of 85 and 79.

With Jephcott and Bickley gone, and Treloar, although sprightly, climbing towards fifty, there was need to reinforce the attack. Tony Clapp and Stuart Munday joined in 1965 and Jerry Pitts-Tucker in 1967. But the prince was Jack Davey.

Here was the man who, in the light of his subsequent cricket career, must be said to be the finest player who ever represented the club. His first-class career for Gloucestershire was to stretch from 1966 to 1978 and between those years he played 175 first-class games and took 411 wickets, scoring also 918 runs as a tail-end batsman. He belonged to the Bannawell Street family that had already provided the club with two of its stalwart performers and servants in his grandfather Glanville and his father Eric. Like them, Jack was a bowler. A left-armer, some people thought that his future was as a spinner, but he was determined to bowl fast, and that is what he did.

He played his first game for the club on August 6th 1961, when he was a month short of his seventeenth birthday, and took his first wicket in a match against Paignton later in that month. It was in the middle of the following summer that his performances began to catch the eye. In one week in June 1962 he played in three games, in the first of which he took 6 for 27, all his wickets being clean bowled. In the following two matches, as well as taking wickets, he showed his value as a tail-end batsman, first by putting up the shutters to earn a draw, and then by scoring 24 not out to bring about a most unlikely 1 wicket victory. A 6 for 28 and an 8 for 9 followed soon after.

In the 1963 season, when he was eighteen, he bowled 458 overs and took 81 wickets at 11.2 each. Towards the end of that summer selection came for Devon Colts, for whom he took 5 for 21 against Cornwall Colts at Liskeard. In 1964 he bowled 465 overs and his 87 wickets cost 11.6 apiece. Selected for the county in two minor county games, he topped the Devon averages. The next logical step, if he was to become a first-class cricketer, was to interest a county in the idea of a trial, and this came in April 1965 at Worcester. Two games for the Worcestershire Second Eleven followed, but the anticipated contract did not materialise. In October of that year, Gloucestershire snapped him up, offering him a one year contract for 1966. The rest, as they say, is history.

If an attempt were to be made to describe the essence of a typical Tavistock Cricket Club eleven, it would surely include two features. There would be three or four all-rounders and no spin bowler. Both these characteristics were evident in the sides that represented the club in the 1960s. It was almost a club tradition that one of the batsmen would deploy a bit of part-time spin, and Gerry Parsons, in filling this role, was more skilled and profitable than most of his predecessors. A specialist off-spin or leg-break bowler, however, simply did not emerge. The tradition of all-rounders, particularly those who combined the duties of middle-order batsman and first-change bowler, was, on the other hand, firmly established. Of those in this category, Roger Quick was already a fixture and Len McEntyre was still on the scene. They were joined, in 1960, by David Ewings. Here was a cricketer of talent and flair who could, more than anyone else in the side during that period, turn a game by delivering the unexpected. In his first few seasons he was seen primarily as a bowler, a reputation grounded in a debut performance of 3 for 8. By 1962 he was an integral part of the pace attack, a position secured on the back of two early-season displays when, on consecutive Saturdays, he took 6 for 15 against Yelverton and 8 for 24 against Bovey Tracey. Perhaps his most lethal spell was in early 1964 when, in an away game, he destroyed the Liskeard batting with figures of 7 for 6. The power of his batting took a little longer to develop, but by 1967 he had already given evidence of what his effective, if unconventional, methods could achieve. Eric Jarman promoted him up the order, and in 1967 he opened for a while. In this position he scored, in four consecutive games, 57, 23, 46 not out, and 71. A few weeks later he opened with George Clements in pursuit of a 156 victory target. They were home by 9 wickets in 72 minutes, with Ewings on 112 not out. He had reached his century in 65 minutes, with thirteen fours and four sixes.

Two young all-rounders joined the playing staff in 1963. Both were local schoolmasters, and one was to follow the other in the captaincy at the end of the decade. Evan Kemp, reliable and thoughtful, was the sort of player who never failed to make an impact on a game in one way or another, either by taking 3 for 25 or by holding up the middle order with a valuable 40, or by both. He had, as a student, played in the formidable St. Luke's College side. Bob Quick had first encountered Tavistock cricketers when he made 51 against them, and took 2 of their wickets, in the same game at Budleigh Salterton in 1960 that also featured Eric 'Budleigh' Davey. Quick was a dashing player, impetuous, talented, popular, and committed. In his debut season he scored 531 runs, some of them as Eric Jarman's opening partner. Bowling usually the second change, he took useful wickets, the highlight here being his 5 for 7 against Bovey Tracey after Jack Davey had bowled a spell of 0 for 33.

In 1965 Derek Pethick took his first bow at The Ring. Following the family tradition (Alec was his second cousin) he was a fine all-rounder, who was to serve the club well. A distinctive contribution was his spin bowling. He was the only practitioner of the art to play regularly in the late 1960s. 'Derek Pethick's match' is remembered as being the one against a touring side in August 1967, when, batting at number 7, he scored 72 not out to lift a modest total to a level that allowed a declaration, and then proceeded to take the middle out of the visiting batting with a spell of 4 for 5.

In the 1950s Tavistock had not had a settled wicketkeeper. That such a specialist job had tended to be passed around had created some problems, and had been unsettling for some of the bowlers. John Perkin had acquitted himself very creditably in the role in the late 1950s, and in 1960 Maurice Craze first appeared as a wicketkeeper-batsman, though his main value to the side was as a run-getter. And then on July 31st 1960, Geoff Husband played his first game. He soon established himself as both wicketkeeper and opening bat. His skill behind the stumps quickly became apparent, and observers were soon talking about his sureness of touch and speed of reaction. One of the features of his performances over the years was the extraordinary number of stumpings that he achieved, and these were not confined to bowling of a particular kind. Take, for instance, the home game against Filleigh on June 9th 1963. Five of the visiting batsmen were stumped, three from the leg-break bowling of Gerry Parsons and two from the pacy swing attack of Doug Treloar. In addition he took two catches. He was, over a long career, to prove himself to be the best wicketkeeper ever to represent Tavistock. On the batting side he had both good technique and an appetite for runs, so that over the years he was to be one of the club's most substantial and consistent run scorers. When he first arrived at The Ring he had a reputation for being rather impetuous and taking too many risks. This was probably because he tended then to come in at Number 4 or 5 in situations where quick runs were required. Graduating to opener brought different priorities, and his style became more sober and restrained, as he saw his chief role as a foundation-laying one. The capacity to make such adjustments is part of the armoury of the thinking cricketer, as another Geoff, making his debut for Yorkshire at about the same time, would no doubt affirm.

Geoff Husband was a schoolmaster, teaching Maths at Tavistock School. He was also an instinctive missionary for the game and the club, so that he spread the word among both colleagues and pupils. Among the members of the Tavistock School staffroom who played for the club at some point during the 1960s were Geoff Beynon, Brian Civil, Tony Clarke, Evan Kemp, Bob Quick, and Harry Tilton. In addition, John Gelsthorpe, Ken Saxby, and Hilton Jones taught in the area.

Half a century before, it had often seemed that Kelly College schoolmasters dominated the scene at The Ring. Now another school was, thanks partly to Husband's recruiting skills, providing the core of a new young side that was emerging from the changes of the late 1950s. Not that, as some may have suspected, teams were selected at secret gatherings in Crowndale Road broom cupboards. There was a properly constituted selection committee consisting of the captain and vice-captain and four other central figures including one non-playing member. They were elected annually, but the formula varied little from year to year. They met each week during the season, on either a Sunday or a Monday evening, to make decisions for the following weekend's matches. This involved a long series of meetings, because the season seemed to stretch almost from Easter to Goose Fair. In 1969, for example, the first match was played on April 13th, and the last one on September 28th.

A New Look at the Fixtures

One constant, and welcome, feature of the pattern of fixtures in the 1960s was the entertainment of touring sides. Caius College Cambridge made regular post-term visits. A number of sides from Kent appeared, as a result of contacts made when Tavistock toured that county in 1962. One of the attractions of such fixtures was that you never knew who you were going to meet. For example, when a Lancashire club paid a visit in the middle of the 1964 season, their players included Roy Cheetham of Manchester City, Maurice Setters of Manchester United, and Nobby Lawton of Preston North End. These three shared between them the 5 Tavistock wickets that fell, but did not make a big impact with the bat, Cheetham being bowled by Davey for 0, Setters getting himself run out for 13, and Lawton being stumped by Craze off Roger Quick for 10.

Further examples of the attractiveness of the unusual were provided both by benefit games, honouring the likes of Bill Alley and Geoff Lomax, and by the occasional festival affair, such as the one in September 1962 in which Godfrey Evans scored 102 not out.

Perhaps the most popular fixture that went on through the decade involved the Mendip Acorns. This was a North Somerset based club which always included a number of past or present county players. Each season they played home and away matches against Tavistock, the former at the County Ground, the latter at The Ring. Regular participants included Bill Alley, Brian Langford, Graham Atkinson, Roy Virgin, and Peter Wight. There was never any question of these games degenerating into a festival romp. They were hard-fought and competitive, and often produced close finishes, like the one in May 1964 at Taunton, won by the Acorns by 1 run.

The 1965 fixture list may be taken as typical of the programmes of the period. There were five games against touring sides, three from Kent, one from Monmouth, and one from the Isle of Wight. Two matches were against locally-based Old Boys' sides, two against Mendip Acorns, and three against Plymouth clubs. Fixtures against Exeter University and St. Luke's College provided, as they always did, stiff opposition. St. Luke's in particular always seemed to come away with the spoils, even in situations when the Tavistock players felt they had a real chance. It was remembered, for instance, that in the previous year Davey had hustled the first two batsmen out for ducks and the College had stood on 0 for 2. Two hours later they declared on 179 for 2, and went on to win by 94 runs.

There were no games in 1965 against regimental or naval sides: those days were over. The rest of the fixtures were against other club sides: Okehampton, Bovey Tracey, Ashburton, Tiverton, Yelverton, Plymouth, Plymstock, Dartington, Plympton, Torquay, Paignton, Exmouth, Buckfastleigh, South Devon, North Devon, St Austell, Penzance, Liskeard, and Weston-Super-Mare. One omission in that particular year was Crediton, who were being punished for cancelling the 1964 fixture on the morning of the match.

It must have been tempting at that period to speculate on the possible futures of some of the potential stars met on the club circuit. David Shepherd of North Devon was, for example, to play for Gloucestershire, Jeff and Roger Tolchard of Torquay for Leicestershire, and John Solanky of Plymouth for Glamorgan. Harold Bird of Paignton was at the other end of a first class career. Messrs Bird and Shepherd were to become in the 1980s and 1990s the best known umpires in England, and, perhaps, in the world.

In a playing season that included more than 40 weekend matches the case for organising mid-week fixtures did not seem strong. Since such additional games would be played at The Ring, there was also the question of the pressure on the square and the number of wickets that could reasonably be prepared in a season. There were, on the other hand, two compelling reasons for retaining some framework of evening matches. One was the responsibility that was felt towards village sides to maintain long-standing arrangements, an obligation which, incidentally, was not without self-interest when one thinks of the number of players recruited from such sides who became central figures at The Ring. The other factor was the continuing, and regularly-lamented, lack of a second eleven to serve as a conduit for young players.

In the 1960s the latter need was finally met. The innovation began somewhat hesitantly, in spite of the determination shown by some, particularly by Geoff Husband. During his first year with the club, Husband urged that the project should be launched, at least on a limited scale. In late 1962 a handful of games were played, using the opportunity of the availability of The Ring while the first team was away on tour. The next step was the convening of a special meeting in April 1963 to discuss the feasibility of the idea. An attendance of eighteen was a heartening sign, and the meeting responded to Husband's invitation to decide in principle to establish a second eleven. The only substantial reservation seemed to be the cost that might be involved, particularly of travel. The enterprise was put in hand, fixtures were organised, and a captain was appointed.

Jack Taylor, when he took up his duties, was forty-seven years old. He was a newcomer to the area, having spent his life hitherto, much of it playing cricket, in the midlands. He brought down with him his life-long passion for the game, and offered his services and experience to the Tavistock club. He was always proud of the fact that his playing career at Tavistock began with a wicket from the first ball he bowled. It was a full-toss down the leg side, and Husband did the stumping. Age, and a knee injury, meant that he was unlikely to hold down a place in the first team, but the discussions that were then going on about the possibility of a second team offered an opportunity for him to carve out a niche. He later recalled the genesis of the undertaking:

> 'The man most concerned with its inception was Geoff Husband. But he was still a young and active member, and a regular playing member of the first team. So he got fixtures, prepared wickets, and set most of the games up. I was still landed at the weekend with the running of the games. It was early days to interest many senior players, and it usually meant Geoff scouring the school for the best of the lads to complete the team'.

The enterprise got off the ground in 1964, when 31 games were played, 14 being won and 14 lost. In the next two seasons, respectively 33 and 34 matches produced 17 victories in each season. Jack Taylor continued to skipper the side down to 1970, when he handed over to another veteran, Doug Treloar.

Treloar had already, in 1967, taken over the fixture-making chores from Geoff Husband, who had laid the foundations in the first three crucial years. Apart from the captain, the member of the second eleven who had the strongest personality, and the greatest cricketing experience, was Ken Saxby, for three years vice-captain. Saxby was a schoolmaster who had recently migrated from Kent, and from 1965 he was a pillar of the second eleven, while also sometimes playing, and making a substantial number of runs, in the first team. Both of these men were to give considerable service to the club in other capacities later on. Three other players who were very effective performers in the second team in those early years, and who also showed themselves able to hold their own in first team company when selected, were Len Rule, Barry Chappell, and Les Curate.

The successful launch of the second eleven was one of four significant innovations in the 1960s that affected the structure of the playing season. Two others were linked. The idea of the week-long August tour was revived in 1962 after a gap of eleven years. The first of the six scheduled games at Rye set the pattern for a highly successful week. Tavistock made 165. The home side seemed to be cruising to a comfortable victory as they sailed past 100 with 2 wickets down. Then Dave Ewings struck. His 6 for 46 included a hat trick, and the visitors shaved it by 5 runs. A happy party returned at the end of the week with a record of four wins and two draws. Two years later the enterprise was repeated with a similar itinerary and outcome.

There followed, before the end of the decade, three more tours in which the focus was switched from Kent to Sussex. In the 'in-between' years, starting in 1965, lest the players should be at a loose end during the third week in August, cricket weeks began. These complemented the tours, providing similar daily fare, but with the club acting as hosts instead of guests.

One other development which has affected the club's programme in the modern era had its roots in the 1960s. The Devon Club Cricket Association, to which Tavistock was affiliated, operated a knock-out cup competition, which was sponsored by Rothmans, with whose name it inevitably became associated. The format consisted of an area tournament of two or three rounds, followed by further county-wide rounds. The area phase involved matches of 18 overs per innings, while the later stages allowed for 40 overs per side.

Tavistock's first swim in these unfamiliar waters came in 1966, and resulted in a first round defeat at the hands of Plymouth. In 1967 victories in the first two rounds brought a place in the area final, but again Plymouth got in the way. The third attempt took the club one stage further, surviving all the area stages but losing to Exeter St. Thomas by 6 runs in the semi final. In 1969 there was again a narrow defeat, this time by 3 runs at the hands of Callington.

This was the period when cricket, at different levels including the first-class game, was learning to come to terms with the consequences of the limited-over revolution. When, in May 1966, Tavistock played its first limited-over game and entered a structured competition, it was entering a new phase in its history. Some players welcomed it as bringing more excitement, more motivation, and a general increase in the level of competitiveness. Others felt that the 'new cricket' would soon elbow out the traditional game, with its friendly fixtures and its greater concern with time than with the number of overs. Some new learning was obviously necessary. No one could have foreseen how far the revolution was to go. But clearly things would never be quite the same again.

The Sixties: A Record of Success

One of the arguments used by supporters of limited-over cricket was that it would reduce the number of drawn games. Insofar as this contention implied criticism of players, and particularly captains, it was unfair, to the extent that it overlooked the fact that the weather was responsible for more inconclusive outcomes than over-cautious or negative cricket. Some of us would go further and claim that drawn games have featured among the most interesting and exciting that we have played in or watched. Nevertheless there were many in the 1960s who agreed with Eric Davey's observation that he was 'rather concerned at the number of drawn games'. Over the decade, of the 422 games that were played, 162, or 38%, were drawn. The 'worst' season, from this point of view, was 1967, when 58% of games were drawn. The 'best' was 1961, when the figure was 22%.

Of more significance than the pattern of drawn games was the record of matches won and lost. Of the 422 fixtures, 183 were won and 73 lost, a ratio of victories to defeats of 2½ to 1. The proportion of victories achieved season by season ranged from 54% in 1963 to 29% in 1967. The proportion of defeats sustained ranged from 31% in 1960 to 5% in 1963. The statistics lead inevitably to the conclusion that the 1960s was, from the point of view of results, one of the most successful periods in the club's history. Gordon Parry had said at the 1961 A.G.M.:

> 'I feel sure that if we can keep together the young side we were able to put into the field at the end of last season, our prospects are bright'.

He was thinking of men like Bickley, Craze, Ewings, Husband, and Jephcott. The lowering of the average age of the team improved the fielding, and this contributed to the success. But of more significance was the fact that there was an attack with a cutting edge, or rather with four or five cutting edges.

In the early part of the decade, matches tended to be low-scoring, with the damage being done, for Tavistock, on a 'perm any two from four' basis. In 1961, Treloar bagged 94 wickets, and Jephcott and Bickley 81 each. In 1962 Ewings was a central figure. Taking, at random in that season, three successive games, Bickley won the first one with 6 for 28, Jephcott the second with 6 for 24, and Ewings the third with 6 for 25. The Tavistock batting tended in these years to be somewhat overshadowed by the performances of the bowlers. But Parsons, the Jarman brothers, and Husband were batting well, and the side was strengthened in 1961 by the addition of Eric Davey and the return of Roger Quick.

By 1963, with the further accession of Evan Kemp and Bob Quick, a well balanced side had emerged, in which there were even glimpses of spin bowling as Parsons wheeled his leg-breaks. Jack Davey was now an integral part of the side, and in that season he and skipper Treloar bowled 898 overs between them, 246 of which were maidens, and took 166 wickets for 1923. When the side, on July 20th, travelled to Torquay to face a side that included five county players, they took with them an unbeaten record. The record went that evening, when Doug Treloar was caught off the fifth ball of the last over, and Tavistock slid to a 42 run defeat. Revenge was taken, in the form of a two-wicket victory, six weeks later.

Through the whole of the season, which featured 43 matches, there were only 2 defeats. The following year, with much the same side, the season took a similar course though the results were less spectacular, with 7 defeats in 42 games. A settled batting line-up had by now emerged, in which Gerry Parsons and 'Budleigh' Davey played key roles. In that summer of 1964 they scored 2405 runs between them. There was one disaster, and that was in the game against Plymouth on August 1st. The previous four games had seen the batsmen in form, with 608 runs being made and only 11 wickets falling. And then, facing the challenge of scoring 148 to beat their old rivals, they were blown away for 34.

The next season, 1965, brought some significant changes to a settled, successful, side. There was a hand-over of the leadership from Treloar to Jarman, which brought to an end an extraordinary three-year reign in which there had been only 15 defeats. Parsons, Bickley, Jephcott, and Davey, all either moved on or joined the irregulars. Replacing them were Peter Earl, Stuart Munday, and Derek Pethick. The appearance of the latter in a side that also included an Eric Davey may have triggered off some memories. Readers of the local papers in the second week of August may have wondered whether they were waking from a long sleep when they read that a Tavistock victory on the previous Sunday had been secured by a not-out century by Davey, followed by a spell of 7 for 34 from Pethick. There were two particular team triumphs in that summer. One came in the game against Plymstock, who had not suffered a Saturday defeat for two years. A partnership of 124 in 63 minutes by Husband and Ewings opened the way for a declaration at 190 for 3, and a comprehensive victory by 113 runs. In the same month an attempt to overhaul a modest Plymouth total of 90 seemed to be faltering as Tavistock fell away to 25 for 6. Enter Ewings and Clements, with an unbroken stand of 67 to bring about the first victory over Plymouth for many years. The result was 'greeted by a salvo of tooting car horns'.

The 1966 season saw no major changes in personnel. The batting had by now solidified, and, on the shoulders of some impressive opening stands, there were a series of impressive performances. Against Liskeard in July Eric Jarman and John Gelsthorpe put on 136 in 67 minutes to set up a total of 211 for 5 declared, achieved in only 127 minutes. Two weeks later, at Exmouth, the home side ran up a total of 235. Jarman and Husband responded with 69 in 30 minutes, and the momentum was maintained as the score reached 150 for 3 in 70 minutes. The middle order, however, subsided, and the visitors were left 14 runs short and with 2 wickets in hand. A further two weeks on and, in the first match of the Sussex tour, Jarman and Davey provided the platform for an assault on a modest victory target of 111. It was left to Kemp and Ewings, batting down the order, to clinch victory after some earlier wobbling. A week later, and back home at The Ring, Husband and Davey put on 112 in 80 minutes to set up a comfortable victory against Plymouth YMCA. The season was characterised by a higher-than-normal number of close finishes. On Whit Monday, Plymouth won at The Ring by 3 runs. The following weekend a victory was secured against South Devon when Kemp scored the winning run off the third ball of the last over. In the first week of July, under a hot Paignton sun, Husband made 108 not out, and Tavistock raced to 198 for 2 in 115 minutes to overtake, in the dying minutes, the formidable target set by the home side. A few days later they failed by 8 runs in a similar chase against a touring eleven. The last weekend of August brought two close finishes. On the Saturday a victory against Plymstock had to wait until the penultimate ball. The Sunday game was even tighter. Buckfastleigh scored 189 for 7 declared, leaving Tavistock 130 minutes to make the runs. When it came to the last over, 6 were still needed. Five came off 5 balls, so that the score stood at 189 for 6. An attempt to scamper a quick single off the last ball led to a close run-out decision and to a final tying of the scores. The season ended, appropriately, with a 3 run victory at North Devon, on the only ground that could, for grandeur, possibly rival The Ring.

And so to 1967, a season of wet weather in which 26 of the 45 games were drawn, but which produced some fine performances, particularly by the all-rounders. Pethick, Rule, Kemp, Ewings, and the Quicks, shared between them a healthy proportion of both runs and wickets. Pethick's strongest performance was against Brookweald, when he first scored 72 not out in a total of 161, and then took 4 for 5 when the tourists batted. Kemp's match was against Crewkerne. He closed their innings by taking 4 wickets in the last over to finish with 5 for 17, and then scored the winning run. Again there were close finishes. Tavistock lost to South Devon by 3 runs, to Old Colfeians by 1 run, and to their bogey team St. Luke's College, though the latter only scraped home by 3 wickets in the last over. The Plymouth saga continued. In a rain-curtailed match, the old foe, in chasing quick runs to reach a victory target of 111, nearly lost, and were in the end happy to escape at 68 for 8. And so to Instow in late September, where, it seemed, fate always provided a theatrical finale to the season. This time Tavistock needed 3 to win from the last ball. George Clements scored 2.

The 1967 season ended on October 1st. The 1968 one began on April 14th. The principal addition to the playing staff this time was another all-rounder, Hilton Jones. Two impressive team performances, in contrasting situations, gave early-season indications of the strength and balance that the side had now achieved. Far from being over-awed by playing at the County Ground, the batsmen scored 256 for 6 declared in 156 minutes against the Mendip Acorns, to set up a winning position. And in the Whit Monday local derby they found themselves, in reply to Plymouth's 197, at 64 for 9 with forty minutes left. Ewings and Munday did the needful, and the match was drawn. In another series of tight finishes, the one involving South Devon was the most memorable, because of an extraordinary final twist. Tavistock were set 141 for victory in 110 minutes. An innings of 84 by Jones helped to keep them in touch, and when the final over began they needed 18. The first five balls of the over realised 13 runs. At that point the umpire called over and stumps were drawn, with 4 runs the difference between the two sides. In a home game against Buckfastleigh later in the season there was further last-over tension, although this time the umpire counted correctly. With Tony Clapp on strike, the home side needed 14 from the last six balls. Clapp hit the first one for six. There were then two singles, leaving a margin of only 6 for victory from three balls. Cricket does not, of course, always provide fairy-tale or heroic endings. The innings ended with three dot balls.

This was the first of Evan Kemp's two seasons in the captaincy. In the second, the summer of 1969, the composition and balance of the side remained similar, and the results continued to be encouraging. The batting did, however, show qualities of brittleness – 73 against Plymouth and 55 against St. Luke's – which had not been so evident in previous seasons. Nevertheless the decade ended with a sense of justifiable satisfaction. Ten years earlier it may have been fashionable to have thought of the club as relying too much on the strength of the pace bowling. What the 1960s had shown was that opponents could also expect to meet strength in depth in both the batting and the fielding departments.

The Sixties: Developments Behind the Scenes

In the 1950s the annual number of fixtures averaged 35. In the 1960s this had increased to 42. More than half of these games were played at The Ring. When to this was added: the requirement of the second eleven for some twenty wickets each year, the pressure on the square became considerable. The club was fortunate to have, at that time, someone with both the skill and the commitment to take on, in practice if not in name, the role of curator. Ken Saxby had brought this expertise, and a love of the game, with him from his native Kent. No one except Gordon Parry has been more assiduous in carrying out the invaluable duties of pitch preparation.

Two innovations in the early part of the decade proved helpful. In 1961 a water pipe was laid to the edge of the square, thus dispensing with the need to have water fed from the pavilion through hose-pipes. In the following year a mechanical roller, 'Ivan', was purchased for £100.

The transfer of the manorial rights of The Down in 1964 from the Bedford Estate to the local council had no significant impact on the club. As before, issues occasionally arose which raised questions about areas of responsibility, but these were usually settled amicably. The club had, for instance, to take on board the need to 'abate' any 'nuisance' that might result from the propensity of the sewage pit to overflow occasionally. The question of access to the ground remained a rather vexed one. Warren Lane was the traditionally favoured route, but some residents became upset as the number of vehicles increased. The outcome of that was to be a clear directive, aided by a sign on the Whitchurch Road, to use Chollacott Lane.

Much interest had been concentrated in the 1950s on the major improvements to the playing area. In the 1960s the focus of attention became the pavilion. The building that stood in 1960 was essentially the structure that had been erected in 1873. It had originally been described as 'commodious', but over the years, in spite of improvements such as the provision of mains water, of toilets, and of a kitchen, it had increasingly come to show signs of its age. Between 1960 and 1962 there were a series of major developments which together served to modernise the building. The old lead piping carrying water was replaced by a polythene pipeline. An additional changing room was added, and a larger kitchen provided. At the rear a more roomy storage shed was erected to house the machinery and implements, including the new mechanical roller. Electricity was installed at a cost of £150. And a bar appeared.

The latter project was first discussed in 1960, when reservations about responsibility and risk were countered by arguments about the value of the income that it would generate. A decision in principle was taken in September. There followed detailed discussion, in which Maurice Jago offered his considerable experience. Geoff Husband became the bar secretary, the first in a line that was to include the long-serving Len Jackman. In the first ten years of its operation, the bar saw sales of £7509 and profits of £1199. Bar affairs took up, understandably perhaps, a disproportionate amount of the time of the committee at meetings in the early 1960s. Thus, on April 7th 1965:

> 'The secretary asked if members present would discuss the type of keg beer to be stocked in the bar for the coming season, and it was the unanimous decision of the meeting that it should be Whitbread's Tankard'.

Other refinements, such as a fruit machine and a dartboard, followed, and, for heating water, electricity replaced calor gas. These were all important and positive improvements. They did not, however, address the fundamental problem of size. More floor space was needed, and this could only be achieved by adding a major extension to the front.

The familiar facade, a wooden-shuttered frontage with a central door and an overhanging roof providing a verandah-like area for benches and seats, had to go. In 1965 the club committed itself to such an extension, and to the expenditure of some £2000 on it. Ground collections, proceeds from dances, and profits from other fund-raising activities, were earmarked for this major project, but it was not to be done without borrowing. A five-year interest-free loan from the National Playing Fields Association helped the scheme along. The final cost was £2700, but when the extension was opened in 1967 it provided considerably more floor space, some of which could be used for a secretary's office, a score box, and a new bar area. Walter Spry, chairman and former player, could, at the opening ceremony, welcome the new facilities by saying that 'we have looked forward to when our accommodation would match our playing achievements'. Doing the honours at the opening was Albert Goss, then in the twenty-second and penultimate year of his presidency. A match accompanied the ceremony, and the captain of the visiting Old Colfeians presented the club with a tankard to mark the event. It was an occasion for real, and justified, self-congratulation. And Spry had surely hit the nail on the head. Belatedly, the club had brought its accommodation in line with its achievements.

Those who felt the benefit of these improvements were not only the players but those who worked behind the scenes. These included the long-suffering tea ladies. A rota arrangement had by now bedded down, together with a convention that the captain's wife – he was obviously expected to have one – would play a major organisational role. No one shouldered this responsibility more conscientiously than Enid Jarman. The provisions for teas were the responsibility of Maurice Jago, the manager of Underwood's, the town-centre grocery store. His contacts and his experience in this field, and in the wider area of social activities, proved invaluable to the club.

In the same way that it was helpful to have the understanding support of a grocery manager, it was useful, particularly at certain times, to have the sympathetic backing of an accountant like K. Lamerton Robins and a solicitor like John Barker (the latter a symbol, surely, of the unbreakable Chilcott connection). As for the men in white coats, the retirement of Bertie Goss opened the way for such former players as Maurice Avery, Eric Davey, and Frank Millman.

Two of these featured in contrasting ways in a game against Paignton in July 1960. Avery was standing. During the Tavistock innings he was hit by a fierce shot from Gerry Parsons, an incident which, after a moment of confusion, led to the retirement of both umpire and batsman, the latter having been run out. Eric Davey, who had travelled with the team, substituted, and proceeded to call one of the home bowlers for having a suspect action. (This, it will be recalled, was the season in which Geoffrey Griffin, the South African fast bowler, was, amid extraordinary scenes, no-balled in the Lords Test Match.) A later generation of umpires was to include Bill Manners, Len Jackman, Tony Miller, John Gauler, and Tony Davies, as well as Clifford Alford, who, in the mid 1970s, was to gain inclusion in the minor counties umpires list.

The Annual General Meeting, held in March, remained the set-piece business occasion of the club's year, and provided useful pre-season publicity. An attendance of twenty-five at the 1962 meeting in the Magistrates' Room suggested that a larger room was required, and in the following year the venue was switched to the U.D.C. council chamber. Large attendances, such as the thirty-two in 1965, reflected very clearly an atmosphere that prevailed at the time.

It has often been observed, usually in a spirit of despair, that it is difficult to involve members of sports clubs in administration, their interest being confined to playing. This was clearly not the case with the Tavistock Cricket Club in the 1960s. The key factor here is that things were being done, and matters were being decided, which affected very directly the rank-and-file member, whether it was participation in cup cricket or the provision of a bar and an additional changing-room.

Perhaps there was another factor that worked in the direction of sustaining a high level of direct involvement in the business side of the club. The membership included during that period a significant number of strong personalities, with firmly held views and a determination to express them. Given this situation the big decisions were not going to be made by nods, winks, and three-line whips. Discussion was sometimes discordant, and debate occasionally fractious. It all added to the level of interest.

Attendance at an A.G.M. might be a useful barometer of interest. The routine work remained with the committee, which met regularly in either the Cornish Arms or the pavilion. Finance occupied a good deal of attention. The most substantial source of annual income at the beginning of the decade was the profit from the Christmas draw, an exercise in which a great deal of energy was understandably invested. By 1970 it had been discovered that a bar and a couple of fruit machines could produce equally lucrative returns. Income from subscriptions, with the full fee of one guinea being levied only on playing members over twenty-one, remained a relatively small budget item.

Financial considerations obviously affected other matters that the committee had to consider. There was the question of the annual social event. This had for some years been held in the Red Barn and had taken the form of a New Year's Party. In 1963 the decision, and the risk, was taken to alter the format. The annual dinner was restored. For the rest of the decade the venue was either the Lewtrenchard Hotel or the Town Hall. The committee had also to monitor such matters as the transport arrangements, where, in the 1960s, there was a mixed pattern which included both coach-hiring and reliance on private cars.

And there was always the possibility of something coming up out of the blue and requiring a decision or at least an expression of opinion. How do you respond when the secretary of the town hockey club writes to tell you that they want to sell their field, and that they would favour an amalgamation of the two clubs and the joint use of The Ring? Well, you call a meeting of three representatives from each club. It met in September 1964. Discussion had scarcely begun when two of the hockey club delegates declared themselves unaware of any proposal to dispose of their ground, and said that 'they were perfectly satisfied with their present position'. The minutes of the meeting ended laconically: 'In view of these remarks, and others, the meeting was abandoned'. The issue did, in fact, re-surface four years later, by which time the hockey club had, indeed, sold its ground, but the prospective marriage never materialised.

The activities of the club, both on and off the field, expanded significantly during the 1960s, and there was a consequent growth in the responsibilities of the officials. This in turn led to three ad hoc developments. A precedent was created in 1962 when the secretary received an honorarium of £25. Additional officers, such as an assistant treasurer and a fixtures secretary, were appointed. And new sub committees, responsible for the bar, the pavilion, and the social programme, were established. By 1970 it had become necessary to bring together these various constitutional innovations and to codify them in a re-written version of that section of the club rules that dealt with the responsibilities of officials. This was done at the 1970 A.G.M. What emerged was a more streamlined administration. But, of course, as every clubman knows, whatever the refinements of the constitution and the rule-book might be, the effectiveness of any organisation depends ultimately on the quality of the personalities occupying the key posts.

Eric Davey had been secretary since 1947. In that role he was resourceful, determined, and forceful. The improvement schemes owed much to his drive and persistence. They were also, as it turned out, to be his legacy, because in 1967 he died, at the age of fifty-nine. It was not only the cricket club that felt his loss. He was a well-known figure in other contexts, and had worked for Ward and Chowen since 1940. Over 300 attended his funeral, and the *Tavistock Gazette* paid tribute to 'a striking example of conscientiousness and courtesy'. At The Ring there was to be a permanent monument to him. On September 29th 1968 his son Jack, now an established Gloucestershire player, unveiled a clock on the pavilion which remains a memorial to a great servant of Tavistock cricket.

The secretaryship came to Walter Spry, but he fell ill at the end of 1970, and Doug Treloar stepped in as acting secretary. Meanwhile Albert Goss, the quiet man who had been president since the war, died in 1968, and was replaced by Maurice Avery, who retained, with the help of an assistant in Clifford Alford, the post of treasurer. Avery was the most popular of clubmen. The same easy-going and jovial bonhomie that had characterised his approach to playing and the captaincy was also a feature of his career as an official, and particularly of his occupancy of the club's highest office. His promotion to the presidency left a vacuum as chairman, which was filled by Jack Taylor. This was a curious office, with no roots in the constitutional history of the club and only an intermittent occupancy. It was to have a more significant role in the future.

The loss of two such pillars as Bertie Goss and Eric Davey gave to the late 1960s a decidedly end-of-an-era character. This became even more pronounced when in 1970 Gordon Parry died after a long and distressing illness. Parry's association with the club had begun just half a century before. Over the years as player, ground curator, and administrator, he had remained at the heart of the club's activities. No one could rival either the length of his service or the depth of his commitment. Recognition of this by the club had come in 1964 when he was the first person to be offered honorary life membership. It was an honour that he appreciated and valued.

His passing, and that of the other two stalwarts, seemed to coincide with a change in wind-direction in local cricket, the gusts of which could be felt round the draughty corners of The Ring. Two events, both in 1969, seemed to point the new direction. The Plymouth club flew a kite on limited-over cricket which was couched in a general frustration at the number of drawn games. From Callington came a proposal for a Sunday League to consist of sixteen clubs in the area. The first approach drew a cautious response from Tavistock, while the second elicited a firm rejection. But the winds were blowing, and before long they were to prove irresistible.

The Quick Era

In 1970 the captaincy of the First Eleven passed from Evan Kemp to Bob Quick. Quick led the side in the 1970 and 1971 seasons. A popular skipper, and a players' player, he was a seasoned club cricketer, and a knowledgeable, if sometimes unpredictable, leader. His philosophy was a cavalier one: cricket was a game to be played for enjoyment. Tactically, he was imaginative, and, to some, over eager in pursuit of experiment and novelty. On one aspect of his captaincy there was unanimity of view. He under-rated his own individual abilities, neither bowling himself enough nor putting himself in the top half of the order, where both his record and his skill suggested he should be. His opening attack was usually in the hands of two of Evan Kemp, Stuart Munday, Les Curate, Len Rule, and Tony Clapp.

Kemp set a pattern of economy and reliability in the 1970 opener by turning in figures of 15 overs, 9 maidens, 15 runs, 5 wickets. But something was missing for the first half of the season, and the Old Colfeians discovered what it was on June 13th when Dave Ewings chalked up, on his return, 7 for 26. A notable feature of the attack at this time was the availability of spin and the readiness of the captain to use it. On June 5th 1971 Derek Pethick bowled 12 overs of his off-spin to take 5 wickets for 16. On the following afternoon he took 4 for 24 while Hilton Jones returned figures of 5 for 39 bowling at the other end. For nine visiting wickets to fall to spin was a rare occurrence at The Ring at any period in the club's history. Some members tut-tutted at the terrible risks being taken in bowling spinners on such a scale, and if the game had been lost, instead of being won by 8 wickets, the captain would no doubt have been strung up. Given the experience of the bowlers concerned, the gamble was, perhaps, not so enormous. Pethick had, since his debut in 1965, shown himself to be a consistently effective all-rounder. Jones had joined the club in 1968, and had from the first shown match-winning abilities with both bat and ball. A Plymouth-based teacher with an easy-going manner and an ample frame, he could both hit prodigiously and turn his off-spinners a long way. The day that established him as a local hero was in May 1970 in the annual encounter with St. Luke's College, a fixture that had gone the way of the college every year since 1953. This time Jones bowled to such effect (he took 5 for 28) that the students were limited to 146. Tavistock's reply had subsided to 90 for 6 before Jones with 23 helped the tail to wag, and victory was achieved with three minutes to spare.

One of the qualities that was not so evident in the performances of the early

1970s was consistency. Three weeks before the historic triumph over St. Luke's, the side had been bundled out for 56 by Exeter University. On the day after this they had scored 178 in 130 minutes on a soft wicket against Dartington Hall. In the home game against Plymouth on May 25th 1970, Tavistock declared on 226 for 8, and were beaten by 7 wickets. Two weeks later they entertained Weston-Super-Mare, who made 157. The home side in reply fell away to 95 for 8. Tony Clapp, who had earlier taken 6 for 55 now held things together with Numbers 10 and 11, and he and Bob Quick steered Tavistock to the most unlikely of wins in the final over.

The second eleven during the early 1970s enjoyed a period of conspicuous success. Over the three seasons beginning in 1970 they won 44 of their 88 games, drawing 21, losing 22, and tying 1. It was a record that reflected the balance of the side with its combination of wise old heads and strong young arms. Doug Treloar captained the side in those three seasons, and clearly enjoyed the opportunity of a final challenge to round off an illustrious career.

There was another direction in which he hoped there would be an expansion of the club's playing activities, and at the 1971 A.G.M. he was able, as acting secretary, to give the first hint of the possibility of a youth team. 'We hope', he announced, 'to arrange colt matches during the August school holidays'.

Meanwhile the evening eleven continued to play its dozen or so mid-week games each season, and to win most of them, and there was even enough confidence to inspire some discussion on the possibility of the formation of a third eleven. This proposal was put on the back boiler, not so much because of doubts about numbers, as on account of worries about pressure on a square which was already being required to provide pitches for something like fifty games each summer.

Supporters and critics alike of limited over cricket were bound to agree that a lot of excitement in the 1970 and 1971 seasons was generated by Tavistock's cup campaigns in the county knock-out competition. The highest rung that had been reached since the first attempt to climb this particular ladder in 1966 had been the semi final. In 1970 all began well with a victory over Launceston, followed by a tense second-round tussle with Yelverton Bohemians, which went to the last over before Derek Pethick hit a boundary off the penultimate ball to win the game.

It was then an area final match against Callington at The Ring. The home side looked beaten at 45 for 6, but rallied with 28 from Captain Quick, and 18 off the last over, to post a final score of 112. Callington, after an opening stand of 50, succumbed to the pressure, there were two run-outs and a stumping, and the visitors arrived in the last over with runs still to make and without wickets in hand. When Ewings prepared to bowl the last ball they needed 2 to win with the last pair in. The batsman charged, Geoff Husband made his second stumping, and the game was won by the narrowest possible margin.

The quarter-final, played two weeks later against Plymouth, proved a sad anti-climax. There was a large crowd at The Ring, and the home side was enjoying a run that had brought nine successive victories. The bubble burst.

The Tour Party. Sussex, August 1968.
Standing: Maurice Avery, Roger Quick, Bill Colling, David Rowe, Brian Crawford, Stuart Munday, John Perkin, Maurice Craze, Jerry Pitts-Tucker, Len Jackman, Piers Bickley, Coachdriver, Clifford Alford. *Middle Row:* Mesdames Colling, Quick, Avery, Treloar, Pitts-Tucker. *Front Row:* Evan Kemp, Doug Treloar, Peter Earl, Derek Pethick.

Gloucestershire, holders of the Gillette Cup, came to The Ring in July 1974.
Arthur Milton and Ron Nicholls, who between them played 1119 times for the county, prepare to open the innings. They were to put on 58 for the first wicket, watched by a crowd estimated at 2,000.

ABOVE: 1963
Standing: Barrie Maunder, Roger Quick, Evan Kemp, Jack Davey, Maurice Craze, Geoff Husband, Bob Quick, Clifford Alford. *Seated:* George Clements, Eric 'Budleigh' Davey, Doug Treloar, Eric Jarman, Gerry Parsons.

BELOW: 1969
Standing: Peter Earl, Hilton Jones, Geoff Husband, Tony Clapp, David Ewings, Don Palmer. *Crouching:* Les Curate, Maurice Craze, Evan Kemp, Eric Jarman, Bob Quick.

ABOVE: 1971 - The cup-winning side before the final tie at Paignton.
Standing: Derek Pethick, Tony Clapp, Steve Callow, Hilton Jones, David Ewings, Phil Treseder, George Forbes (scorer). *Seated:* Geoff Husband, Maurice Craze, Doug Treloar, Tim Redman, Eric Jarman, Ray Treseder (twelfth man).

BELOW: 1979.
Standing: Robin Wilson, David Dilleigh, Peter Coombe, Derek Pethick, Chris Louden, Neil Sherrell, Tony Miller (umpire). *Seated:* Tony Clapp, Graham Kelly, Bill Pruce (captain), Andrew Jarman, Robert Jarman.

The first Colts' Presentation Evening, 1977. Mr and Mrs Tucker, donors of the trophy, present it to the first Colt of the Year, Neil Sherrell. Tony Miller and John Montgomery, pioneers of the initiative, complete the picture, along with sixteen fellow-colts.

Tony Clapp, popular club captain in the late 1970s, earned the highest honour in cricket by being made the subject of a cartoon. This how he was seen by Jacken of the *Tavistock Gazette*.

All out for 68, Tavistock went under by 7 wickets. There was disappointment, but a persistent feeling that the team, or one very similar to it, had the makings, with a bit of luck, of a cup-winning side.

The theory was put to the test in 1971. The first round, played at The Ring on June 14th, brought an easy six-wicket victory over Okehampton, who had been dismissed in 16 overs for 77. Two further wins, and, as in the previous year, a quarter-final place was secured. History repeated itself by giving Tavistock a home draw against Plymouth. But there was to be no repeat of the earlier humiliation. Plymouth were bowled out for 86. Tavistock, with Eric Jarman making 45, knocked off the runs for 4 wickets.

The Ring was to be the setting for the semi-final, by which time the competition had moved to a weekend and a forty-overs-a-side format. On a showery Sunday afternoon in late July, North Devon made 134, with Ewings and Clapp taking 4 wickets each. With just a few heart-flutterings among the 200 or 300 spectators, the home side reached the target to win by 3 wickets. And so to the final. Paignton were the opponents, and they had home advantage.

The match was played on Sunday August 22nd in front of a crowd of 800. Tavistock batted first. After 12 of their allotted 40 overs they were 25 for 4, with Redman, the former Somerset Seconds player who was captaining the side, Husband, Jarman, and Pethick, all back in the pavilion. A middle-order recovery led by Jones, Clapp, and Ewings, pushed the score up to 48 for 5 at half-time, and to 96 for 6 after 34 overs. The final total of 135 all out looked modest, but certainly gave Tavistock something to bowl at.

Steve Callow, reputed to weigh in at 18½ stones, proceeded to send back the Paignton openers for 1 and 0. Meanwhile, at the other end, Doug Treloar, at the age of fifty-five, bowled his nine-over stint for 12 runs and 1 wicket. The opening pair of bowlers had done their job, and Ewings and Clapp came on at 42 for 4. Ewings proceeded to take 4 for 20, and Pethick, brought on to mop up the tail, did just that with 2 for 2. The total was 92, and the margin of victory 47 runs.

It was a famous victory, and clearly the highlight of a season which had otherwise produced a large number of draws. There were two immediate effects. One was the inevitable boost to the morale and the reputation of the club, and to its image as a local institution. The other was the encouragement it gave to those who favoured going further down the road towards a more competitively structured pattern of club cricket. This was to come rather sooner than many observers had imagined.

League Cricket Takes Hold

In 1972 the captaincy fell to Geoff Husband, who was playing his thirteenth season for the club. With the bat, he had just enjoyed a particularly productive and consistent season, scoring over 1000 runs, while his performances behind the stumps were now on the plateau that earned him the reputation of being the best club keeper in the south-west.

A particular feature of the season was to be the number of big opening stands, involving Husband and either John Gelsthorpe or Tim Redman. Gelsthorpe was the keen-eyed, sprightly jack-in-a-box, whose improvisation and appetite for the short single could be expected to keep the scoreboard moving. He ended a ten-season stretch with the club in 1973 by moving back to his original club, Yelverton, which was conveniently nearer to his home base. Redman, a class batsman of minor counties standard, played from 1970 to 1976. In 1972 he scored two centuries. There were one or two holes to fill. George Clements retired at the beginning of the season, and Evan Kemp moved away at the end of it. Husband characteristically managed to plug some gaps by exercising the instinct for improvisation that often bewildered those around him, and that made his predecessor appear, by comparison, almost cautious.

The most significant acquisition of 1972 was to secure the services of the new police inspector. Peter Anderson's impact was such that by the end of the summer, in spite of his missing the first six weeks, he had scored 735 runs. The number was only exceeded by Tony Clapp, who scored 742 as part of another fine all-round performance.

As the season started, attention inevitably focused on whether Tavistock were going to be able to produce a cup run to compare with that of the previous summer. In the first two rounds, Launceston and Yelverton Bohemians were swept aside, with the bowling honours going successively to Treloar with 3 for 7 and to Kemp with 6 for 16. A comfortable victory against Plymstock followed, and this opened up a semi-final tie at home to Barton, in mid August. Tavistock won by 100 runs, and in so doing gave the kind of impressive team performance that might have induced some supporters to feel that the cup was already won.

Two weeks later the final was played against Exeter on Paignton's ground. Exeter batted well, and set a formidable target of 199. Tavistock, in spite of a good start and strong contributions from Anderson and Pethick, were always a little behind in both time and wickets, and the final margin of 29, significant enough in the context of a 40-over game, brought the dream to an end. In the six seasons that followed, Tavistock were not to proceed beyond the stage of the area final, and in three of these years there were to be first-round knock-outs.

The interest and publicity that attended the cup campaign in 1972 tended to obscure other important aspects of the club's playing activities. The second eleven under Doug Treloar, and the midweek eleven under Ken Saxby, both did well, and the early foundations of a colts team were laid with four late-season fixtures. There was no tour, following weeks in Sussex in both 1970 and 1971, but, in line with convention, a cricket week was held. For the next few seasons these two contrasting week-long festivals, at home and away, were to alternate in the club's programme. There was, however, as the events of 1972 showed, to be little relief from the gathering pressures leading towards a cricket environment of a more structured competitive kind.

In January 1972 proposals for the creation of a Devon Senior League, which had been the subject of discussion for some time, re-surfaced with the support of powerful clubs like Plymouth. A series of meetings between representatives of the county's twelve most successful clubs showed a clear majority for pushing ahead. The Tavistock view, presented at those early meetings by Eric Jarman, Geoff Husband, and Ken Saxby, was the minority one. It was fully representative of the membership, both playing and non-playing, in its opposition to the idea of league cricket. The case rested partly on resistance to the principle embodied in the proposals, and partly on the argument that radical innovations were being pushed through too hastily and without sufficient thought to some of the practical implications. Among the latter were cited the question of player-registrations and the thorny matter of neutral umpires.

By April the mood at The Ring was one of resigned acceptance that nothing could be done to halt the juggernaut. The plan was to launch the league on the back of a structure of fixtures already negotiated between the twelve participating clubs. For Tavistock to pull out at the last minute would, it was argued, put a whole set of fixtures at risk. It was a time for swallowing hard and accepting the inevitable.

On Sunday April 30th 1972, Messrs Husband, Redman, Budge, Jones, Pethick, Clapp, Gelsthorpe, Kemp, Baker, Treseder, and Treloar, took the field at The Ring against Exmouth in the first league game in the history of the home club. The visitors, whose opening batsman was out hit-wicket for 99, made 192 for 5, and the home side replied with 170 for 8.

The dividends to be derived from such a drawn game depended, according to the rules of the competition, on who enjoyed the balance of advantage at the end of the match. For Exmouth this was a 'winning draw' and attracted three points, while for Tavistock the reward for a 'losing draw' was one point. If either side had won the game the prize would have been five points. The maximum duration of a game was 92 overs, the side batting first being limited to 46 overs, and their opponents being provided with the incentive to bowl them out, rather than simply to contain them, by being offered the prospect of additional batting time. Thus, if you could dismiss a side in 40 overs you had up to 52 overs to reach the required target.

Such were the ground rules of the new competition into which the club drifted, almost like a sleepwalker, at the beginning of 1972, and from which she emerged at the end of the season occupying a position of eighth out of twelve. In October the players held a special meeting. Fifteen of them attended. When it came to a vote on the principle of league cricket, thirteen expressed their opposition and the other two abstained. This view, unanimous and clear, was taken to a meeting of the participating clubs in January 1973. The Tavistock delegates found themselves in a minority of one. Such isolation left the club with the most stark of choices. Either you stuck to your guns, reflected the gut feeling of the players, and withdrew from the competition, facing the almost certain consequence of losing fixtures against all the top county clubs, or you gritted your teeth, accepted league cricket as a fact of life, and came down on the side of a reluctant involvement rather than a principled detachment. There was never any real doubt about which way it would go.

Neither the doubts about the league, nor the record number of defeats (19 in the 40 games played) created a mood of pessimism as Geoff Husband's year in charge came towards its end. The skipper scored 1310 runs, and earned his first, well-deserved, county cap, when he was selected for Cornwall against Dorset. There had been a good cup run, and an enjoyable cricket week, and four players, Eric Jarman, Tony Clapp, Dave Ewings, and Stuart Munday, were invited to tour Gibraltar with a Mendip Acorns side.

The most significant addition to the playing strength had come with the arrival in mid-season of Peter Anderson, and he was, unsurprisingly, chosen to captain the side in 1973, when Husband moved away to play the first of two seasons with the Callington club. The Anderson reign was to last for three seasons. Strictly speaking, in 1973 and 1974 he shared responsibility with, respectively, Derek Pethick and Tony Clapp, who captained the side on Sundays leaving Anderson to lead on Saturdays. There was, however, no doubt who the dominant personality was during these three years.

Inspector Anderson brought to his cricket the same sense of authority and self-confidence that drove his professional life. He was a brilliant bat, adding to the already formidable battery of openers at The Ring. He was also a more-than-useful change bowler. In particular he developed a fruitful relationship with Tim Redman which produced a succession of impressive opening stands, most notable of all the 186 against Bovey Tracey. His skill and consistency brought him a number of Devon caps, and he also represented the police at national level. Along with Redman, and with Tony Clapp and Hilton Jones, he formed a quartet who scored the bulk of the runs during this period.

In the bowling department the wicket-taking honours were shared roughly equally by a dozen players. The exception was Hilton Jones, whose career as an all-rounder struck a particularly rich vein during the middle years of the decade. He took 73 wickets in 1974 and 64 in 1975, a year in which he also scored 867 runs at an average of 38. His value to the side was considerable.

Of the new faces, Andrew Scott and Alan Stevens were, like their captain, in the police force. The former, a pace bowler who won county selection, showed his ability in one of his first matches at The Ring when he shot out six Chudleigh batsmen for 24. Not to be out-done, Stevens had, before the end of the same month, taken 6 for 11 against Plymstock. He was to play for only one season, Scott for three.

Other new arrivals included local businessman David Rees, a wicketkeeper-batsman who had played a good deal of club cricket before moving to Tavistock in 1971, and had had a trial for Glamorgan. For two seasons he captained the midweek eleven. Robin Wilson, a left-arm spinner, took 4 for 43 in his debut game in 1975. He was, over the years, to lend welcome variety to the attack, and to combine with playing duties in both first and second elevens a commitment to working with young players, particularly in the development of fielding skills.

The infusion of new blood, especially in the form of the trio of policemen whose arrival brought a challenge to teaching for the top slot in the club's occupation-table, was particularly helpful at a time when Maurice Craze and

Bob Quick were retiring from the scene, and Len Rule and Ken Saxby were being required to invest their experience in building up the second eleven.

There occurred also in 1973 a sudden, unexpected, and tragic loss. The deaths, in the previous year, of Frank Millman and Rex Parry had caused sadness and had evoked memories among older generations of players and supporters. The death of Doug Treloar was, however, different, because he was not yet one of yesterday's men. He had just completed yet another full season of cricket, culminating in a bowling performance of 8 for 28, and, although fifty-seven years old, he appeared fit and youthful. He had taken over the secretaryship from Walter Spry, and had, on the evening on which he died, attended a committee meeting. His sudden departure from the scene was received, first with stunned disbelief, and then with a deep sense of loss.

Douglas Treloar had, in the last year of his life, become the eighth man to have received the club's ultimate accolade, the granting of life membership. The distinction had been first bestowed, in 1963, on Gordon Parry, and in the following year Rex Parry, Eric Davey, Maurice Avery, and Frank Millman had been similarly honoured. In the early 1970s the recognition had gone to Walter Spry, to K. Lamerton Robins, the club's auditor, and to Francis Charles Doidge, president of the Devon Club Cricket Association and a former Tavistockian who had played for the club between 1927 and 1929.

Treloar now joined the illustrious ranks. The first two recipients, the Parry brothers, were in 1973 also commemorated by a clock inside the pavilion. The only one of these pioneers to still be alive in 1974, apart from F. C. Doidge, was Maurice Avery, and in that year, to celebrate his fiftieth season as a member, there was a special ceremony in his honour, and a presentation. A picture of the scene appeared the next week in the last edition of the old *Tavistock Gazette*, a paper that had faithfully reported the doings of the club for more than a century. By 1980 the depleted ranks of surviving life members had been replenished by the addition of Clifford Alford and Len Jackman in 1974, Eric Jarman and Ken Saxby in 1975, and Jack Taylor in 1978.

Maurice Avery's golden jubilee summer featured, on Sunday July 21st, a game against Gloucestershire. The Gillette Cup holders brought down an impressive team as part of the benefit programme for John Mortimore, Ron Nicholls, and Arthur Milton. The publicity was good, the crowd was large, and the organisation was effective. Over 400 runs were scored and there was general satisfaction at the success of the day, and particular pleasure at seeing Jack Davey back at The Ring. The only slightly sour note was struck by a Down Road resident who subsequently complained that 111 cars had gained access to The Ring by driving across the Down from the top of Down Road, ignoring the advice to use Chollacott Lane.

After the two great efforts of 1971 and 1972, the club made little impact in the cup competition for the rest of the decade. Attention therefore tended to be focused on the league, which continued to produce teething troubles and disharmony. With control of fixtures still with the clubs, there was always the potential for the kind of disagreement that occurred when South Devon turned up for a fixture with two key players missing, and requested that the game should be classified as a friendly rather than a league match.

Radical proposals for centralised fixture-making and for the creation of two divisions with promotion and relegation were postponed until 1977. Meanwhile controversy continued on such matters as the movement of players between clubs and the system of points allocation. Tavistock came out of each league campaign with only modest success, occupying ninth position in three successive seasons. A number of the monthly awards offered by the sponsors for individual or team achievements did, however, come to The Ring. The 239 for 8 against Exeter St. Thomas was recognised, for example, as was Hilton Jones's 8 for 34 against Chudleigh.

In the early part of 1975 there were some sharp disagreements involving Peter Anderson and other club officers. These mainly concerned the best use of bar profits, and the authority of the captain to sanction certain expenditures without recourse to the committee. Some feeling was generated. In mid-season a sudden and dramatic resignation announcement brought his captaincy to an end. He continued to play for the rest of the summer at the end of which a move to Hong Kong brought to an end his association with the club. His involvement with cricket in the south-west did not end there, however, for in the 1990s he became chief executive of the Somerset County Club. Taking into account all the games played by the first eleven during the 'Anderson years', covering league, cup, and friendly fixtures, the record reads: Played 131, Won 48, Drawn 34, Lost 49.

Tony Clapp came from Bere Alston and was a British Rail employee. By the mid 1970s he was a seasoned club cricketer. A popular clubman, he had performed consistently over the years with both bat and ball, and had also had some experience of captaincy during the Anderson years. He was the natural person to take the reins in 1976, and he held down the job for two years. He enjoyed the support of the estimable Jones, who continued to turn in a succession of strong all-round performances, of which that against Dartington, when he top-scored with 53 not out and then took 4 for 15 in 10 overs, was typical.

There were welcome appearances from such newcomers as Nigel Day, David Dilleigh, and Graham Kelly. Individual players enjoyed their red-letter days, none more so than Barry Chappell, who, having been recalled to first team colours after a long period with the seconds, opened the batting in a league encounter and proceeded to carry his bat to end with 106 not out. There was a welcome back for the prodigal son as Gerry Parsons, after a gap of twelve years, returned to The Ring and, as far as run-getting was concerned, picked up where he had left off. And Bill Pruce, an effective and consistent opening bat as well as a committed and loyal clubman, came onto the scene.

On the other side of the equation, Tim Redman played irregularly in 1976, and not at all thereafter. Dave Ewings did not bowl after his knee injury in 1973, and retired in 1976. Gerry Parsons played in only seven games in 1977, and Hilton Jones in only ten. The Treseder brothers, Phil and Ray, who had played a good deal throughout the decade, both moved on in 1977. And at the end of that season Geoff Husband also packed his bags. Clearly there was something wrong. How far was the decline in club morale, if that is what it was, related to the players' experience of league cricket?

The league, launched over-hastily in 1972, was subjected to its first overhaul in 1977. A central arrangement of fixtures and a concentration on Saturdays, leaving clubs free to arrange friendlies on Sundays, were innovations that had long been foreshadowed. Neutral umpiring represented a sad, but perhaps inevitable, departure. (Clifford Afford, incidentally, reported that the Umpires' Association had noted reports from its members of a significant increase in gamesmanship and bad sportsmanship since the advent of league cricket.) But for Tavistock, who had lurked in the lower reaches of the league since its inception, the threat was the creation of two divisions.

The trap-door opened in 1977. In the first year, the club fell through. Two principal reasons were offered. The bowling had lacked consistency and penetration and wickets were expensively bought. And, as it was reported to the members at the 1978 A.G.M.: 'So many players only make themselves available spasmodically'. The valiant efforts of Tony Clapp in leading from the front. (He took, in the season, more wickets (51) and scored more runs (732) than anyone else) were not enough.

In 1978 Tavistock found itself playing in the second division. The experience did not produce the hoped-for bounce-back. Only 3 of the 18 games were won, and the club ended the campaign occupying the eighth of the ten rungs on the second division ladder. By this time the captaincy had passed from Tony Clapp to Bill Pruce. But the playing record overall remained modest. Over the three seasons from 1976 to 1978 inclusive, 127 games were played. (There were fewer than average in 1976 because the domestic season had to be aborted at the end of August as a result of the effects that the drought had had on the playing surface.) Only 33 of these produced victories, and there were 51 defeats.

The 1970s was the decade in which the momentum towards league cricket, at various levels of the game, increased. No doubt, as with so many other innovations, good and bad, there was a conscious desire to follow the pattern being set at the top, and the counties had, in 1969, launched their Sunday League. As we have seen the Devon Senior League was born in 1972. In 1976 there followed a league for second elevens, in which Tavistock, led successively by Eric Jarman, Maurice Luke, and John Doidge, participated. After a year of modest results in 1977 the side was, like the first team, relegated.

The mid-week eleven continued its more corinthian progress, though even here it was decided in 1979 to compete in the regional Isaac Foot Cup competition. The captaincy of the Wednesday team during these years alternated between Robin Wilson, the perennially youthful doctor, and Andrew Jarman, one of the two talented cricketing sons of Eric.

Wilson it was who, in 1976, gave a further kick-start to the initiative of setting up a youth team, an idea which had become becalmed after first being floated at the beginning of the decade. In 1977 John Montgomery took the matter in hand, and, with the support of Tony Miller, managed to develop a programme of fixtures over the next few seasons which included, inevitably, participation in a Tamarside Colts League. In a period when, for various reasons, cricket was in full retreat in schools, the club was able to nurture such talents as Stephen Doidge, Andrew Rich, John Rich, and Neil Sherrell.

Slightly older, and playing first eleven cricket while still at school, Tim Harding took 100 wickets in the 1978 season, and was presented with an engraved stump for his labours. The development of Tavistock School to community college status helped the club's youth programme in one practical way. The sports hall, built on the campus in 1973, could be hired by members of affiliated organisations; in return for a membership fee the club could, and did, use it for winter nets.

It took the club establishment some time to appreciate fully the value of the initiative that John Montgomery took in 1977 and sustained over a period of ten years. By the early 1980s there had developed a pattern of fixtures which engaged youth teams in some 30 games per season. And in support there emerged a coaching programme using the facilities at the school and under the guidance of two cricketing doctors, Messrs Allenby and Wilson.

An annual presentation to the Colt of the Year was inaugurated when Mr and Mrs Tucker presented a trophy for that purpose to the club, in recognition of the financial support that the club had given to the area society for the mentally handicapped. Two other awards were also established at the same time. The Douglas Treloar Cup, first presented in 1975 as a fielding award, went, successively, to Maurice Luke, Peter Coombe, and Robin Wilson. The Maurice Avery Trophy, given by the president himself for particular service to the club, was first presented to Tony Clapp. Later recipients included Maurice Luke and Bill Pruce.

'Keeping the Club Together'

The most intractable problem that the club and its officers faced, in these, as in earlier times, was the care and maintenance of the ground. Most club members found it a chore to participate in some kind of rota scheme, and the issue, when raised, could be relied upon to generate some ill-feeling. There had been periods when difficulties had been obscured, and cracks papered over, by the willingness of an individual to take on what was in all but name the post of curator, and this was true, for some years, of Ken Saxby.

In 1973 Saxby made it clear that he would have to reduce the amount of time he could spend at The Ring, and he urged the committee to recruit a part-time, paid, groundsman. The suggestion was taken up, and the post advertised. There was no response. Saxby agreed to carry on until an appointment could be made, and in 1976 he was officially designated the curator. Some disagreements and tensions did, however, develop, and, by the end of the decade, there had been a parting of the ways, and Graham Kelly had taken over the ground duties. The fundamental issues remained unresolved.

One distinct improvement, from the club's point of view, came about in

1974, when, for the first time, following agreement with the council and with the Whitchurch Commoners, the square was fenced off for the duration of the playing season. This was a sensitive matter, and was handled with skill and tact by the officers of the club, who recognised the public concern that was expressed about the interests of ponies, dogs, and people, in that order.

Equally diplomatic was the response, in the same year, to the doubling of rates, for which the club was liable. The club's case, that 'the playing area was common land and not used exclusively by the club' was accepted. A challenge along the lines that this argument conflicted with the policy of fencing was easily deflected, on the dual grounds that the fencing was not intended to establish all-year-round exclusivity of use, and that the area involved, the square, was but a part of the playing area, to most of which access was unrestricted. The increase in the levy was abated.

The question of access to the ground remained a subject of controversy. The use of the route from the top of Down Road had been highlighted by Mrs Wedd's careful count of 111 vehicles having taken this course on the day of the game against Gloucestershire. The Council's response here was to control access by means of a locked gate, which could be used only on special occasions or at moments of emergency. The club was given the code of the combination lock. At the same time some of the residents of Warren Lane lodged a formal objection to the amount of cricket traffic passing their gates and negotiating the narrow road. The club was happy to underline the fact that access from the top of Warren Lane to the pavilion was for pedestrians only, and that everything should be done to encourage the Chollacott Lane route as the only means of through vehicular access. When this message was reinforced by a sign on the Whitchurch Road, at the foot of Chollacott Lane, there was a reaction from the Lane's residents, on the grounds that their modest throughway could not adequately handle the pressure that was imposed on it on match days.

In all such matters the difficulty that the club faced, and the price it had to pay for operating in such a delightful setting, was that it had to deal with statutory bodies and pressure groups, public and private, between whom lines of responsibility were not necessarily clearly drawn. This required, at times, careful tact, and, sometimes, graceful concessions. When the Council insisted that the club was responsible for maintaining the toilets at the rear of the pavilion, the point was accepted. The case that was argued was that the toilets formed part of the pavilion complex. And there was no doubt what the lease said about responsibility for maintaining the pavilion: the club was to keep it 'in a reasonable state of repair to the approval of the landlords', and the landlords were the Tavistock Town Council.

There was, in fact, no complaint about the way the club had discharged its responsibilities in this area. A great deal of attention had been focused, and a great deal of money spent, on improvements to the pavilion. In 1974, with the loan that had been raised to pay for the earlier extensions now repaid, a further scheme was discussed. Over the next year, at a cost of £5955, a new roof and a new kitchen were added, showers were installed in the dressing rooms, and a new electricity cable was laid. At the same time curtains were added, a telephone installed, and a new scoreboard provided. The bar continued to be a popular feature, under the stewardship of Len Jackman. The level of sales rose from £1179 in 1970 to £2708 in 1978, and the margin of profit over the same period increased from £230 to £609.

There were some significant signs of acknowledgement of the improvements that had been carried out to both ground and pavilion. Requests to hire the pavilion for social events increased, but had to be carefully monitored because of security and access considerations. One activity that found a home there was table tennis. Geoff Husband had been responsible for launching a team, under the auspices and patronage of the cricket club, in the 1960s, and it had first played at the hospital. From 1978 it was based at The Ring. The dominant personality in its development and progress was Barry Chappell. There were also approaches from three other sports clubs in the town, hockey, squash, and rugby, anxious to explore the possibilities of sharing the enhanced social facilities.

But the approach that brought most pleasure and satisfaction came from the Devon County Cricket Club, and resulted in 1976 in the arrangement of a two-day minor counties fixture between Devon and Dorset. It represented a clear pat on the back for the club, a belated recognition for the historic old ground, and a welcome distraction for members from some of the disappointments then being experienced in the club's playing record.

As the 1970s came to an end, the leadership of the club presented a mixed picture. On the one hand there was the continuity provided by the active and involved presidential figure of Maurice Avery and the cool, wise, and experienced chairmanship of Jack Taylor. In other areas there was change. Avery retired as treasurer in 1978, and was succeeded by Chris Louden. The secretary's job, left suddenly vacant in 1973 by the death of Doug Treloar, fell to John Doidge, who had played for the club in the 1950s before serving the Wayfarers Club for some years as player and administrator.

For four years he proved to be a conscientious and hard-working officer. In an effort to communicate more effectively with the membership, he introduced the idea of a regular newsletter, which proved a welcome innovation. His resignation in 1977 for personal reasons brought in Bill Pruce, who also captained the side for one season in 1978. A quiet, unassuming servant of the club, he performed, during a difficult period, a variety of duties in an inconspicuous way. His professional work with Plymouth City Council helped him to make a contribution to the maintenance of the ground, and he also became, in terms of administration, the club's work-horse. As captain, his style was effective, albeit undemonstrative and rather self-effacing. He was succeeded, for the last summer of the decade, by the father of the house, Eric Jarman.

By that time the list of officers had lengthened considerably. The players, at a special meeting, continued to choose the captain and vice-captain of the first, second, and midweek elevens. The other posts were filled at the A.G.M. They included the president, vice-presidents, chairman, vice-chairman, secretary, fixtures secretary, team secretary, colts secretary, bar secretary, social secretary, treasurer, assistant treasurer, auditor, press officer, ground curator, and community college representative. Only two, the secretary and the curator, received honoraria, the level of which, in 1979, stood at £75.

As office holders in any organisation will know, it is usually considered unfair to burden A.G.M.s with too much decision-making, and it is expected that a committee will have, to some degree, 'sorted out' the appointments beforehand. Such civilised arrangements applied as much in the case of the cricket club as with other bodies, and so the wheels were oiled. The only significant change to the pattern of these meetings, apart from an occasional change of venue, arose from the decision in 1979 to meet in the autumn instead of the spring. The immediate result was to offer to members, for one year only, the enticing prospect of two A.G.Ms for the price of one.

The routine administration of the club remained the responsibility of the main committee which, while happily delegating certain functions to sub-committees, insisted on retaining ultimate authority. It met, normally each month, in a room at the Cornish Arms kindly made available by a well-disposed landlord, Mr Bert Wood. Finance inevitably occupied much of the time, particularly during a period of inflation. It was important to ensure that income, whether from subscriptions, fund-raising events, the bar, the collecting tin taken round the ground on match days by Mr Jack Collacott, or any other conceivable sources, should keep pace with the ever rising expenditure on administration, travel, maintenance, insurance, repairs, and gas and electricity. The full adult subscription, which stood in 1970 at £2.10p, or two guineas in the language still understood by most members, was increased five times during the decade, reaching, in 1979, £6.50, a figure which reflected the final abandonment of any attachment to the lost and lamented guinea.

At the second of 1979's two A.G.Ms, three of the posts remained unfilled. There were no nominations, or volunteers, for the offices of team secretary, bar secretary, or groundsman. Some observers took this as evidence that all was not well in the club. They were right. The problems went back two or three years. There had been the waves, and occasional storms, over the maintenance of the ground and the preparation of wickets. Then there had been the controversy over the league, followed by the souring experience of relegation. In 1977 there was the first in a series of on-field incidents, this one involving two senior players whose conduct was reported to the committee by the umpire. Both subsequently apologised to the chairman, and to each other, and the record of the incident was later deleted from the minutes. But it left behind it some bad feeling.

Shortly afterwards Bill Pruce, the captain, called a players' meeting to discuss 'several points of contention'. It became clear at the meeting that, in the immediate aftermath of relegation, there were differing views about whether the club should remain in the league. There was also a sideswipe at some players whose loyalty was said to be questionable, and a demand that 'team selection should be limited to players who only played for Tavistock'. Pruce did his best throughout 1978 to maintain a sense of unity, and earned as a result the compliment from his president that he had 'kept the club together'.

But the troubles continued. Geoff Husband, eighteen years after his club debut, went off to play for Lanhydrock. There followed a succession of the kind of incidents that tend to occur when success is proving elusive and morale is suffering. A nasty on-field spat, again involving senior players, led to recriminations and a committee hearing that only partially restored the situation. Another long-standing member was accused of sulking throughout a game after not being invited to keep wicket. What was described as a 'fracas' took place between two members in the pavilion. And a committee member resigned following an 'unauthorised' interview with a local radio station.

Efforts were made to keep spirits up. The success of the colts' initiative began to be appreciated and celebrated, and the talents of such young first-team players as Robert Jarman and Tim Harding (990 runs and 100 wickets respectively in 1978) were recognised. An award evening was instituted. Gloucestershire came again, this time as part of the benefit programme for David Shepherd and Jack Davey. There appeared, as well as the two local heroes, Andy Stovold, Zaheer Abbas, John Childs, and Mike Proctor. And a new flag was presented to the club by two of its vice-presidents, Major General Leech Porter and Mr Cyril Prance. All-in-all the picture, as the 1970s came to an end, was that while cloud persisted there was no shortage of silver lining.

The season that brought down the curtain on the decade brought only modest success, but produced some memorable games. The veteran Eric Jarman, who had settled into elder statesman second-eleven duties, was recalled to the colours to lead the club on the field. He saw it as a short-term expedient, and accepted it as such. Jack Davey's illustrious county career had come to an end, and he was back on his ancestral patch, running a pub at Princetown and readjusting to club cricket. He would be ready to take over the captaincy in 1980. Meanwhile Eric Jarman, in his twenty-seventh season at The Ring, held the fort, leading a young, largely inexperienced side.

One game in particular lives on in the memory, and not only in the folklore of the Jarman family. It was the opening match of the summer's campaign, a friendly against Yelverton. Tavistock's innings quickly subsided to 8 for 3, at which point the skipper's son, Robert, came in. A further early wicket brought father Eric striding to the wicket through the debris. Advice, along the lines of 'you just stay in; I'll get the runs', was offered, though in the opposite direction to the one that might have been expected. The stand became worth 97, of which Eric scored 14. Robert was finally out for 108, enabling his captain to declare on 143 for 8. And, just to make the family's day out complete, the skipper's elder son, Andrew, proceeded to bowl 9 overs of leg-spin for a mere 14 runs. Meanwhile, his mother, one of the wonderful breed of long-suffering cricket wives, contemplated the prospect of another summer of washing whites and brewing gallons of tea.

Part Six: 1980–1999

The Age of Opportunity

The Saviour Returns

It is a familiar theme in novels and films. Local boy finds fame and success on the wider stage, but returns finally to his home town, where his talents and experience bring great benefit to an appreciative community. Jack Davey's reappearance may not have been seen by Tavistock sportsmen as the return of the messiah, but it certainly gave to the club a much needed fillip. In the thirteen seasons that he had been in county cricket he had played in 175 first-class matches, and had taken 411 wickets at 28 apiece. He had earned his benefit, had 'retired' to run the Devil's Elbow at Princetown, and was ready, at the beginning of the 1980 season, to take over the club captaincy. Miracles might not be expected. But there was a good deal of anticipation that the flock might be led out of the desert of Division B into the top division, where the milk and honey flowed.

As there were twelve competing teams in the B Division, and only one promotion place, the task that Davey set himself in the first year of his captaincy was a formidable one. Nor was it forgotten that, while league cricket was the priority, other fixtures constituted a larger component of the season. In that summer of 1980 the first eleven played 47 games, of which 22 were league matches. There was some confidence that the batting, with a combination of experience and youth, would be up to the task.

At the core were four hardened competitors. Tony Clapp and Bill Pruce were both former captains. David Dilleigh and Robert Jarman had both been playing since 1974. In the event, the four were to score, between them, 2994 runs in the season, with Pruce topping the list for aggregate with 936, and Jarman for average with 33.3. Others did more than simply chip in. Jim Allenby scored useful runs, as did Robin Wilson, whose contributions as an opener led to him being considered much more as a genuine all-rounder than as a spinner who could bat a bit. Barry Chappell contributed regularly and usefully in the lower order. The captain himself made runs; he scored 79 not out, for example, in a match against Chelmsford when, in a tight situation, a lot was left to the tail. The two 'fathers of the house', Husband and Parsons, batted three innings between them and scored 174 runs for once out.

As to the attack, Davey bowled 325 overs in the season, of which 92 were maidens. He took 66 wickets for 604, at an average of 9.1. Strongest support came from Graham Kelly and Mike Crocker, with 65 and 60 wickets respectively, and from Neil Mort in his first season, and Stuart Munday in his sixteenth, who took 26 and 25 respectively. Tim Harding, one of the early graduates of the colts nursery, had a good season. There was a good deal of pleasure at the success of two spin bowlers, both of whom were well known to followers of Tavistock cricket. Derek Pethick contributed both runs and wickets, an early-season 4 for 24 in 12 overs being a highlight. The same was true of Hilton Jones. In his first game of the season, on July 19th, he bowled 9 overs and took 5 for 18, to secure a 13 run victory, achieved, as Tony Miller's press report had it, 'in the gloom, to the accompaniment of carnival bands in the town below'.

It was a very rare event, in that 1980 campaign, for the first four in the batting order to all fail on the same day. More often they each fired on all cylinders. Against Plympton a target of 169 was reached with only 1 wicket down, Dilleigh, Pruce, and Clapp scoring the runs. Always, it seemed, at least one of the principal batsmen scored heavily. Against Torquay Corinthians a modest-looking goal of 116 for victory suddenly looked very formidable when Tavistock subsided to 52 for 5, with Dilleigh, Pruce, Jarman, and Wilson back in the pavilion. Clapp's 63 not out saw them home.

The bowling performance of the season was by Stuart Munday in a remarkable match at Paignton. Tavistock batted first and collapsed from 21 for 0 to 65 for 9 before a last-wicket stand, and a top-scoring 21 not out from Crocker, brought the total up to 96. The Paignton innings took an almost identical course, falling away from 20 for 0 to 71 for 9 before a last-wicket stand brought them to 95. And there it ended, one run short, with Munday taking the last wicket, to finish with 8 for 45. The only other bowler likely to rise to these heights was Munday's old schoolmate and current business partner, who was also his captain. Davey's most impressive spell of the summer was against Exeter St. Thomas in August, when he bowled 17 overs and took 6 for 23.

The most interesting games seemed to come in the second half of the season. On July 9th Chudleigh entertained a Tavistock side missing three of its key players. The home side made 88, with Hilton Jones, in only his second game of the season, adding 4 for 14 to his previous day's 5 for 18. Tavistock, in reply, were 19 for 6 and then 33 for 7, before Barry Chappell joined Bill Pruce, who had gone in first. There followed an unbroken stand of 56 and a victory of 3 wickets. Pruce's fine knock left him undefeated on 60.

A fortnight later saw an entirely different game when tourists from Wavertree visited The Ring. Facing a total of 245 for 1 declared, the home side made 230 for 8. In 77 overs, 475 runs had been scored and 9 wickets had fallen. No wonder batsmen whose clubs planned tours of Devon or Cornwall clamoured to have Tavistock included in their itinerary! And it wasn't only grockles who gorged themselves at the crease on hot sunny afternoons. Exmouth responded to a challenge of 179 for 1 by scoring 180 for 1. In five hours of cricket, 81 overs were bowled, 359 runs were scored, and only 1 wicket was taken by a bowler all day.

The season moved to its close with, on the one hand the heaviest defeat, and on the other the most meaningless result. The former was the outcome of a one-sided game at Plymouth in which the visitors were shot out for 49. The latter was the festival game against a star-studded Gloucestershire eleven, for who Mike Proctor took 66 runs from 38 balls. When the curtain came down, in late September, Tavistock had won 24 and lost 8 of their 47 matches. And Moses had done it. Promotion had been achieved.

If the principal task in 1980 had been to get into the A Division, the main purpose in 1981 was to establish a presence there. This was to be attempted with few changes of personnel. Neil Mort had moved on, and David Dilleigh did not play until late in the season. On the other hand there was more of Jim Allenby and Frank Corbridge, and Kevin Rees made his debut. The most significant addition was Bobby Luffman, an experienced all-rounder formerly with Plymouth. He was, over the season, to score more runs than anyone except Jarman and to take more wickets than everyone except Davey. With Bill Pruce and Tony Clapp again scoring heavily and consistently, with Graham Kelly acting as the work-horse of the attack, and with the skipper taking 71 wickets at an average of 10.7, there was an overall record of 24 wins and 9 draws in 46 games.

In the league, competing among the twelve top senior clubs in the county, Tavistock finished the season as runners-up. Only Exmouth produced a better record. It was an impressive team performance, but one in which Davey's contribution had been crucial. His value was well illustrated in an away match against South Devon on June 14th. The visitors had been reduced to 96 for 7 when Davey came in to bat. He scored 26, stiffened the tail, and brought his side to 147 for 9 at the closure. This gave him something to bowl at, and he proceeded to operate throughout the home side's innings, taking 7 for 20 in 18 overs, 8 of which were maidens. It was vintage Jack Davey, on a day when you felt that his father and grandfather were both smiling down on him.

The 1982 campaign saw Tavistock without David Dilleigh, who had played for eight seasons, and Tony Clapp, whose contribution to the club on and off the field, over a playing career that had stretched from the mid 1960s, had been a very considerable one. In came Paul Monk and Maurice Babb. Monk, who had previously played for Plymouth, scored 76 not out in his first game for Tavistock, and proceeded to clock up a season aggregate of 1302 runs, and an average of 42. With Babb, Luffman, Pruce, and Jarman also scoring heavily, the top five batsmen totalled between them 3757 runs. This proved to be the main factor in the first eleven's success.

The team became very dependent on Davey and Luffman to take wickets. They responded magnificently, pocketing 116 between them, but apart from Kelly with 18, no one else ended the season with more than 14 scalps. Overall there were 19 victories and 16 defeats in the 49 games played. The league position was third, behind Torquay and Sidmouth. Individual feats of note were recorded by Paul Monk, who added three centuries to his startling debut performance, and there was a sparkling undefeated 83 from Jim Allenby against Exeter. Robert Jarman and Bob Luffman both scored centuries. Two poor team performances against North Devon, long seen as Tavistock's bogey team, probably cost the club the championship. Nonetheless there was considerable cause for satisfaction, and as the three-year Davey reign came to its end with the close of the 1982 season, the record was there for all to see.

One of the rules of the county league gave rise to occasional misunderstanding on the part of the more casual observer. This related to the provision of competition among second elevens. The arrangement was that a parallel structure should operate alongside the one that accommodated first teams. Thus, if the performance of a club's senior team entitled it to Division A status, then its second eleven would automatically, irrespective of its own record as a team, occupy a place in the top division of the parallel league. This was the context in which the Tavistock second team found itself in the early 80s. Under the experienced captaincy of men like Eric Jarman and Barry Chappell they improved year by year, and the contributions of Mike Crocker, Graham Kelly, and Robin Wilson gave the side an increasingly solid appearance.

Wilson also captained the mid-week eleven. Given the typical composition of the Wednesday side, with its sprinkling of first and second team players and its combination of experience and rawness, this was an exacting duty, and one which the young doctor carried out, through the rest of the decade, with enthusiasm and with a high level of attention to the importance of the quality of the fielding.

The initiative to establish a colts' section of the club had been taken in 1977 and implemented in 1978. John Montgomery was the secretary of the section from its inception. He, and others, saw the danger presented by the decline of cricket in schools, and decided that clubs should attempt to fill the vacuum. Weekly sessions of indoor nets became a regular feature of the winter months, proving more popular among the 10–16 age range than with their more senior club colleagues. In the early 1980s an average of 28 games a season were being played by four teams at different age levels. The exercise was acclaimed on all sides. It could be justified in its own terms as providing recreational opportunities for a large number of local boys. It could also be seen, in club terms, as supplying a valuable source of talent for the senior teams. For John Montgomery and his small group of helpers, including Tony Miller, it involved a good deal of work, and in 1982, after five seasons, Montgomery suggested that responsibility should be redefined by the establishment of an administrative framework including officers, committee, and team managers. A meeting of parents in December supported the idea and it was implemented. An area of ambiguity was allowed to remain over the extent to which the new organisation could act autonomously, and the extent to which it would need to keep referring back to the parent body. This was to present the occasional difficulty in the future.

Throughout the three years of the Davey period the presidency and the chairmanship remained in the hands of the club's two father-figures, Maurice Avery and Jack Taylor. Bill Pruce was the secretary and Chris Louden the treasurer. As fixtures secretary Tony Clapp was succeeded in 1982 by Robert Jarman, and successive social secretaries were Stuart Munday and Mike Crocker. A new appointment, that of press secretary, was filled by Tony Miller, and this led to improved newspaper coverage of matches. The treasurer, Chris Louden, was able to present a healthy balance each year, of £919, £2305, and £269, the latter appearing modest only because it had been necessary to spend £1499 in that year on repairs to the pavilion. Profits from the bar, now run by Len Jackman, totalled £6776 over the three years. Compared with this, income from subscriptions constituted only a small part of the annual revenue. The rate in 1981 was £7.50, with lower levels for younger players. Since 1979 the rule had applied that subscriptions not paid by mid-season would be levied at a higher rate.

One other source of income had been introduced in 1981. This was the 200 club. Members and supporters were encouraged to contribute regularly to a fund which would both support the club and generate prizes in regular draws. It was to prove something of a struggle to sustain it, but it got off on the right foot because it was linked to an ambitious scheme to replace the pavilion by a two-storey building with expanded facilities. It was a project that was to re-emerge, alongside a similar fund-raising plan, in 1997. This was, of course, an objective that could not be speedily realised.

In the meantime, remedial measures had to be taken to keep the clubhouse in a reasonable state. Hence the new carpet and the repairs to roof and kitchen. Similarly, money had to be spent on equipment for use on the ground. In 1980 it was a new roller, and in 1982 a slip cradle. In between came an artificial wicket, bought at a cost of £2100, the bulk of the money coming from gifts and grants. Meanwhile Bill Pruce demonstrated again his commitment to the club by taking on the duties of ground curator.

The club's administration, with its General Committee serviced by six sub-committees with specific areas of responsibility, operated, for the most part, effectively. There were, however, undercurrents which sometimes inhibited the smooth running of the operation. Personal vendettas led to incidents that clouded the atmosphere at committee meetings. One on-field disagreement between two senior players in 1981 was so serious as to require a special meeting to attempt to bring peace.

On a different level, the captain criticised players for not taking full advantage of the availability of winter nets on Sunday afternoons. He also reported, in August 1982, that:

> 'the first eleven are not playing very well, and many players are not making themselves available for selection.'

He had told Jack Taylor, at the beginning of that season, that for business reasons he would be giving up the captaincy at the end of the season, and he must have hoped that his final summer of leadership at The Ring would have brought the league championship to Tavistock. It was not to be. Nevertheless, as Jack Davey retired from the captaincy at the end of 1982 to well-deserved applause, it was clear that he had restored the club to a position where it was once more a power in the land.

The Mid Eighties: Cricket, Colts, Committees and Controversy

In 1983 the captaincy passed to Paul Monk. He had proved himself to be a class player and a prolific run-maker. He did the job for two years before being succeeded by Kevin Rees, who was captain for the 1985 season. During these three years, from 1983 to 1985, the club registered league positions of eighth, ninth, and eleventh in the twelve-team table. As there was only one relegation place, the position in the senior division remained secure. There was, however, clearly a falling-off from the heights of the early years of the decade.

The 1983 campaign had started well enough, with Davey still playing, and by mid June Tavistock were chasing the division leaders. The departure of Davey to his new home and business in Exeter brought a change of fortune, and towards the end of the season the attack found itself toiling to take wickets on good pitches. The two matches against Sidmouth reflected the way things went. In May, in the away fixture, Bob Luffman took 6 for 17 in 18 overs in a tied match. In July, at The Ring, the visitors were put in, and proceeded to make 230 for 6. The attack came under increasing pressure.

Meanwhile the batting held up well. Robert Jarman topped the overall aggregates with 838 runs, including a 133 not out when Tavistock overhauled a touring side's 230 for 2 to win by 6 wickets. Paul Monk and Bill Pruce scored 813 and 717 runs respectively, and both featured among the list of top ten batsmen in the division. It was not surprising that when it came to selecting the recipients for club trophies, presented for the first time in 1983, the batting award went to Monk, and the bowling award was withheld. Among those who made significant contributions during the season were Chris Ollerenshaw and Maurice Babb with the bat and Andrew Luffman and Mike Crocker with the ball.

Three promising young bowlers, Ian Piper, Paul Farnham, and Martin Crocker, caught the eye. In mid June Robin Wilson bowled 14 overs of left arm spin and took 4 wickets while conceding only 5 scoring strokes. Bob Luffman continued to chip in with both runs and wickets, and Kevin Rees and Robert Jarman shared the wicket keeping duties.

Attempts to strengthen the side in 1984 brought in a number of new faces. Keith Donohue, destined to win a county cap in 1989, arrived from Plympton, as did Alan Pattenden, who scored 98 not out in his debut game but did not stay for the whole season. David Tall, from Plymouth, took 8 for 75 in his first league match, and former Falmouth player Phil Stephens made an undefeated century against Plymouth. Alan Grayson joined the club after moving down from Berkshire.

Once again the batting proved strong, with Maurice Babb scoring over 900 runs to win the club batting award. The burden of the attack was carried by the new duo of Donohue and Tall, who bowled over 500 overs between them. The lack of consistent support bowling showed itself in the results: in the 49 games played there were 17 draws and 18 defeats. In the league there were 3 victories and 9 defeats in the 22 fixtures, but relegation, which had appeared a possibility until the last weeks, was averted, and the final position was eighth. For the second season running, a tie was recorded. This was against the Old Colfeians on June 21st. The visitors, their last two wickets falling to stumping by the evergreen, if now occasional, Husband, made 143. The last Tavistock wicket fell at the same total, after a last wicket stand of 18.

Paul Monk stood down from the captaincy for the 1985 season, but continued to play. With no significant change to the balance of the side, it was always likely that the league campaign would be a struggle. Wicket keeper Kevin Rees took over the leadership. Monk, Babb, and Donohue constituted the nucleus of the batting, with Tall and Donohue leading an attack that overall was again exposed as lacking both consistency and variety. The final league position was eleventh, and they were thus one place clear of the relegation spot, occupied by Plymouth.

There were compensations. Overall more matches were won than lost. And there was a triumph in the county knock-out cup. Here, victories in the first two rounds, against Cornwood and Yelverton, led to a tie against Bideford, which was won by 2 runs. In the semi-final Sidmouth were defeated by 18 runs, and on September 8th the final was played at Newton Abbot. The opponents were Paignton, who displayed, at the top of the order, two Twoses and two Tolchards. Tavistock scored 128, with Bob Luffman scoring 36 runs from 26 balls. Paignton, in the 18 eight-ball overs allowed by the rules of the competition, fell 7 short of their target, and Rees and his boys had lifted the cup. It was sweet revenge for a mid-season meeting of the two sides when a Twose and a Tolchard had demolished the Tavistock attack and engineered an emphatic nine-wicket victory.

By the mid 1980s the Devon Cricket League, sponsored by Mod-Dec Windows, had expanded to five divisions, labelled A to E. Competition in the top three, Divisions A to C, accommodated clubs who also fielded second elevens. Since Tavistock's first eleven played in the top division, its second eleven enjoyed a similar status, irrespective of its playing record. During these years, under the captaincy, successively, of Trevor Harris, Eric Jarman, and Mike Crocker, the team just about held its own in the top flight, finishing tenth in 1983 and ninth in 1984 in the twelve-strong league. In 1985, however, they finished bottom. The usual combination of seasoned veterans, colts, and players on the edge of the first team, made up a standard team. In the first category were Gerry Parsons and Geoff Husband, in the second John Rich and Tim Cashell, and in the third Terry Burnside and Graham Kelly. But it was difficult to get a settled side, and to achieve regularly the kind of balance that was needed for sustained success. In the 1985 season, for example, 33 players were called on for the league programme.

There was a good deal of success for the other sides that represented the club in the mid 1980s. The Under-21 team, playing in the Launceston League, reached the play-off stage and won the runners-up cup. Meanwhile the Colts' Section prospered under the new structure inaugurated in 1983. Under the overall guidance of the three wise men, John Montgomery, Tony Miller, and Jack Taylor, the administration was streamlined, and a Presentation Evening was introduced. Each of the five teams had a manager. In the first year these were Bill Tynan, John Gauler, Peter Thistlethwaite, Don Anderson, and John Gosling. Chris Louden was also involved, and Steve Hodge did a lot of coaching. In 1983 the Under 16s won the Cornwall Cup. In 1984 county honours were won by Christopher Cashell, Darren Chappell, Adrian Towl, and Stephen Montgomery. And in 1985 the Under 13s were the winners, and the Under 15s the runners-up, in their respective leagues.

The chairman of the committee that co-ordinated the activities of the Colts' Section was Tony Miller. Among his other club commitments was umpiring. He shared these duties with Len Jackman, and, in the middle years of the decade, with Bob Elliott, John Plested, and John Doidge. In later seasons, Rodney Brown, Neil Scruton, Tony Davies, and Clifford Alford were to officiate.

One of the joys of wearing the white coat is that just occasionally you are called on to examine matters that raise deep philosophical issues. One such appeared in 1985, when Tony Miller raised with the committee the question of what would happen if the ball, in play, struck an animal that had inadvertently strayed onto the playing area. Apart from all the moral and legal issues raised, there was, of course, the overriding consideration of whether the batsman in such circumstances was entitled to 5 runs under Law 41. These were deep waters. The jury may still be out.

If umpires are a special breed, as they are, then the same may be said of scorers and groundsmen. In the former category the club was well served by a succession of bright young men, like Mark Lovell, Richard Kelly, and Lee Easton, who gave to the task the detailed attention it required. As for the job of curator, the period after Graham Kelly and Bill Pruce belonged to Bob Newton. He was helped by a group of mainly young players, led by Robin Wilson, and was paid for his work, on an hourly basis.

Meanwhile the cricket house continued to produce worries, the secretary reporting to the 1985 A.G.M. concerns about 'a leaking roof, rising damp, and general dilapidation'. It was decided to aim for an ambitious project of renovation. Meetings were held with the Town Council and an architect was briefed. Much of the finance would, it was hoped, come from grants, but even if applications were successful there would still be a need to generate matching funds. It was therefore a disappointment that the 200 Club, launched with such hopes, had to be reduced in scale and then closed down. An attempt to revive it was made in 1985.

The adult subscription level was, in 1983, raised to £10, but this source of income never constituted a major part of the club's revenue. The bar, responsibility for which passed in 1983 from Len Jackman to John Gauler, produced annual profits in the next three years averaging £1894. And Clifford Alford, who was treasurer for those three years, was able to show a healthy surplus at the end of each year. He had taken over from Chris Louden in 1983. At the same time there had been a change of secretary, with Patrick Cashell succeeding Bill Pruce. Among the secretary's many duties was that of servicing the committee and preparing for its monthly meetings, held occasionally in the clubhouse but more often in the West Devon Club.

These meetings were sometimes, during this period, conducted in a difficult atmosphere, though this did not come through to the minutes or to press reports. Chris Louden in 1984, prior to leaving the area, offered the thought that 'with such dissent over recent years the committee cannot be said to have fulfilled properly its functions'. His remedy was to streamline the administration and slim down the committee to nine members, a proposal defeated at the subsequent A.G.M. He also referred to ill-discipline and bad language by some players on and off the field. This latter point was taken up at the same time by a newcomer to the club, Alan Grayson. He felt that a major cause of the dissension in the club lay in the procedure for selecting teams. Too often, he argued, merit was ignored and decisions were made on the basis of personal friendships on the one hand and fears of potential personality clashes on the other. Trevor Harris and Graham Kelly were cited as examples of second team players who regularly performed well but were rarely offered a first team place. At the same time Tony Miller resigned from the committee in protest at the behaviour of some of its members, complaining of 'outbreaks of daft quarrelling'.

Small incidents occasionally blew up into major issues, as they tend to do when there are some deep-seated personality clashes. At the same time, ill-feeling was generated by the reluctance of a number of players to make themselves available for friendly fixtures. As these non-league games tended to be on Sundays, it meant that the club on that day would often be putting out weakened sides for both first and second eleven matches. The problem was highlighted in an embarrassing way when Tavistock cancelled a game against Hatherleigh at the last minute because it could not raise a team. The recriminations that followed brought to the fore again all the old arguments about league cricket.

Two connected themes helped to fuel the discontent that occasionally surfaced in the club's affairs. One was related to a condition that has been shared by many comparable organisations at various times. The other arose from some features distinctive to the Tavistock club,

In many associations, sporting or otherwise, there are members who join to share in the common interest or activity but are reluctant to participate in the wider range of tasks and responsibilities that have to be carried out if the organisation is to survive. A member who turned up at The Ring once or twice a week to enjoy his game but was not prepared to help to maintain either the ground or the pavilion provoked ill-feeling and gave rise to complaints of unfairness. The fact that a player was effective on the field did not, of course, lessen the sense of grievance.

But there was a second, and a complicating, factor. The recruitment of Plymouth-based players was not a new phenomenon in the 1980s. The club had benefited over the years from a succession of players of quality who, for one reason or another, had been drawn to The Ring. The danger was, of course, that, while they might be thanked for raising standards on the field, they might at the same time be criticised for not showing the same level of commitment to the club as the home-grown members. There were many cases where such charges were grossly, and self-evidently, unfair. But in the very nature of the situation there existed the potential for dissension, even at the level of the sound-bite phrase, uttered loudly enough for everyone to hear, either from a committee seat or from first slip.

It would be wrong to think of the club during this period as being unable to operate effectively because of the undercurrent of discontent that was revealed by occasional incidents. Some players and supporters remained quite oblivious of what was going on. Others were surprised at a clutch of resignations over a short period, and alarmed at the strength of feeling shown by one officer who said that:

> 'members resigning were running from the club and not facing the unpleasant fact that there was a bad element whom they ought to be working to either remove or to discipline'.

This was the summer of 1984, towards the end of which a special meeting of playing members was called. Its recommendations, forty-one in all, indicated clearly enough what was on people's minds. There was a call for a 'fairer' selection procedure, and a suggestion that part of the problem here had been the fact that there had been six second eleven captains in as many years. There was also a request for the setting up of a Disciplinary Committee to deal with charges of misconduct against members. And behind these positive suggestions were pleas to stop fighting old wars, whether on the issue of league cricket or on the basis of a long-standing vendetta, and to end the 'quarrelling and recurrent wrangles between members on and off the field'. Time would tell whether these were more than forlorn hopes.

Apart from the cricket itself, the middle years of the decade brought, for the club, one momentous, and overdue, improvement. The Ring had remained, for all its charm, one of the least accessible of venues. Whitchurch Road is, as everyone knows, flanked by the graves of those who, over the years, have died while trying to find the ground. In 1985 all was changed. The agreed and accepted policy of advertising Chollacott Lane as the access route was strengthened by a county council notice at the foot of the Lane directing traffic up it from Whitchurch Road. The cost was £147. The authority was originally disposed to limit the words on the sign to 'Cricket Club', but it was persuaded to add 'Tavistock' to avoid possible confusion with the Whitchurch Club. The subsequent A.G.M. was the occasion for self-congratulation:

> 'Our Tavistock Cricket Club sign may have annoyed residents of Chollacott Lane, but has been appreciated by those of Warren Lane, as well as a considerable number of visiting clubs who have found their way more easily'.

The first three seasons of the decade, the years of Davey's captaincy, had seen an overall playing record on the part of the first eleven which was statistically impressive. On the 142 games played, 67, or 47.2%, were won. Of the remainder, 38 were drawn and 37 lost. In the following three year period, covering the seasons 1983, 1984, and 1985, there were 43 victories from 134 matches, a success rate of 32.1%. Two games were tied, 52 were drawn, and 37 were lost. The two captains during this latter period, Paul Monk and Kevin Rees, both made important contributions to the side by their own performances, as respectively opening bat and wicketkeeper-batsman. They had few worries about the batting, in terms of either depth or consistency.

The real difficulty, after Davey's departure, lay with the bowling. Significantly, the fixtures show little change in the proportion of games lost; the real difference was that matches that were being won at the beginning of the decade were now being drawn. It was a problem inherited in 1986 by the new captain, Bob Luffman. An experienced cricketer and a genuine all-rounder, Luffman led the club into a season that was to see a good deal of success. Overall, the 47 matches produced 19 victories and 17 defeats.

In the league the club ended the season in a comfortable mid-table position. And there was again a good cup run, only ended by Paignton in the final. The bowling, further weakened by the departure of David Tall, who returned to Plymouth to help his former club cope with the consequences of relegation, was heavily dependent on the efforts of Keith Donohue, who bowled 318 overs, taking 49 wickets at 20.3 apiece. In the League, a revitalised Stuart Munday forced his way into fifth position in the overall A Division averages, with a record that ran: 186 overs, 42 maidens, 516 runs, 34 wickets, 15.2 average. Not surprisingly, he won the club's bowling award.

The batting honours went to Steve Luffman, the skipper's son, who scored 910 runs at an average of 32.5. In the league, Paul Monk again proved a model of consistency, compiling an aggregate of 584 and an average of 30.7. The fielder of the year was Peter Steward, and Bob Luffman took the all-rounder award. The two second eleven honours went to representatives of two different cricket generations: Gerry Parsons and John Rich.

Two clouds darkened the summer skies. One resulted from a display of an on-field dissent by the Tavistock captain in a game against Brockhampton on July 14th. The committee decided to impose a penalty of two weeks' suspension. Luffman was to renew his playing career on August 9th, making his come-back by scoring a sturdy middle-order 45 not out. He did not, however, resume the captaincy. This had passed to the vice-captain Stuart Munday. He was to keep it for two-and-a-half seasons. The meeting of the committee that dealt with this was attended by the president. It was Maurice Avery's last service to the club.

He had been, in one capacity or another, a part of the scene at The Ring for more than sixty years, and it was, even for the oldest members, difficult to imagine the club without him. His widow Dot was to keep alive the Avery presence by her continued interest and enthusiasm. At the end of the season the traditional President's Day game became a memorial match, and, in the most appropriate way, Maurice was remembered by the presence of old players like Tim Redman and Jack Davey, of well known figures like David Shepherd and Sadiq Mohammed, and of fellow members who had shared with him at least a part of the long Avery era.

The 1986 season saw, in addition to the star-studded President's Match, some other special occasions. A strong team of 'Old Boys' provided the opposition for the annual encounter for the Gazette Cup, an award presented by the local newspaper to mark the contribution to the club of Jack Davey. There was also a match against the Plymouth Argyle Football Club, whose team included Geoff Crudgington, later to became a regular feature of the landscape at The Ring.

But the most memorable moments included the first afternoon of the season, when Monk, Rees, and Parsons posted 180 before the second wicket fell in the 34th over. Or Steve Luffman's 86 as in as many minutes against Plympton, an innings that contained only nine singles. Or, for sheer drama, there was the league encounter with Plymstock at The Ring on August 16th. The visitors were dismissed for 130, Derek Pethick taking 5 for 44. Tavistock, at 93 for 3, seemed to be cruising to a comfortable victory. Then wickets tumbled, and the innings fell away to 118 for 9. With one over to go the score stood at 123 with John McGahey and Stuart Munday, Numbers 10 and 11, at the crease. Tavistock needed 8 runs for victory, and Plymstock needed 1 wicket. Stuart Brace, who had bowled throughout the innings, came up to bowl his twenty-third, and last, over. Munday took a single off the first ball and McGahey hit the second one for four. Three runs were now required from four balls. A dot ball was followed by a single. Munday then scored one, and off the last ball the winning run was scrambled. A potentially nasty incident was avoided in the last over when the bowler, in an attempt to check some over-enthusiastic backing-up, brought his arm over but, instead of releasing the ball, removed the bails. The Plymstock captain saved the situation by ordering that there should be no appeal.

As well as the obituaries of Maurice Avery, there were, in 1986, occasions for other tributes. John Montgomery stood down as Colts' Secretary after nine years in the vanguard of an enterprise that he had himself launched; Margaret Wood and Robert Carr were added to list of Life Members in recognition of their contributions to the well-being of the club; and Sandra Chappell received the Clubman of the Year award for her work in organising the refreshments so effectively that the profits ran annually into four figures.

This enterprise was, in fact, one of the most important sources of revenue. The profit from that other refreshment-dispenser, the bar, amounted in 1986 to £2236, while the subscription level was raised to £15. At the same time an issue that had given rise to some controversy in the past was put to rest. Various schemes to pay travel expenses for away games had been tried, and had often been felt to be unfair in their application as well as burdensome for the club (the bill in 1985 was £563). From now on, players were to be responsible for making mutually acceptable arrangements.

One other matter engaged attention in 1986. Cricket lovers are traditionalists by instinct. They have had to swallow, in recent years, a number of innovations. For a generation that learned its cricket by batting on cart-tracks against bowlers who earned their livings as blacksmiths, the arrival of the helmet seemed to confirm all our prejudices about the softness of the modern cricketer. The Tavistock committee decided to spend £90 on helmets. They did it without much enthusiasm. There were four in favour, one against, and four abstentions.

Varying Fortunes

Stuart Munday assumed the captaincy by accident in 1986. In 1987 he held the post in his own right. He could by now be considered a veteran, and was certainly an experienced club cricketer, whose service to Tavistock went back to 1965. It has always been a feature of English cricket at every level that specialist bowlers have become captains far less often than their batsmen-counterparts. And Munday was a bowler, with no pretensions to being anything another than a natural tail-end batsman. He was the thirty-fifth captain of the club, and only the ninth bowler to fill that role. He had been at the centre of some of the controversies within the club, and, while he had friends and supporters, he also had opponents. A strong personality, he was always at pains to remind everyone that, while he might now be a Plymouth resident, he was, by birth, upbringing, and allegiance, very much a Tavistock boy. There was never any doubt in anyone's mind, whether you agreed with him or not, that he maintained, throughout his career, a fierce loyalty to the club, and to its interests as he saw them.

In playing terms, the 1987 season turned out to be one of mixed fortunes. Overall, the first team won 13 and drew 11 of their 40 matches. In the league, there was at one point a threat of relegation, but this was averted, and the record at the end of the year was 5 victories and 6 draws in 20 games. The tradition of cup success was maintained with a good run up to the semi-final stage. The captain carried a good part of the burden, bowling, for instance, 233 overs in league matches. The only other significant wicket-taker was Keith Donohue, who turned in a fine all-round season-long performance. Bob Luffman continued to show his value as change-bowler and middle-order batsman, while newcomers Simon Stevenson, formerly of Plymouth Civil Service, and Tony Bosustow, from RNEC Manadon, made their marks.

The second eleven featured some noteworthy individual performances, with John McGahey, a second-generation clubman (his father, J. M. McGahey, having been a regular player from 1936 to 1939), making 167 not out in an early-season match, and John Rich turning in figures against Torquay of 18 overs, 10 maidens, 18 runs, and 6 wickets. The most consistent batsman was Gerry Parsons. The season also brought the level of success in the colts area that was by now almost taken for granted. The Under-16 team gave the clearest possible evidence of the value of the exercise of winning their league with a side that had played together since they had been under-13s.

The ambitious project to overhaul the clubhouse received a helpful boost in

1987, the year in which gas was installed. The Town and Borough Councils both made substantial grants. Together with a record-breaking bar profit of £2704, the club was able to respond positively to the challenge of re-roofing the building and carrying out some major internal improvements.

Close observers of the scene at The Ring showed some signs of apprehension as the 1988 season approached. At first glance the side that faced up to the challenge of maintaining the club's status in the top division appeared to be well balanced. The batting, with established run-makers like Kevin Rees, Tony Bosustow, and John McGahey, was bolstered by the addition of opener Steve Wright. Stuart Munday, in the second year of his leadership, was operating in harness with the hard-working Keith Donohue, and they were supported by all-rounders like the evergreen Bob Luffman. Also the promotion of such home-grown talent as Adrian Towl, Paul Tynan, and John Rich, helped to disarm those critics who were arguing that a Plymouth-based skipper was unbalancing the team by bringing in too many imports.

There were, however, some fundamental weaknesses, particularly the one that was highlighted in an early-season encounter with Exmouth at The Ring. The home side made 253 for 3, with Wright scoring 130 not out, in their 46 overs. In most situations, such a target would have proved to be out of reach for the side batting second. Exmouth got there in the penultimate over. One possible consequence of losing a match that you seemed set to win is that morale can be sapped. By the end of the season, Tavistock had lost 13 of their 19 games, and were relegated.

The blow was not softened by again reaching the final of the county cup. Nor did it help much that the second eleven finished fifth, with Phil Mitchell topping the league averages with 67. They, as the rules of the league dictated, would also go down. Good news, like the continued form of veterans Husband and Parsons, and the success of the latter in captaining the Devon Over-50s to the national title, lifted the gloom a little. And there was a memorable mid-season encounter with the Lord's Taverners, when a large crowd was entertained by Sadiq and Mushtaq, not to speak of Richard Kershaw, Gary Newbon, and William Rushton. This occasion required considerable organisation. A financial commitment to the Taverners, together with expenses, could only be met by large-scale sponsorship, extensive publicity, and feverish ticket selling.

The colts again brought success and distinction to the club. John Gosling captained the County Under 14 side; Nick Blythe, grandson of Douglas Treloar, won county honours, and Darren Chappell, son of Barry, scored a century in an Under 15 game. All this was good news but it could do little to sweeten the pill. Relegation had revealed some weaknesses, particularly in the bowling.

Stuart Munday was accurate, economical, and reliable, but was not primarily a strike bowler. The attack had leaned heavily on Keith Donohue, who played well enough to earn the club awards for both batting and bowling, but this over-reliance was exposed at the end of the season, when he decided to end his five-year career at Tavistock, and to move on in order to continue to play A Division cricket, and so hope to catch the eyes of the county selectors. This kind of situation would, of course, become a major problem for

Tavistock if they remained long in the second division. Not surprisingly, the club at its first opportunity moved an amendment to the rules of the league to double the number of clubs moving between divisions, from one to two. The change was approved. Meanwhile the fall-out from the season included Mike Crocker's resignation after two years as secretary, and a sharp disagreement over the purchase of new furniture for the pavilion, which led to the departure of Bert Wood.

A Brace of Crockers

The last year of the decade saw a number of changes to the leadership of the club. This did not apply to the two highest offices. Jack Taylor had been the obvious, and popular, choice to succeed Maurice Avery as president. Meanwhile David Rees had taken over the more pressing and difficult duties of chairmanship that Taylor had carried for so long.

Elsewhere, there was change. Clifford Alford, that amiable and wise work-horse, who had already shown his willingness to further the club's interests in any capacity in which he was needed, was happy to hand on the accounts to Peter Ayres; Stuart Munday filled the secretarial vacancy created by the resignation of Mike Crocker; and the captaincy changed hands. The new man in charge, who had led the second team for the past four seasons, was also the Social Secretary. His name was Mike Crocker. He was based in Plymouth, and was a friend and neighbour of Stuart Munday, who had introduced him to the club, as he had many other Plymouthians over the years. There had, of course, to be some way of differentiating between the two Mike Crockers, both of them playing a central role in the life of the club on and off the field. Unfortunately for those trying to follow the fortunes of the club, this difficulty was often overlooked by scorers, reporters, correspondents, and minute takers. Sometimes a distinction was made by adding a home base to a name, so that the man who in 1989 was club captain and social secretary and former second eleven captain was M. Crocker (Plympton), while the current second eleven captain and former secretary was M. Crocker (Tavistock). More usually, as will be the case here, the former was referred to as M. A. Crocker and the latter as M.H. Crocker.

Each in his own way showed a high degree of commitment to the club, and worked tirelessly in its cause. On the field, M. H.'s main contribution came with his left arm bowling, while M. A., although no stylist, was an effective run-getter. As an added complication, M. H.'s son Martin also featured during these years as a very promising young player.

Under M. A. Crocker's captaincy the first team launched its campaign to regain senior status. After a promising start, in which victories were secured by scores of 229 for 1 and 182 for 0, the season fell away, and the club had to be satisfied with a modest seventh position. Overall, 50 games were played, 15 of which were won and 17 lost. The pattern of fixtures pursued, for the most part, a well-established pattern, with a combination of league, cup, and friendly matches, punctuated by the odd game to mark a special occasion or the reception of a touring club.

The team again made plenty of runs, with regular contributions coming from Steve Luffman, who averaged 63 in league games, and Phil Stephens, returning after a long absence, along with Steve Wright, John McGahey, and the captain. Geoff Husband played regularly. Newcomer Stephen Larder's efforts with both bat and ball augured well for the future; he seemed to be filling the Donohue shoes as the side's principal all-rounder. The attack was again rather stretched. Support for Stuart Munday and John Rich came mainly from M. H. Crocker who, although he had been originally appointed to second team captaincy duties, was regularly required to bowl for the first team, and took 43 wickets in league matches.

One innovation in the fixture list, seen as a recognition of the club's traditional success in cup cricket, was an invitation to contend for the Cockspur Cup, a national inter-club competition. No such competitive edge was involved when friendlies were played, or so it might be thought. But even here a will to win just occasionally spilled over into something else. Most scorebooks include on each page a box headed 'Type of Match'. The Tavistock scorer having entered, on this particular day, the word 'friendly', an unknown hand subsequently added 'ish'.

While the senior team was enjoying only a modest season in the new surroundings of the second division, the second eleven won their league by a wide margin. John McGahey had taken over the captaincy after M.H. Crocker had been drafted into first team duty. Among the young players, John Rich and Andrew Gauler performed particularly well. The team could obviously have done itself justice in more distinguished company, but the rules of the league did not allow it.

Elsewhere, the colts continued successfully, as did the mid-week eleven. The latter, a hybrid team recruited from the club members ranging from first team players to colts, performed regularly on Wednesday evenings in limited overs games against sides in the immediate area. Local derbys against Whitchurch were a particular feature of their programme. The captain of such a side required particular qualities of both tact and cricketing nous. It was fortunate for the club that the duties were borne, throughout the whole of the 1980s, by Robin Wilson.

Financially, the decade came to an end with the club appearing to be in a sound position. A record bar profit of £4287 in 1989 helped to pay for the re-furnishing of the pavilion and for the installation of a burglar-alarm system. The bar secretary, Bert Wood, was certainly felt to be worth the £300 honorarium that he received. (The only other honorarium was the £100 that was given to the secretary.) He was made a life member in 1989, as was Stuart Munday. The death, in that year, of Len Jackman, a former bar secretary and a faithful servant of the club, was seen as a sad loss by everyone at The Ring. It was in a situation of some uncertainty, and of mixed fortunes, that the club prepared for the 1990s.

The new decade, and the club's 142nd season, began with a new captain in charge. Not everyone, however, realised that there had been a change. The name was the same. M. H. Crocker replaced M. A. Crocker. The latter had

ABOVE: Jack Davey.

BELOW: The team Jack Davey led in 1980.
Standing: Len Jackman, George Richards, Ron Ball, Neil Mort, Graham Kelly, Peter Coombe, Mike Crocker, Robert Jarman, Robin Wilson, Tony Miller (umpire), John Doidge (secretary). *Seated:* Derek Watson, Tony Clapp, Jack Davey, Stuart Munday, Bill Pruce.

The club's two senior sides show, in 1984, interesting variations in both age and hair length.
ABOVE: The First Eleven.
Standing: Robert Jarman, Chris Ollerenshaw, Kevin Rees, Bob Luffman, Stephen Montgomery, Trevor Harris, Mark Lovell (scorer). *Seated:* Maurice Babb, Stuart Munday, Paul Monk (captain), Bill Pruce, Jack Davey.

BELOW: The Second Eleven
Standing: Len Jackman (umpire), Keith Wiley, Andrew Luffman, Steve Hodge, David Endacott, Mike Crocker, Graham Kelly. *Kneeling:* Andrew Gauler, Tim Cashell, Patrick Cashell (captain), Terry Burnside, John Rich.

The average age has fallen a little, and the haircuts have become more standard.
ABOVE: The First Eleven 1997.
Standing: Steve Bray, Dave Jeffery, Bobby Ancil, John McGahey, Matthew Smith, Mike Tremellen(scorer), Dave Manning. *Seated:* Steve Johns, Mike Crocker, Andrew Gauler (captain), John Gosling, Geoff Astle.

BELOW: The Second Eleven 1996
Standing: Dave Manning, Paul Mackenzie, Bobby Ancil, Mark Lovell, Matthew Smith, Geoff Astle, Tony Davies (umpire). *Seated:* Andrew Rich, Clive Johns, Geoff Crudgington (captain), Stuart Munday, John Rich.

ABOVE: A special celebration in 1993 to honour two club stalwarts, Clifford Alford and Dot Avery, as they clocked up, respectively, fifty and sixty years service to the club. Chairman Jack Taylor (left) and Treasurer Peter Ayres (right) record the scores. Looking on, Michael Crocker and Stephen Larder, captains of the Second and First Elevens.

BELOW: The 1995 Colts Under-17 Cup winning side.
Standing: Nathan Godwin, Chris Ancil, Paul Daymond, Mike Ancil (team manager), Robert Coombe, Steve Vanstone, Chris Daymond. *Kneeling:* Richard Newnham, David Manning, Andrew Alford (captain), Ross Hann, Francis Fletcher.

been described by the chairman, David Rees, as 'a popular leader on and off the field who encouraged the chances of our younger players'. He was also an effective recruiting agent, bringing a number of Plymouth-based players into the club. He and his wife had, moreover, contributed a great deal to the club off the field, in the organisation of social events and of the catering.

Following his year in office he concentrated on the second eleven, and gave to that side something of the stability that it had lacked in previous years by captaining it through the next five seasons. His successor was a former second eleven captain and former club secretary, who had established a reputation for commitment to the club generally, and in particular to the maintenance of the ground and the clubhouse. On the field he was, regularly, one of the principals in an attack that, over a period, was over-reliant on two or three performers.

The league campaign remained the main focus of attention for the new captain, and for the club generally. A restructuring carried out in 1990 followed the fashion of the age by re-designating the top division as 'the premier league'. Tavistock, in the second flight, found itself in Division A. The club, naturally, supported the idea of a two-up and two-down transfer between the two top divisions, as had hitherto been the case, but a special meeting of the league voted to reduce the numbers to one each way.

The quest for that one place began promisingly enough in the early stages of the 1990 season. Two defeats in early August finally halted the momentum, and the season ended with the club occupying fifth place in the table, having won 10 and drawn 5 of the 22 league games. Of the 30 friendly fixtures, 12 were drawn, an outcome that reflected the continuing difficulty in bowling sides out. A total of 244 for 5, as was achieved against Budleigh Salterton on May 26th, should, in most circumstances, have been enough to, at least, avoid defeat. Budleigh knocked off the runs.

Stephen Larder took 40 league wickets in the season at 16.7 apiece, and skipper Mike Crocker took 31 at 22.5 each, but no one else took more than 15. Robin Wilson's left-arm slows gave him, on a rare outing, 5 for 50 against Buckfastleigh. The batting, by contrast, prospered throughout the summer. Phil Stephens's 754 runs at an average of 44.3 featured two innings of 144 and 123, both not out, and gave him second place in the league averages. Stephen Larder scored 597 in 20 league matches, and Stephen Luffman and John Gosling also scored heavily. Kevin Willcocks performed consistently with both bat and ball.

The 1991 season followed a very similar pattern to that of the previous summer. There were some impressive individual performances, with young players like Darren Chappell, John Gosling, and Adrian Towl making their marks alongside Phil Stephens, Stephen Luffman, and Stephen Larder. There were high spots, including a tour, based at Brighton, which was successful in playing terms and was a welcome revival of an old tradition.

There were also lows, notably an undistinguished exit from the cup competition when, following a three-wicket victory over Plymouth achieved on the back of a century stand between Gosling and Stephens, the club was eliminated following a failure to submit a results sheet. Overall the record was disappointing, with only 5 league victories, and only 14 in all matches. Far from challenging for promotion, the club seemed to be facing the prospect of decline and the threat of further relegation.

Phil Stephens took over the captaincy for the 1992 season. Now living at Chillaton and teaching at Mount House School, he was an experienced club cricketer, and there was no doubt that he was a class act. But the quality of the batting had not been the problem. Even the loss of Stephen Luffman, who moved on to pursue an ambition to play at a higher level, did not stem the flow of runs. Stephens and Larder both scored heavily and consistently. In June they created a new league record with a partnership of 209 (not 299 as the secretary subsequently reported). Larder finished with 163 not out. But the season ended with a dismal league record of only 3 victories. It meant relegation to Division B.

The problems that beset the first team during the first three years of the decade did not inhibit the performance of the second eleven. In 1990 they finished third, after leading the table for much of the season. In 1991 they were runners-up, only four points behind the champions, in a season in which John Rich performed the hat trick twice. In 1992 they again finished in second place, with Chris Cashell and Clive Johns both scoring centuries and David Hill taking 50 wickets. The midweek side, meanwhile, experienced some difficulties in raising teams on a regular basis, even after the incorporation, in 1990, of the Under-21 side.

Umpiring duties during the early 1990s were mainly in the hands of Tony Davies, Clifford Alford, David Endecott, and John Gauler. Anthony Warrington was the scorer. In 1992 the club committed itself to the replacement of the scorebox, and at the end of the year planning permission was obtained for a larger, wider box. There still remained a number of other features of the clubhouse that needed improvement. The overdue refurbishment of the kitchen was carried out in 1992, while outside the space to the rear of the pavilion was flattened to provide a net area, and plans went ahead to replace the all-weather wicket. Eric Willcocks took over from Bob Newton as ground curator in 1990. At the same time an attempt was made to tackle a perennial source of grumbles by employing a pavilion cleaner, who was to be paid £25 for a spring clean and £5 for a weekly shift during the season.

Bert Wood, sadly was not around to participate in some of these improvements. He died in 1992, a year after he and his wife Margaret had received special presentations in appreciation of their services to the club. They were both, of course, life members, and in 1992 the committee decided to recommend to the A.G.M. that there should be two more recipients of this particular honour. They were John Gosling and Mike Crocker. When David Shepherd, now busily combining the duties of test match umpire and postmaster of Instow, was subsequently added to the list, the role of honour had, by the middle of the decade, come to include thirteen names. The new names went alongside those of the six who had been given the distinction during the 1980s, Mesdames Avery, Jarman, and Wood, and Messrs Pruce,

Carr, and Munday, and the four who had been honoured even earlier, Messrs Robins, Alford, Jarman, and Saxby.

There was also a significant addition to the club's collection of trophies. In addition to those given in recognition of achievements on the field, a cup had been presented to be awarded annually to the Club Person of the Year, and to bear the name of the club's former president Maurice Avery. In 1990 a second trophy, given this time by Maurice's widow and carrying her name, was added, with the stipulation that it should go 'to the person who had made the most significant contribution to the club over the year'. Dot Avery's affection for the club, and her long-standing devotion to its service and interests, were thus commemorated in an appropriate and lasting form.

The annual turnover of the club in the early part of the nineties approached five figures. Taking altogether the first three years of the decade, there was an average annual income of £9316. The largest element of this, £4047, or 43.4%, came from profits from the bar. Subscriptions contributed 13.7%, and the surplus on refreshments brought in 12.7%. Other significant sources of revenue were local government grants at 7.6%, draws at 6.3%, and sponsorships at 6.8%.

The scale of sponsorship arrangements, though still only contributing a small proportion of total income, had grown appreciably over the years. The idea of inviting local firms and organisations to sponsor home fixtures had been launched in 1979, and in that first year thirteen games were supported. Over the next few years the net spread more widely to the point at which all home matches were being sponsored. By the end of the 1980s such arrangements were bringing into the club annual amounts between £700 and £800. Here was yet another example of cricket at club level, pursuing both economic necessity and the example set in the game at higher levels, bringing in innovations at which earlier generations might shudder. In this case, it must be said, the operation remained locally focused and the amounts involved were modest. Advertising hoardings at The Ring remain a distant, and surely unwelcome, prospect.

Over the three year period in question, annual expenditure ran at an average of £8566. Of this, £3251 or 38% was earmarked for maintenance, repairs, or replacements to ground and pavilion. A further 11.4% went on rates and services such as water, gas, and electricity, while 10.2% covered the costs of the telephone and secretarial expenses. Depreciation accounted for 14.3%. One item that disappeared from the accounts in 1992, after figuring at a very modest level for some years, was that of honoraria. The club was never in a position to finance major projects from the small balance that remained after essential bills had been paid. This situation had always produced differences within the club between those whose outlook was above all cautious and those who favoured a bolder approach. It was not the only, or even the most significant, source of disagreement during these years.

Predictably, the smouldering embers were fanned into flame under the pressures of the 'relegation summer' of 1992. Again it was alleged that some clubmen from out of town were not pulling their weight. David Rees put the blame at the door of a small group who:

> 'unable now to blame the Plymouth contingent (who have mostly left, and considerably weakened the playing strength of the club) turned on other members of the club.'

Feeling himself to be one of the targets of criticism, he resigned the chairmanship. The last part of Rees's six-year tenure had been made more difficult by the frequent absence from meetings of Stuart Munday, the secretary, whose work had taken him to London. At about the same time there was an unfortunate misunderstanding which led to Jack Taylor feeling that he was being elbowed out of the presidency, a position that he valued and that he saw as one for life. And all this at a time when the first eleven was struggling to retain its 'A' division status.

At the end of the season, Stuart Munday put forward in candid terms the issue that lay behind many of the conflicts of personality that had beset the club. Was Tavistock to remain a strictly local, almost parochial, club, or was it to encourage talent from outside? The retiring secretary, who had done more than anyone to bring fresh blood to The Ring, had no doubt what the answer should be. 'The way forward to me', he announced in his last secretary's report, 'is we have to look to recruiting new players if we want to get promotion'. 'I know', he added, 'that this will not be accepted by a lot of members'.

One difficulty, at least, seemed by 1992 to have been partially overcome. In 1989 relations with the local newspaper had broken down. The club felt that it was not getting the kind of coverage that its status and achievements justified, and the wider charge was made that the sports editor was unsympathetic to the game generally. Such situations, not unknown in the history of other sports clubs and other societies, are good for neither side. They usually end in a compromise which recognises their mutual dependence. By 1992 the paper was sponsoring a match at The Ring and advertising in the club's fixture leaflet. As the club faced up to the challenge of making a rapid return to 'A' Division cricket, there could at least be some confidence that the recovery effort would be given fair publicity.

1993: A New Dawn?

The 1993 campaign, seen by many of its well-wishers as a crucial test of not only the team's ability but the club's ambition, was preceded by some significant changes. For the first time there was a club sponsor. Historically, there could scarcely have been a more appropriate patron than Chilcotts, the firm of solicitors. The playing membership differed little from that of the preceding year. John Gosling had moved to play for Plymouth. Jimmy Hargreaves from Plymstock, a seasoned campaigner, joined what otherwise remained a very young team. Phil Stephens, who was unlikely to play as regularly as heretofore, gave up the captaincy, which fell to Stephen Larder.

The secretary's job, vacated by Stuart Munday, passed into the hands of Clifford Alford. David Rees was succeeded as chairman by Peter Ayres. He in turn handed on the finances to Tracey Larder, the wife of the captain, who, together with Margaret Alford, became the first woman to sit on the committee. Jack Taylor remained in the presidency for life, as had his predecessor.

Such changes as there were among the officers of the club did not disguise the fact that an attempt was to be made, as the 1993 season opened, to turn the fortunes of the club round with a team almost the same as that which had failed to avoid relegation just a few months earlier. Whatever else the club was to be involved in during the coming summer, the focus would, inevitably, be on the first team's league performance. There was a certain novelty about the new campaign, which saw the club's baptism in the Bowring Insurance Devon Cricket League Division B. Games against the likes of Babbacombe, Chudleigh, Thorverton, and Cockington had not previously featured in Tavistock's programme, and some opponents had never visited The Ring in their history.

There were twelve clubs competing for two promotion places. A complex points system included bonus points for both batting and bowling as well as a range of points dependent on the result, 10 for a win, 6 for a winning draw or an abandonment, 5 for a tie, and 2 for a losing draw. Tactically, the side winning the toss almost always batted second. An analysis of the 1993 results showed why. Taking all the teams in the division, the number of games won batting second as against victories in games batting first was 55 to 21. In the case of Tavistock the figures were 10 to 0. A team batting first earned, on average, 9.7 points, as against 12.4 if they were chasing a total. In the case of Tavistock the corresponding figures were 9.3 and 16.2. Insertion was, then, the name of the game.

The distinguishing feature of the new league season for Tavistock was again some excellent batting performances. Phil Stephens played in 12 games, scored 523 runs, and clocked up the extraordinary average of 130.7. Darren Chappell averaged 44.5, and compiled a remarkable season aggregate of 1243 runs, including four centuries. Steve Larder and John McGahey also batted well, as did Kevin Rees, returning to the side in the wicketkeeper-batsman role and travelling regularly from his West Cornwall home. The attack leaned heavily on the efforts of skipper Larder, with solid support from pace bowler Adrian Towl and off spinner Steve Bray. The battle for promotion was an exciting one, with the outcome remaining in doubt until a late stage in the season, but Larder's pre-season claim that Tavistock were the best side in the division was finally vindicated by events, and amid prolonged celebrations at The Ring the championship was secured by a margin of 13 points.

Of the 22 fixtures, 10 had been won, 8 drawn, 1 tied, and 3 lost. It was, in fact, part of a double triumph, because the second eleven also ended the season as champions of their division, having led the table from the first day. Captain M. A. Crocker headed the batting tables of both the club and the league, and Clive Johns proved to be a model of consistency. Geoff Crudgington,

Plymouth-based former professional footballer, also came into the side and made a lot of runs, while young players like Bobby Ancil, Richard Potts, Dominic Nott, and Matthew Smith made their marks.

The bowling showed a happy combination of experience and youth, with Jim Hannaford, M. H. Crocker, and Jim Hargreaves in the first category, and Matthew Nott and Jonathan Rowan in the second. The colts, as always performed with credit, the Under 13s, under the leadership of Brian Hulme, coming first and second in cup and league competitions. The other managers were Alan Smith and Mike Ancil; the latter had also taken over the duties of colts' secretary.

In view of the resounding successes that the season had brought, it was not surprising that Clifford Alford had a very up-beat message to deliver when he gave his first secretarial report to the following A.G.M., an occasion now established as being held in the Parish Centre in the first half of January. Confirmation that a new era had dawned seemed to come with the news that grants had been secured to cover the cost of the new scorebox. The magnificent Dot Avery had marked the sixtieth year of her active support for the club by giving £1000 towards the new protect.

One other feature of the summer of '93 deserves a mention. The fixture programme of the first eleven gives an interesting picture of the club's annual playing commitments at this stage of its life. There were 61 games. Of these, 22 were league matches. Thus, in spite of the natural concentration of attention on the league campaign, it accounted for fewer than half of the total number of fixtures. Three of the others were in cup competitions. That left 36 friendly games. Of these, 15 were against other clubs either in Devon or, as in the case of the Mendip Acorns, from slightly further afield. The remaining 21 were against visiting sides on tour from such places as Great Yarmouth, Northampton, Sheffield, Chelmsford, Swindon, and even Hong Kong. The west country tour was an established feature of the programme of many clubs, the last part of the season being particularly favoured, and Tavistock remained, for a whole range of understandable reasons, a part of many of these programmes. Such a preponderance of home games (only 15 of the 61 were away) put a strain on the club to provide pitches. It did, on the other hand, continue to reinforce the reputation of the club for hospitality and good cricket, provided in a congenial setting.

The death of Jack Taylor on Christmas Day 1994 marked the end of an era. He had been president since 1986, and before that chairman since 1969. His deep love of the game and his loyalty to the club had been manifest over a long period, and his loss was deeply felt. He was, appropriately, succeeded by the only member who could match this record of service. Clifford Afford was now asked to put the honorific office of the presidency alongside the burdensome duties of being secretary. He brought a range of qualities to both tasks. A universally popular and respected figure, he showed qualities of patience and understanding, was conscientious and assiduous in carrying out a wide range of duties, and enjoyed the advantage of having been closely involved in the affairs of the club for the best part of half a century. In the whole of its history there have been few who have served the club with such distinction, and who have been held, on all sides, in such high regard.

The Alford family involvement did not end with Clifford, Margaret became treasurer in 1995, and made a heavy commitment in time and effort to the affairs of the club, including the organisation of match teas, and Andrew contributed significantly, not only on the field, but in working on the ground. He also, as a graduate of the colts' section, became involved in managing a side, and in 1997 he took on the responsibility of being colts' secretary, a post that had been filled for the previous five years by Mike Ancil.

The middle years of the decade had, in fact, seen some welcome stability in this, and in other club offices. Peter Willetts and Clive Johns were chairman and vice-chairman, the latter also acting as fixtures secretary, John Gauler remained in charge of the bar. Only in the case of the ground curator were there rapid changes. Eric Willcocks was doing the job in 1993, but following his resignation Bob Newton was reappointed. By 1995 the duties had come to Peter Ayres.

The Contemporary Scene

The captain of the first eleven in the 1994 season was Peter Jones, who replaced Stephen Larder when the latter moved out of the area. Jones was a second generation clubman, the son of the estimable Hilton. He lived in Plymouth. Under his leadership the team had a very successful campaign, finishing in third position in the league and missing promotion by only a narrow margin. Phil Stephens averaged 96.2 in the 10 innings that he played, and young Duncan Roke topped 50 in 9 of his 20 innings to finish with an aggregate of 890 and an average of 55.6. Steve Bray took the principal bowling honours with a haul of 41 wickets at 16.3 each.

The season saw two interesting developments, both of which were clearly signs of the time. One was the extent to which league cricket had come to dominate the club's programme, not in terms of the number of games played but in the sense that friendly games were increasingly seen as being in a different category to the league fixtures. This was reflected in the quality of the side selected. The trend was acknowledged, and formalised, in 1997, when the fixtures booklet provided, for the first time, two separate lists. The other sign of changing times was the appearance of the players in shirts dominated by the principal patron, Chilcotts, and bearing the name of the sponsor. In the middle of the decade sponsorship was bringing in over £1000 a year.

The impressive showing of the first team in 1994 was matched by the second eleven. They ended the season as runners-up in their league, with M. A. Crocker and Geoff Crudgington scoring heavily and M. H. Crocker and John Rich sharing the principal bowling honours. The following season, which was M. A. Crocker's last as captain, underlined how closely the fortunes of a second eleven are tied to those of the senior side. Crocker had to call on no fewer than 37 players to carry out his league commitments. And the reason was because the first eleven was not a settled side. Some of the promising youngsters, like Duncan Roke, Matthew Smith, and Edmund Hulme moved on to universities, and neither Phil Stephens nor Peter Jones could play a full season. John Gosling was back in the fold, but suffered from injury. He did, however, manage to average 45.7 in his 10 games, while M. H. Crocker bowled more overs than anyone else, taking 35 wickets and winning the club award. It was heartening to see former colts like Bobby Ancil, Andrew Alford, and Chris Ancil finding their feet in senior cricket.

Peter Jones's partial indisposition meant that a new captain was needed. The choice fell, in his nineteenth season with the club, on Andrew Gauler. The difficulties in team selection made it a rather difficult summer for him, but in the end the results were quite satisfactory, and relegation, which had at one point threatened, was avoided by a significant margin. It was, moreover, a source of considerable satisfaction that in the report submitted by league umpires, Tavistock came second in the table that measured the conduct of players on the field.

If the playing record of the club in 1995 reflected a rather unsettled picture, the achievements of 1996 suggested a more secure basis. Andrew Gauler grew in confidence in the second year of his captaincy. As the season opened his side seemed to hit the ground running. In the first month John Gosling clocked up scores of 50, 66, 75, and 113. His opening partner, Mark Lovell, scored 100, 56, and 49 in his first three games. Useful contributions were to come, with consistency, from John McGahey, from Peter Jones, and from the captain himself. And, in the second half of the season, returning from his studies, Duncan Roke caught everyone's eye, including that of the county selection committee. He rounded off the season with an innings of 189 out of a total of 272 for 6, made against a touring side from Hampshire.

The bowlers responded well to the opportunities they were given to defend large totals. Steve Bray set a pattern by capturing 5 for 33 in 23 overs in his first outing of the season, while Crocker and Munday, neither any longer in the first flush of youth, bowled with perseverance, cunning, and consistency. Others, like Gauler and Gosling, bowled useful spells from time to time. Overall the attack was good enough to bring a reasonable harvest of victories. But the absence of a real strike bowler, let alone two, continued to affect results. On many occasions a clear superiority was not turned into a victory because of a failure to bowl the other side out.

There was one other obvious inhibition. Many clubs with whom Tavistock were competing for league honours hired professionals. Tavistock were in no position to follow suit. Indeed, as the nineties proceeded the reliance on local talent became increasingly evident. It was in the light of factors such as these that the achievement of fourth position in the league table generated considerable satisfaction. And, as tends to happen, the success of the senior team, particularly if it is sustained over the season, affects the performance of the other teams representing the club. The second eleven were convincing champions in their league campaign. And the colts, in Mike Ancil's last year as secretary, collected a range of awards including, for the first time, the Bob Whitburn Cup, a county-wide Under-16 competition.

One Saturday afternoon in the middle of the 1997 season there was a welcome visit to The Ring from Bill Tucker, into the ninety-third year of his life and the fiftieth of his retirement from cricket. Of the changes that had come about in the previous half-century, he was particularly interested to note the extent to which league performance had become a dominating factor in the life of the club. At that point, mid-way through the campaign, there was a good deal of unease on this account, because players and supporters were still awaiting a first victory. It came, finally, on July 5th. The achievement, on that day, of a six-wicket win over Bradninch was made possible by an innings of 93 not out from John Gosling that included six sixes. It also helped that Andrew Gauler, after thirteen successive wrong calls, had won the toss.

From that point on there was never any real fear of relegation, although victories proved elusive. At the end of the season, Tavistock occupied ninth place in the twelve-club table, having won 3 and lost 8 of their 22 games. The batsmen had, overall, acquitted themselves well, with John Gosling playing the starring role by scoring more than twice as many runs (669) as anyone else. The only other player to equal his average was Peter Jones, who unfortunately only played in five matches. The other chief contributors were Andrew Gauler, John McGahey, Edmund Hulme, and Matthew Smith.

Again, the bowling attack lacked the cutting edge that might have turned some of the winning draws into victories. Andrew Gauler topped the averages, so confirming his value as an all-rounder, Steve Bray took most wickets, with 27. On only three occasions did a bowler take 5 wickets in an innings: Paul McKenzie did it twice and Andy Gauler once. The overall record for the season was modest, in that only 12 of the 50 games were won. Much encouragement could, however, be drawn from the performance of some of the younger players, like Edmund Hulme, Matthew Smith, and the fifteen-year old Paul Tomkies. Two sets of brothers, Martin and David Manning, and Bobby and Chris Ancil, made their marks, Bobby chalking up some kind of record by scoring two 98s in one week, in mid-July.

The 1998 A.G.M. was the 140th in the history of the club. Only the two world wars have interrupted a pattern of regular meetings in winter or spring, and their format and content have remained fairly constant. This one saw the decision to confer life membership on Peter Ayres, a recognition of his contribution both as ground curator and as the holder of other offices over a number of years. Clive Johns, who had taken over on Peter Willetts's resignation, was confirmed in the chair, with Geoff Crudgington as vice-chairman. Both were respected elder statesmen, who had served the club well, and who, on the field, continued to supply a steady flow of runs for the second eleven.

The other major change was in the first team captaincy. Andrew Gauler stood down after three seasons in charge and John Gosling took over. Andrew had been a popular leader and an able all-round cricketer. In handing over the reins after three terms he was following the tradition of rotating the captaincy frequently. It should be emphasised that this convention had only become established since the Second World War. Since 1950, no captain has held office for longer than three consecutive years. The contrast with earlier periods is striking. During its first hundred years the club was led by 18 captains. There were the same number between 1970 and 1998.

The twelve clubs that made up the 'A', or Second, Division of the Devon League in the mid-1990s played 22 league matches per season. All the matches could not be played on Saturdays, and one weekend a month became an occasion for a 'double header' with games on both Saturday and Sunday. In 1998 the league authority decided to respond to a growing desire among the clubs to confine the league fixtures to Saturdays. They did this by reducing the size of the divisions. It was decreed that of the twelve clubs contesting the Division A competition in 1998, five should be demoted to Division B at the end of the season. The decision cast a shadow over the 1998 season at The Ring. The record of the club in recent campaigns had suggested that the avoidance of relegation under these new conditions might be beyond them. And so it was to prove.

Four defeats and four draws in the first eight games meant that the writing was, by mid-June, already on the wall. A recovery in the second half of the summer, that brought three victories in the last month, came too late to turn the tide. A position in the top seven at the end of the season was required in order to maintain 'A' Division status. Tavistock finished in ninth spot. Significantly, the Second Eleven also managed a striking late-season revival in their league fortunes. An emphatic ten-wicket victory on the last day of the programme gave them a final position of seventh, and ensured that they would be playing again in the 'A' Division in 1999. Meanwhile, ambitions for the senior team centred on the need for a quick bounce-back in time for millennium year.

The 1998 season suffered more than most from the weather, and there were a number of abandonments. This, together with the fact that some of the players were not available throughout the season, led to some inconsistency in performance. Peter Jones and Steve Larder, for example, played only occasionally. Matthew Smith became available in mid-season, and quickly tapped a rich vein of runs that did not dry up before the end of the season. The late-season opening stand between him and Paul Tomkies of almost 200 was a good augury for the future; they clocked up only thirty-six years between them. At a different point on the age-scale came a mid-season extravaganza from one of the club's longest-serving players, an innings described by the *Tavistock Gazette* as 'a calypso-style 35 from a rejuvenated John Perkin'.

David Manning established himself with an early-season century, and thereafter scored heavily to confirm earlier promise of his potential as a wicket-keeper-batsman. Of the regulars, John McGahey, and the stalwart openers, John Gosling and Andy Gauler, made regular and significant contributions. Gosling and Gauler also carried a good share of the bowling burden, along with Steve Bray. Paul Mackenzie and Matthew Smith also bowled well. The attack often proved to be an effective weapon of containment. What was missing was an opening bowler with a high strike record.

On the second eleven front, the captaincy of John Rich, an able and committed cricketer and a member of one of the club's outstanding dynasties, was a powerful factor. The veterans in the team performed with distinction. Looking to the future, the most eye-catching performance was by fifteen-year old James Vincent, who took eight wickets in a league match in June.

Because performance in the league had become a consideration of such overwhelming importance, those entrusted with the welfare of the club had to address a range of anxieties and questions. Was it, for example, inevitable that the path taken by so many other clubs in the county should be followed and a professional be appointed? Many players and supporters considered that such a route was the only one likely to lead to a speedy improvement in league status. If this were to happen it would, of course, be not a novelty but a return to the practice of a century earlier, though in the modern age the paid mercenaries would be more likely to come from the sugarcane fields of Barbados than from the coalfields of Nottinghamshire.

A wider issue lurked behind the headline-catching controversy over professionalism. Should the club concentrate mainly, or even exclusively, on home-grown talent, bearing in mind that the fostering of such talent was now, for the most part, not a burden that clubs were able to share with local schools? Or should efforts be made to bring in players from further afield? This was an old controversy that had been a source of division within the club at times in the past. Its echoes would continue to be heard because it was essentially a debate about ambition. To what levels should the club realistically aspire?

Such heights could, of course, be gauged in playing terms. Equally, other forms of measurement could be applied, like the quality of the ground, the resources, and the pavilion. In any case, considerations of cost would continue to occupy the minds of those responsible for the club's welfare. And here, the announcement of a new sponsorship arrangement was very welcome. Largely through the efforts of Stuart Munday, a two-year deal was struck with Chaplins of Plympton Ltd. It offered the prospect of greater financial stability, at least in the short term.

Future generations of club players, officials, and members, were to be faced with a range of issues and questions, some of them new and some of them recurrent themes through the club's history. In addressing them, they could expect to enjoy three advantages, the value of which can hardly be over-estimated. The first of these is a tradition, stretching back to the earliest days, which has provided, at successive stages, a band of dedicated clubmen who could be relied upon to carry out the essential work. Cometh the hour, cometh the Tom Chave, or the Gordon Parry, or the Clifford Alford.

The second immeasurable advantage that the club enjoys is the place. The Ring has changed little over the years. The pavilion, as a dated stone high up in the northern wall reminds us, remains fundamentally the edifice that Daniel Westaway built in 1873. So much about the building, and the area, would be immediately recognisable to the pioneer cricketers in Victorian Tavistock. And the guardians of this unchanging mood are the stones. Sixty-one of them mark the boundary. The metal chain-holders that surmounted them have long been redundant, but are still in place. On average, each stone shows about three feet of itself above ground, and is twenty feet from its neighbours on each side. There is a gap, in front of the pavilion. It is likely that three additional stones originally stood here, and completed 'The Ring'; they were removed, probably at the time of the construction of the pavilion. Among the sixty-one survivors, one impostor shares the scene. The odd man out is a short, squat figure on the opposite side of the ground from the pavilion, looking for all the world like a crouching wicket keeper in the middle of a wide cordon of lanky slips and short legs. This is an old stone marking an early boundary line between the parishes of Tavistock and Whitchurch, a line that once bisected the ground.

The final source of strength for the club as it faces the challenges of the future is, quite simply, its past. History can be a burden or a millstone. It can equally be a stimulus or a guide. Among the many friends of Tavistock Cricket Club there is the hope, and the belief, that the last 150 years will act as a spur, and that the great game will continue to be played, and enjoyed, at The Ring, for centuries to come.

Appendix One

Presidents

From	*To*	
1849	1858	Richard Gribbell
1858	1887	John Carpenter
1887	1892	Reginald Gill
1892	1899	Reginald Morshead
1899	1901	Thomas Smythe
1901	1906	William David
1906	1907	Francis Freeman
1907	1908	William David
1908	1909	Edward Rundle
1909	1911	Frederick Porter
1911	1913	Frank Campbell
1913	1920	Edward Chilcott
1920	1921	Frank Campbell
1921	1922	Charles Brodrick
1922	1923	Frederick Porter
1923	1926	Leslie Watt
1926	1927	Theo Rowe
1927	1928	Alfred Penny
1928	1929	Edward Chilcott
1929	1930	Leslie Watt
1930	1938	Kenneth Johnstone
1938	1945	Francis Kelly
1946	1969	Albert Goss
1969	1986	Maurice Avery
1986	1994	Jack Taylor
1995		Clifford Alford

Appendix Two

Chairmen

The post of Chairman was not rooted in the club's early history. The pattern was for the President to assume the duties normally associated with the office of Chairman, namely the chairing of General or Committee Meetings. In the 1960s, the increased number of meetings, during the last part of Albert Goss's long presidency, led, for the first time, to the regular appointment of a chairman. Maurice Avery filled that post until 1969. His successors have been:

From	*To*	
1969	1986	Jack Taylor
1986	1992	David Rees
1992	1994	Peter Ayres
1994	1997	Peter Willetts
1997	1999	Clive Johns
1999		Stuart Munday

Appendix Three

Captains and Playing Records

Notes

1. The club had no regular captain between 1871 and 1874.
2. Arthur Hill was the first captain to be chosen by the Annual General Meeting. This was in 1875. Since then the appointment has been made by the A.G.M., often confirming a recommendation made by a pre-meeting of playing members.
3. The results, which include all games of which records exist, are those achieved by the first eleven in all types of matches.
4. Records over the first ten seasons are very thin. Of the 10 results that are known for that period, 5 were victories and 5 were defeats.

Season	*Captain*	*Playing Record*				
		P	*W*	*D*	*L*	*T*
1849	Richard Sleeman					
1850	Richard Sleeman					
1851	Richard Sleeman					
1852	Richard Sleeman					
1853	Richard Sleeman					
1854	Richard Sleeman					
1855	Richard Sleeman					
1856	Richard Sleeman					
1857	Richard Sleeman					
1858	John Carpenter					
1859	John Carpenter	6	5	0	1	0
1860	John Carpenter	6	6	0	0	0
1861	John Carpenter	5	4	0	1	0
1862	John Carpenter	3	2	0	1	0
1863	John Carpenter	4	2	0	2	0
1864	John Carpenter	3	2	0	1	0
1865	John Carpenter	4	0	0	4	0
1866	John Carpenter	2	1	0	1	0
1867	John Carpenter	5	3	1	1	0

Appendix Three

Season	Captain	Playing Record				
		P	W	D	L	T
1868	John Carpenter	1	0	0	1	0
1869	John Carpenter	0	0	0	0	0
1870	John Carpenter	2	1	0	1	0
1871		4	1	0	3	0
1872		5	2	1	2	0
1873		8	5	0	3	0
1874		6	2	0	4	0
1875	Arthur Hill	9	7	0	2	0
1876	Arthur Hill	11	8	0	3	0
1877	Samuel Featherstone	6	4	1	1	0
1878	Samuel Featherstone	3	3	0	0	0
1879	Arthur Hill	14	10	0	4	0
1880	Arthur Hill	10	5	1	4	0
1881	Arthur Hill	12	7	0	5	0
1882	Arthur Hill	16	7	1	8	0
1883	Kingsley Spencer	16	12	2	2	0
1884	Kingsley Spencer/James Wolferstan	20	14	2	4	0
1885	Samuel Featherstone	20	11	6	3	0
1886	Herbert Spencer	14	7	2	5	0
1887	Edward Chilcott	10	2	1	7	0
1888	Edward Chilcott	16	9	0	7	0
1889	Samuel Featherstone	12	7	1	4	0
1890	Samuel Featherstone	16	9	1	6	0
1891	Edward Chilcott	14	9	1	4	0
1892	Edward Chilcott	16	10	1	5	0
1893	Edward Chilcott	19	11	1	7	0
1894	Edward Chilcott	13	8	1	4	0
1895	Edward Chilcott	12	9	0	3	0
1896	Edward Chilcott	17	9	3	5	0
1897	Edward Chilcott	17	8	6	2	1
1898	Edward Chilcott	15	7	3	5	0
1899	Edward Chilcott	21	13	5	3	0
1900	Alfred Penny	22	11	7	4	0
1901	Alfred Penny	22	16	3	3	0
1902	Alfred Penny	22	11	9	2	0
1903	Alfred Penny	20	13	4	3	0
1904	Alfred Penny	21	8	4	9	0
1905	Alfred Penny	27	13	7	7	0
1906	Louis Tamworth	19	4	6	9	0
1907	Louis Tamworth	20	9	7	4	0
1908	Sidney Sone	22	12	1	9	0
1909	Sidney Sone	23	14	5	4	0
1910	Rowland Powell-Williams	27	18	3	6	0
1911	Rowland Powell-Williams	21	13	2	6	0
1912	Rowland Powell-Williams	22	17	1	4	0
1913	Rowland Powell-Williams	24	20	1	3	0
1914	Rowland Powell-Williams	18	10	2	6	0

Appendix Three

Season	*Captain*	*Playing Record*				
		P	*W*	*D*	*L*	*T*
1920	William Snell	8	7	0	1	0
1921	William Snell	20	7	1	12	0
1922	William Snell	21	16	3	2	0
1923	William Snell	19	13	3	3	0
1924	William Snell	14	7	2	5	0
1925	William Snell	15	5	0	10	0
1926	William Snell	24	15	0	9	0
1927	William Snell	20	4	5	10	1
1928	Gordon Parry	21	11	3	7	0
1929	Gordon Parry	23	12	2	9	0
1930	Gordon Parry	19	9	0	9	1
1931	Gordon Parry	15	10	0	5	0
1932	Eric Davey	20	12	1	7	0
1933	James Beale	25	20	2	3	0
1934	James Beale	27	15	6	6	0
1935	James Beale	22	14	3	5	0
1936	James Beale	20	12	5	3	0
1937	Eric Davey	23	11	6	6	0
1938	Bill Colling	21	12	6	3	0
1939	Bill Colling	17	10	2	5	0
1940	Francis Kelly	5	2	1	2	0
1941	Francis Kelly	12	5	1	6	0
1942	Francis Kelly	20	15	0	5	0
1943	Francis Kelly	13	6	3	4	0
1944	Francis Kelly	17	12	0	4	1
1945	Francis Kelly	16	13	1	2	0
1946	Bill Colling	18	13	4	1	0
1947	Bill Colling	40	27	8	5	0
1948	Bill Colling	40	30	2	8	0
1949	Bill Colling	41	20	10	10	1
1950	Bill Colling	31	8	14	9	0
1951	Maurice Avery	34	12	12	10	0
1952	Maurice Avery	34	12	14	8	0
1953	Bill Colling	35	14	13	7	1
1954	Maurice Avery	37	18	12	7	0
1955	Maurice Avery	40	12	13	14	1
1956	Jack Rogers	36	21	9	6	0
1957	Jack Rogers	34	12	12	10	0
1958	Dennis Paull	35	11	13	11	0
1959	Len McEntyre	37	11	13	13	0
1960	Eric Jarman	39	16	11	12	0
1961	Eric Jarman	45	24	10	10	1
1962	Douglas Treloar	43	22	15	6	0
1963	Douglas Treloar	43	23	18	2	0
1964	Douglas Treloar	42	16	18	7	1
1965	Eric Jarman	41	20	14	7	0
1966	Eric Jarman	38	15	13	9	1
1967	Eric Jarman	45	13	26	5	1

Appendix Three

Season	*Captain*	*Playing Record*				
		P	*W*	*D*	*L*	*T*
1968	Evan Kemp	41	16	20	5	0
1969	Evan Kemp	45	18	17	10	0
1970	Bob Quick	42	19	17	6	0
1971	Bob Quick	46	16	18	12	0
1972	Geoff Husband	40	11	10	19	0
1973	Peter Anderson/Derek Pethick	43	17	8	18	0
1974	Peter Anderson/Tony Clapp	42	17	9	16	0
1975	Peter Anderson	46	14	17	15	0
1976	Tony Clapp	35	13	9	13	0
1977	Tony Clapp	46	6	15	24	1
1978	Bill Pruce	46	14	18	14	0
1979	Eric Jarman	46	10	20	16	0
1980	Jack Davey	47	24	15	8	0
1981	Jack Davey	46	24	9	13	0
1982	Jack Davey	49	19	14	16	0
1983	Paul Monk	45	16	19	9	1
1984	Paul Monk	49	13	17	18	1
1985	Kevin Rees	40	14	16	10	0
1986	Robert Luffman	47	19	11	17	0
1987	Stuart Munday	40	13	11	16	0
1988	Stuart Munday	37	11	6	20	0
1989	Michael A Crocker	50	15	18	17	0
1990	Michael J Crocker	52	18	17	17	0
1991	Michael J Crocker	47	14	17	16	0
1992	Philip Stephens	50	9	20	20	1
1993	Stephen Larder	61	24	22	14	1
1994	Peter Jones	51	19	18	14	0
1995	Andrew Gauler	51	17	16	18	0
1996	Andrew Gauler	44	13	16	15	0
1997	Andrew Gauler	50	12	14	24	0
1998	John Gosling	46	11	17	18	0
1999	Andrew Gauler					

Appendix Four

Secretaries

From	*To*	
1849	1870	Thomas Chave
1870	1873	Henry Trigg
1873	1874	George Rench
1874	1875	George Chapman
1875	1876	Thomas Doidge
1876	1877	James Wolferstan
1877	1878	Thomas Doidge/John Northway
1878	1879	Thomas Doidge
1879	1883	Arthur Hill
1883	1884	Kingsley Spencer
1884	1889	Joseph Camozzi
1889	1890	Henry Neat/Thomas Doidge
1890	1891	Henry Neat/Francis Stowe
1891	1896	Edward Wilson
1896	1900	Edward Chilcott
1900	1906	Alfred Penny
1906	1908	Louis Tamworth
1908	1909	Kenneth Johnstone
1909	1910	Henry Cole
1910	1911	James Crook
1911	1913	William Snell
1913	1917	Harry Barkell/Thomas Doidge
1917	1921	Harry Barkell
1921	1925	Gordon Parry
1925	1926	Frederick Clutson
1926	1928	Gordon Parry
1928	1947	Frank Millman
1947	1968	Eric Davey
1968	1971	Walter Spry
1971	1974	Douglas Treloar
1974	1977	John Doidge
1977	1983	Bill Pruce
1983	1987	Patrick Cashell

From	*To*	
1987	1989	Michael Crocker
1989	1993	Stuart Munday
1993	1999	Clifford Alford
1999		Colin Piper

Appendix Five

Treasurers

From	*To*	
1849	1861	Richard Gribbell
1861	1870	Henry Allen
1870	1880	Robert Luxton
1880	1885	James Wolferstan
1885	1886	Harold Wolferstan
1886	1894	John Daw
1894	1899	Thomas Doidge
1899	1900	Edward Kay
1900	1901	Thomas Doidge
1901	1903	Edward Chilcott/Thomas Doidge
1903	1908	Edward Chilcott/Frank Jackman
1908	1925	Edward Chilcott/Frank Jolliffe
1925	1931	Frank Jolliffe
1931	1932	Leslie Hender
1932	1940	George Bricknell
1940	1947	Claud Lacey
1947	1959	Bernard Kerswill
1959	1978	Maurice Avery
1978	1983	Christopher Louden
1983	1986	Clifford Alford
1986	1988	Tony Berthon
1988	1989	Clifford Alford
1989	1993	Peter Ayres
1993	1994	Tracey Larder
1994	1995	Peter Willetts
1995		Margaret Alford

Index of Names